UNDERSTANDING EDUCATION

This book explores undergraduate education programmes in a new way. Written by those at the forefront of teaching and learning, it encourages students to delve beneath the surface of their degree subject and reveals important insights about the how, why and where next for education studies.

With contributions from course leaders, tutors, current students and recent graduates, this book offers insights from nearly 60 authors based in 20 different institutions from five different countries. The chapters offer opportunities for readers to consider their own learning experiences in a wider context, enhance their understanding of the degree course and actively shape the education studies community of the future.

Each chapter is written in an accessible way, with 'questions to consider' throughout and 'recommended readings' at the end to advance readers' thinking and reflections. Chapters cover topics such as:

- Education Studies' development as a degree subject
- Its evolving identity, values and purposes
- Teaching and assessment approaches in undergraduate education programmes
- How the subject develops students' professional aptitudes and transferable skills
- Possibilities for advancing inclusion, equity and justice in education at degree level

These 'behind the scenes' factors are brought to the fore through case studies and examples of how lecturers and students make sense of their teaching and learning. With its unique approach to examining these issues, this book is essential for students of Education Studies at undergraduate level while also being relevant for staff and postgraduate students in education.

Mark Pulsford is an Associate Professor and Director of Undergraduate Studies in the Department of Education Studies at the University of Warwick.

Rebecca Morris is an Associate Professor in the Department of Education Studies at the University of Warwick.

Ross Purves is an Associate Professor of Music Education at the Institute of Education, University College London's Faculty of Education and Society.

The Routledge Education Studies Series

Series Editor: Stephen Ward, Bath Spa University, UK

The Routledge Education Studies Series aims to support advanced level study on Education Studies and related degrees by offering in-depth introductions from which students can begin to extend their research and writing in years 2 and 3 of their course. Titles in the series cover a range of classic and up-and-coming topics, developing understanding of key issues through detailed discussion and consideration of conflicting ideas and supporting evidence. With an emphasis on developing critical thinking, allowing students to think for themselves and beyond their own experiences, the titles in the series offer historical, global and comparative perspectives on core issues in education.

Contemporary Issues in Childhood
A Bio-ecological Approach
Zeta Brown and Stephen Ward

International and Comparative Education
Contemporary Issues and Debates
Brendan Bartram

Psychology and the Study of Education
Critical Perspectives on Developing Theories
Edited by Cathal O'Siochru

Philosophy and the Study of Education
New Perspectives on a Complex Relationship
Edited by Tom Feldges

Sociology for Education Studies
Connecting Theory, Settings and Everyday Experiences
Edited by Catherine A. Simon and Graham Downes

Understanding Education and Economics
Key Debates and Critical Perspectives
Edited by Jessie A. Bustillos Morales and Sandra Abegglen

Understanding Contemporary Issues in Higher Education
Contradictions, Complexities and Challenges
Edited by Brendan Bartram

Education in Europe
Looking out for what the neighbours do
Edited by Tom Feldges

Pedagogies for the Future
A critical reimagining of education
Gary Beauchamp, Dylan Adams and Kevin Smith

Understanding Education Studies
Critical Issues and New Directions
Edited by Mark Pulsford, Rebecca Morris and Ross Purves

For more information about this series, please visit: www.routledge.com/The-Routledge-Education-Studies-Series/book-series/RESS

UNDERSTANDING EDUCATION STUDIES

CRITICAL ISSUES AND NEW DIRECTIONS

Edited by
Mark Pulsford
Rebecca Morris
Ross Purves

Routledge
Taylor & Francis Group
LONDON AND NEW YORK

Designed cover image: © Getty Images

First published 2023
by Routledge
4 Park Square, Milton Park, Abingdon, Oxon, OX14 4RN

and by Routledge
605 Third Avenue, New York, NY 10158

Routledge is an imprint of the Taylor & Francis Group, an informa business

© 2023 selection and editorial matter, Mark Pulsford, Rebecca Morris and Ross Purves; individual chapters, the contributors

The right of Mark Pulsford, Rebecca Morris and Ross Purves to be identified as the authors of the editorial material, and of the authors for their individual chapters, has been asserted in accordance with sections 77 and 78 of the Copyright, Designs and Patents Act 1988.

All rights reserved. No part of this book may be reprinted or reproduced or utilised in any form or by any electronic, mechanical, or other means, now known or hereafter invented, including photocopying and recording, or in any information storage or retrieval system, without permission in writing from the publishers.

Trademark notice: Product or corporate names may be trademarks or registered trademarks, and are used only for identification and explanation without intent to infringe.

British Library Cataloguing-in-Publication Data
A catalogue record for this book is available from the British Library

ISBN: 978-1-032-28469-9 (hbk)
ISBN: 978-1-032-28468-2 (pbk)
ISBN: 978-1-003-29693-5 (ebk)

DOI: 10.4324/9781003296935

Typeset in News Gothic
by codeMantra

Contents

List of contributors	viii
Series editor's preface	xv

1 Introduction   1
MARK PULSFORD, ROSS PURVES AND REBECCA MORRIS

Section 1   Positioning education studies   **5**
Ross Purves

2 Education studies as an undergraduate university subject: A short history   7
STEPHEN WARD

3 An international insight into education studies   15
DAVID MENENDEZ ALVAREZ-HEVIA, ALEJANDRO RODRÍGUEZ-MARTÍN AND EMILIO ÁLVAREZ-ARREGUI

4 Exploring the identity of an undergraduate education programme   21
JENNY ELLIOTT, RUPERT KNIGHT, SHARON CLANCY AND COLIN MORLEY

Section 2   Practices and pedagogies of education studies   **31**
Rebecca Morris

5 Knowing learning matters   33
NICK PRATT, ABIGAIL O'BRIEN, MARLON COLE AND BETHAN CILLO

6 Discovering your philosophy of education through digital storytelling   40
SOPHIE WARD, LAURA MAZZOLI SMITH AND TETI DRAGAS

7 Assessment for transformation: Adopting a humanist approach to assessment and feedback on a BA Education course   48
TRISTAN MIDDLETON, RICK MILLICAN, SIAN TEMPLETON AND LYNDA KAY

8 Student achievement and wellbeing: Understanding motivation through self-determination theory   57
MARK TYMMS

9	Taking a global perspective: The nature and value of comparative and international education (CIE) in UK universities LEANNE CAMERON, RAFAEL MITCHELL, GURPINDER LALLI AND BRENDAN BARTRAM	67
10	Being 'international': The opportunities and challenges of studying education as an international student YUTONG LIU, REBECCA MORRIS, TASHA PEDITTO, LINGXI PENG AND ROSS PURVES	74
11	Learning about research methods: A case study LOUISE GASCOINE AND LAURA MAZZOLI SMITH	83
12	Education for sustainability: Connecting students to outdoor learning via forest school DAVE CUDWORTH	88
13	The role and value of arts-based learning for education studies CHERYL CANE	96

Section 3 Challenge and change in education studies **103**
Mark Pulsford

14	Education and democracy: The public sphere reclaimed for educational study TED FLEMING	105
15	The role of social justice theory in education studies JENNY HATLEY	112
16	Inclusive curriculum matters: Co-creating a decolonised education curriculum through student voices JAWIRIA NASEEM AND ZHU HUA	119
17	Speaking through silence: Embracing fear and shame in anti-racist education HEATHER KNIGHT AND EMMA JONES	128
18	Understanding identity and positionality through student–staff interactions on an education studies undergraduate programme TALITHA BIRD AND RAJVIR GILL	137
19	Men and masculinities on undergraduate education studies degrees MARK PULSFORD, RYAN CAZLEY, ABDULLAH DAYA, ROWAN GODFREY, SHENGHAO LYU AND TAIWO OKUTUBO	144

20 Rebalancing power relations in teacher–student co-creation 153
ROSI SMITH, ROBYN WALL, LUCINDA WHITE, EMMA WRIGHT AND MELISSA VERNON

Section 4 The personal and professional in education studies 169
Ross Purves

21 Employability and pedagogies for employability in education studies 171
DAVID MENENDEZ ALVAREZ-HEVIA AND ALEXANDRA HAY

22 Career identity, employability and placements in education studies 179
CATHERINE A. SIMON

23 Placements as mediational transitions: An opportunity for negotiated, identity-shaping make-belief experiences 185
GISELA OLIVEIRA

24 More than your degree title: Transferable skills, employability and diverse opportunities for education students 191
DAVID THOMPSON, RACHEL HIGDON AND CHARLOTTE BARROW

Index *201*

Contributors

Emilio Álvarez-Arregui is a Senior Lecturer in Education at University of Oviedo. He has participated in numerous projects, working with educative institutions and international agencies in America, Africa and Europe. He is interested in the development of competence models.

Charlotte Barrow is a Senior Lecturer in Education at the University of Central Lancashire. She researches in the area of inclusion in both compulsory and higher education, particularly with regard to gender and special educational needs and disabilities.

Brendan Bartram holds a PhD in Education from the University of Birmingham, and his research focuses on comparative and international education. Previously, he held the position of Reader in Education for Social Justice at the University of Wolverhampton.

Talitha Bird is a Senior Lecturer in Education Studies at De Montfort University. She is currently Programme Leader for the BA Education Studies programmes and is completing her PhD on gender, sexuality and schooling.

Leanne Cameron holds a PhD in Education from the University of Bristol, and her research to date has focused on teacher professionalism, English language teaching and language-in-education policy in sub-Saharan Africa, and pedagogical change. She currently works as a Senior Consultant with Education Development Trust.

Cheryl Cane is an Assistant Professor and Director of Student Experience in the Department of Education Studies, University of Warwick. She has a background in teaching and leadership of arts education in secondary, further and higher education including teacher education.

Ryan Cazley is a final year student on the BA Education Studies programme at De Montfort University. His dissertation is focused on how mispronouncing the names of Black and Asian students affects their educational experiences.

Bethan Cillo is now a LLB (Hons) Law student at the University of Plymouth, having previously completed a Diploma of Higher Education in Education Studies. Her research interests are in family law, specialising in child law.

Contributors ix

Sharon Clancy is the former Head of Community Partnerships at the University of Nottingham and before that was the Chief Executive Officer of Mansfield Council for Voluntary Services. She currently teaches at the University of Nottingham in educational leadership and management and on the BA Education and PGCEi programmes. Her writing and research focus on class, community, adult education and lifelong learning and social justice.

Marlon Cole is in the final year of the BA Education Studies programme at the University of Plymouth. His final dissertation is focused on the ethnic attainment gap of Key Stage 4 students before and after the Covid-19 pandemic of 2020. He has a keen interest in football, both as a player and a coach.

Dave Cudworth is an education consultant and TES pathway tutor on the iPGCE, after recently semi-retiring (May 2022) as an Associate Professor and Head of the Education Department at the HEI where he ran his Forest School and Outdoor Learning Module. He is interested in how engagement in outdoor learning spaces promote learners' mental health, wellbeing and confidence alongside enabling a (re)connection with nature and the development of Education for Sustainability and pro-environmental sensibilities.

Abdullah Daya is moving into his final year of the BA Education Studies Programme at De Montfort University. His dissertation will focus on the role of Teaching Assistants in primary school classrooms and how this has evolved over the last 20 years. Abdullah is a Course Representative at DMU and has trained in Carbon Literacy as part of the Leicester City Council's Sustainable Schools Programme.

Teti Dragas is an Associate Professor in the Durham Centre for Academic Development. Her interests include the development and design of digital storytelling courses for higher education in a wide variety of contexts. She launched Digital Storytelling Durham in 2019 and she has also facilitated, designed and collaborated in digital storytelling workshops with a range of national and international partners.

Jenny Elliott started her career as a modern languages teacher in Germany, Italy and the UK. She is currently the Course Leader of the BA Education at the University of Nottingham and teaches on a number of the BA Education modules. Her research interests include South/North education collaborations, creativity in the classroom, outdoor education and urban agriculture.

Ted Fleming is an Adjunct Faculty member at Teachers College Columbia University, New York. He is also the external advisor to the UNESCO funded Learning City project of the Municipality of Larissa (Greece). He is currently a member of International Expert Panel advising the National Adult Learners Association about policies and practices of including student voice in Ireland's further education system.

Louise Gascoine is an Assistant Professor in Education at Durham University. Louise's research interests include metacognition, intersections between education and psychotherapeutic theory and practice, systematic reviewing, inclusive educational research and participant voice.

Contributors

Rajvir Gill is a Lecturer in Education Studies at De Montfort University. She is currently Year 1 Lead on the BA Education Studies programme and completing her PhD. Her research interests include Higher Education, identities, social justice, intersectionality and technology.

Rowan Godfrey graduated with a first-class honours degree in Education Studies from De Montfort University and progressed to the MA Education Practice programme. Rowan's BA dissertation was a comparative case study of the education systems in England and Finland. His Masters' dissertation seeks to explore how Forest School interventions can support English National Curriculum Goals.

Alexandra Hay is a Senior Lecturer in Education at Manchester Metropolitan University. She spent ten years as a secondary social science teacher, during which time she completed a doctorate in Education. She is currently programme lead for the Education BA at Manchester Metropolitan University.

Jenny Hatley teaches and researches in education in the areas of social justice, global citizenship and international education policy. She views education as a vehicle for social justice across all its forms, both formal and informal, and encourages asking critical questions of education so that it can be transformative for all.

Rachel Higdon is an Associate Professor in Education at De Montfort University. She researches in the creative transdisciplinary themes between the arts, education and industry.

Emma Jones is a Lecturer in Sociology at The Cornwall College Group, where she teaches on access to higher education courses. She has a particular interest in widening participation programmes within education and how these address equality and inclusivity issues. Having been a mature student herself, Emma's current role reflects her passion for this group, facilitating their return to formal learning and progression into higher education.

Lynda Kay is a Senior Lecturer in Inclusion and Special Educational Needs and Academic Course Leader of the MA Education suite and the PGCert National SENCO Award at the University of Gloucestershire. She is Vice-Chair of Directors of Leading Learning for SEND Community Interest Company.

Heather Knight is a Lecturer in Education at the University of Plymouth and has worked in Higher Education for over ten years. She specialises in issues of equalities and social justice, and has a particular interest in critical theory and critical pedagogy. She has a background in community arts and arts for social justice.

Rupert Knight was a primary teacher in London and Nottingham. He currently works at the University of Nottingham, where he has taught on the BA Education, PGCE and a range of postgraduate courses. His interests include dialogic pedagogies, spoken language in classrooms, teacher development and teacher professionalism.

Gurpinder Lalli holds a PhD in Education from the University of Leicester, and his research focuses on the sociology of education and he is actively engaged in research on social justice and inclusion. He currently works as a Reader in Education for Social Justice and Inclusion and a member of the Education Observatory, based in the School of Education at the University of Wolverhampton.

Yutong Liu is a second year BA Education Studies student at the University of Warwick. Alongside her studies, she works on the International Foundation Programme at Warwick, supporting international students with adapting to life in the UK. After her degree, Yutong (Veronica) hopes to join an MA Education course in order to continue exploring educational issues that she is passionate about.

Shenghao Lyu is in the final year of the BA Education Studies programme at the University of Warwick. His dissertation focuses on the reasons why men choose to study Education Studies courses at university.

Laura Mazzoli Smith is an Associate Professor in the School of Education, Durham University. Her research interests include inclusive education and education for diversity, narrative and auto-biographical methods and out of school/lifelong learning. A recent co-edited book is Repositioning Out-of-School Learning: Methodological Challenges and Possibilities for Researching Learning Beyond School.

David Menendez Alvarez-Hevia is a Lecturer in Education at the University of Oviedo. He worked as a Senior Lecturer and educational researcher in UK for more than ten years. He has been involved in teaching, leading and developing different undergraduate and master's programmes in education.

Tristan Middleton is a Senior Lecturer in Education and Academic Course Leader of the MA Education suite and the PGCert National SENCO Award at the University of Gloucestershire. He is Chair of Directors of Leading Learning for SEND Community Interest Company and Editor of the *International Journal of Nurture in Education*.

Rick Millican is a Senior Lecturer in Education and Academic Course Leader of a BA (Hons) Education at the University of Gloucestershire. His interests are education for sustainability, social justice and resilience.

Rafael Mitchell is a Lecturer in Comparative and International Education at the University of Bristol, with a special focus on African and low- and middle-income countries. His research and teaching addresses processes of schooling and school improvement for disadvantaged groups, and inequalities in knowledge production on education.

Colin Morley was a drama and English teacher in the English East Midlands. His interests include the arts with the curriculum and as pedagogic tools. He currently works on the BA and PGCEi at the University of Nottingham.

Rebecca Morris is an Associate Professor in the Department of Education Studies at the University of Warwick. She teaches across a range of undergraduate and postgraduate courses in the department. Rebecca's research interests include social justice and inequalities, widening participation, evidence use in education, assessment and curriculum.

Jawiria Naseem is a Lecturer in Education Studies at the University of Birmingham. She is leading the School of Education's decolonising the curriculum project. She is interested in examining the dynamics of Higher Education and the labour market for minority ethnic graduates and how these may create socio-economic outcomes.

Abigail O'Brien is an Associate Lecturer on the BA Education team at the University of Plymouth, on which she was formerly a student. Her PhD was about Widening Participation in Higher Education with a focus on advocacy and student voice. Her research interests are predominantly in alternatives in education, issues surrounding social class in education and inequalities in education.

Taiwo Okutubo is in the final year of BA Education Studies at the University of Warwick. He has a keen interest in the socio-cultural impact of education in society, a topic which he has spoken on at roundtables with government ministers in the DfE, DCMS and DWP.

Gisela Oliveira is a Lecturer in Education Studies at De Montfort University. Her research and publications focus on socio-cultural explorations of students' transitions between university and the workplace.

Tasha Peditto is a Primary Music Teacher at Garden International School in Kuala Lumpur, Malaysia. She graduated from University College London with a Masters in Music Education. Tasha's main research interests involve supporting the development of 'musical identities' of educators and students from the Early Years up to Key Stage 2 as well as the importance of music and creative arts at an early age.

Lingxi Peng is an international student in the Department of Education Studies at the University of Warwick. Lingxi has a wide range of research interests, including Chinese international students, multicultural identity, second language education, applied linguistics and social justice.

Nick Pratt works as a Senior Lecturer and researcher in education at the University of Plymouth. Originally trained as a primary teacher, he now teaches across a range of undergraduate and postgraduate programmes, including BA Education Studies, MA Education and PhD. His research interests focus on ways in which teaching, at all levels, is affected by assessment and accountability and how this alters students' experiences.

Mark Pulsford is an Associate Professor in the Department of Education Studies at the University of Warwick. He has previously taught on education programmes at the University of Sheffield and De Montfort University. After a first career in marketing research, Mark worked as a primary school teacher in London and Leicester before his university roles. His teaching and research interests are around fatherhood, men, masculinities and education.

Ross Purves is an Associate Professor of Music Education at the Institute of Education, University College London's Faculty of Education and Society, where he contributes to master's, doctoral and secondary PGCE programmes. A Senior Fellow of the Higher Education Academy, Ross was previously Deputy Programme Leader and Employability Champion for BA Education Studies at De Montfort University. Before entering higher education, Ross was a course manager in a large sixth form college and also served as music subject coordinator for a school-led consortium for initial teacher education.

Alejandro Rodríguez-Martín is a Senior Lecturer in Education at the University of Oviedo. He has been a visiting scholar at different higher education institutions and research centres in Europe and America. His research interests include inclusive education, entrepreneurial Training, ICT and innovation.

Catherine A. Simon was formerly Programme Leader (Associate Professor) for Education Studies at Bath Spa University where she was also a Teaching Fellow. With research interests in education policy, school systems and leadership and management, her work has informed both her teaching and supervision. Catherine has written extensively and sits on a number of editorial boards for academic journals.

Rosi Smith is a Lecturer in Education at De Montfort University, having previously worked in teaching, support and research roles in further, secondary and higher education. Her research has principally focused on ideology, citizenship and widening participation in Cuban education.

Sian Templeton is a Senior Lecturer in Education and Strand Leader of the BA (Hons) Education, Education, Special Educational Needs and Inclusion at the University of Gloucestershire. She is also a practising Educational Psychologist for part of her working week.

David Thompson is a Senior Lecturer in Education Studies at the University of Wolverhampton. His research and teaching focus on widening participation, social justice and inclusion.

Mark Tymms is a Senior Lecturer in Education at De Montfort University, Leicester, where he lectures predominantly in the psychology of education and development, adult education and wellbeing. His primary research focus is on person-centred learning and the relationship between individual learners and practitioners and the educational systems within which they act. He has a particular interest in Self-Determination Theory, the role of learner autonomy and existential-phenomenological philosophy and research methods.

Melissa Vernon studied BSc Speech and Language Therapy at De Montfort University, graduating in 2021. She is now a practising speech and language therapist.

Robyn Wall studied BA Education Studies at De Montfort University, graduating in 2021. She has previously worked as a teaching assistant and is now undertaking initial teacher training with the University of Warwick.

Sophie Ward is an Associate Professor in the School of Education, Durham University. Her research interests include the arts in education, creativity and education policy. Sophie's publications include her book, *Using Shakespeare's Plays to Explore Education Policy Today: Neoliberalism through the Lens of Renaissance Humanism*.

Stephen Ward is an Emeritus Professor of Education at Bath Spa University, formerly Dean of the School of Education and Subject Leader for Education Studies. A founder member of the British Education Studies Association, he has published on the primary curriculum, primary music teaching and education studies. His research interests are education policy and university knowledge.

Lucinda White studied BA Education Studies at De Montfort University, graduating in 2021, and began her initial teaching training in the autumn of 2022.

Emma Wright is a Lecturer in Education at De Montfort University, having previously worked as primary school teacher, mentor and school governor. Her research interests include special educational needs and disability, home education and inter-religious relations.

Zhu Hua is a Professor of Language Learning and Intercultural Communication at the Institute of Education, University College London (UCL). She is a Fellow of Academy of Social Sciences, UK and Chair of British Association for Applied Linguistics (BAAL). Prior to IOE, she worked in the School of Education at the University of Birmingham as the School Director of Internationalisation.

Series editor's preface

Education Studies has become a popular and exciting undergraduate subject in many universities in the UK. It began in the early 2000s, mainly in the post-1992 universities which had been centres of teacher training. Gaining academic credibility, the subject is now taught and researched in pre-1992 and Russell Group institutions. In 2004, Routledge published one of the first texts for undergraduates, *Education Studies: A Student's Guide* (Ward, 2004), now in its fourth edition (Simon and Ward, 2020). It comprises a series of chapters introducing key topics in Education Studies and has contributed to the development of the subject. Targeted at students and academic staff at the levels 5, 6 and 7, the Routledge Education Studies Series offers a sequence of volumes which explore such topics in depth.

It is important to understand that education studies is not teacher training or teacher education, although graduates in the subject may well go on to become teachers after a PGCE or school-based training. Education studies should be regarded as a subject with a variety of career outcomes, or indeed, none: it can be taken as the academic and critical study of education in itself. At the same time, while the theoretical elements of teacher training are continually reduced in PGCE courses and school-based training, undergraduate education studies provides a critical analysis for future teachers who, in a rapidly changing world, need so much more than simply the training to deliver a government-defined school curriculum.

Education studies is concerned with understanding how people develop and learn throughout their lives, the nature of knowledge and critical engagement with ways of knowing. It demands an intellectually rigorous analysis of educational processes and their cultural, social, political and historical contexts. In a time of rapid change across the planet, education is about how we both make and manage such change. Education studies, therefore, includes perspectives on international education, economic relationships, globalisation, ecological issues and human rights. It deals with beliefs, values and principles in education and the way that they change over time.

Since its early developments at the beginning of the century, the subject has grown in academic depth, drawing explicitly on the disciplines of Psychology, Sociology, Philosophy, History and Economics (see Chapter 2). But it has also broadened in scope to address the many social and political questions of globalisation, international education and perceptions of childhood. A glance through the list of book titles in the series below reveals the ever-growing range of topics which education studies embraces.

Coming new to the subject, you may rightly be shocked at the number of different topics you need to understand and learn about. The present book offers a wide range of topics from a total of 58 authors with a vast range of sources from the UK and worldwide, from the young and the old, and from a rich range of perspectives: teachers, tutors, education leaders and students. But what is special about the book is the way it makes sense of this wide array by giving us new insights into thinking and ideas, the values and assumptions, that underlie education studies and its development as a subject from teacher training. Through examples and case studies we see in detail why and how topics are important and need to be addressed. Much of the thinking about education studies has focused on its development as a 'pure' university academic subject. But the final section of this book helps you to start thinking about the many options for your future as a graduate. In total, the book gives us the broadest analysis of the growth of education studies as a university subject.

British Education Studies Association (BESA)

Many of the editors and contributors to Education Studies book series are members of the British Education Studies Association (BESA). Formed in 2005, BESA is an academic association providing a network for tutors and students in Education Studies. It holds an annual conference with research papers from staff and students; there are bursaries for students on Education Studies programmes. The Association funds small-scale research projects; the support for the writing of this book was one of those.

The website offers information and news about Education Studies and two journals: *Educationalfutures* and *Transformations*, a journal for student publications. Both are available without charge on the website: https://educationstudies.org.uk/

Stephen Ward, Series Editor,
Bath Spa University

References

Simon, C.A. and Ward, S. (Eds.) (2020) *A Student's Guide to Education Studies*. Abingdon: Routledge.
Ward, S. (Ed.) (2004) *Education Studies: A Student's Guide*. Abingdon: Routledge.

1 Introduction

Mark Pulsford, Ross Purves and Rebecca Morris

This book is primarily for students who are studying, or are thinking of studying, education at undergraduate degree level. It is designed as a critical guide to *what education studies is* as an area of study, rather than being about the topics that make up education studies (there are lots of books that do the latter, and you're reminded to look at the other titles in the Routledge Education Studies Series for some of them). In this book, each chapter addresses something 'behind the scenes' of education studies, whether that be its development as a degree subject; its evolving identity, values and purposes; its teaching and assessment approaches; the ways that it advances students' professional aptitudes and transferable skills; or its current challenges in the wider context of higher education. The book provides case studies that illuminate this dynamic degree subject, offering accounts of critical issues and new directions that are significant to students' experiences on education studies programmes. Each chapter supports considered thought and reflection about this area of study, allowing you to gain a deeper understanding to advance your learning whilst also asking you to think about how your time as an education studies student profoundly influences the way you navigate the wider world and prepares you to manage the professional responsibilities you will come to have.

The book encourages its readers to think deeply about what it means to be a *student of education*. As such it is about you – your interests, your aspirations and your journey through and beyond higher education. It invites you to see yourself as a fundamental part of what education studies can be. Many of the chapters show the possibilities that emerge when students and staff cooperate to examine elements of their education studies courses. In this way, the book can be seen as an example of *doing* education studies – the critical, constructive, collaborative and hope-full analysis of educational phenomena.

Education Studies, at almost 25 years old, is a maturing UK university subject. In that quarter century, the subject has become a well-established and popular choice for UK-based and international undergraduate students, having grown from the theory for teacher training to become a diverse subject area reflecting the varied institutional contexts in which it is taught and mixture of academic disciplines at its heart. In many areas of the world too, undergraduate education courses are flourishing. Our chapter authors bring these varied contexts, disciplinary backgrounds and institutional priorities to the book. Fifty-eight people, 14 of whom are current or former education studies students, contributed to the 23 main chapters. Our authors are affiliated with 20 different institutions and offer perspectives on undergraduate education studies from the UK, across Europe, the USA and China, too. A feature of the book is the joint-authorship of many chapters, whether that is across institutions or national borders, and in several cases staff and students have

DOI: 10.4324/9781003296935-1

written together. This reflects the collaborative ethos of the education studies field and is one way that the book foregrounds the varied perspectives of those at the heart of teaching and learning in education studies.

The chapters in this book will support your studies in various ways. You will find that individual chapters link closely to particular modules, assignments and session topics on your course, as well as to wider debates about the *how* and *why* of your degree subject. Each chapter features 'questions to consider', useful as prompts for individual study and assignment preparation, as well as to frame student discussions and class presentations. The recommended readings will be a great place to start in order to develop your understanding and advance your thinking, perhaps in preparation for an assignment, presentation or seminar discussion.

Whilst dipping into individual chapters may be of most relevance, you should also find it beneficial to read all the chapters in a section as we've tried to group them into related themes or topics. To help make the most of those connections, you will see that we have written brief overviews for each section. The first section, called 'Positioning education studies', is focused on locating the subject in terms of its history, international status and identity, and as such should help you reflect on your own identity in relation to your degree. Section 2 – 'Practices and pedagogies' – explores the varied features and approaches that are often part of undergraduate education courses. The chapters here address perspectives on issues which are central to teaching and learning in our field. 'Challenge and change' is our third section, reminding us of the need to consider education studies' relationship with power, privilege and social inequality. The chapters here ask questions about the perspectives and needs of marginalised groups in education, and consider how education studies can take steps to model more just and equitable educational experiences. The book ends with a fourth section called 'the personal and professional', which will help readers to see themselves in their studies and to understand how the transition to the graduate workplace will involve drawing on personal, academic and professional experience and skills that courses in education studies are often adept at highlighting.

If you've been an undergraduate student of education studies for any length of time, you are likely to have been asked about your plans to become a schoolteacher. The historical legacy of our subject has resulted in a complex identity, something that is explored from many perspectives in the following chapters. Many readers will be planning a career in the school classroom and an education studies degree offers a fantastic intellectual foundation for this. Yet through your studies, you are also likely to have discovered the many other ways that those with a degree in education, who have a breadth of knowledge, perspectives and transferable skills, can contribute to a complex and ever-changing world. Indeed, the 'critical issues' and 'new directions' that we refer to in the book's title have emerged straight from the seminars, lecture theatres, staffrooms and placement settings where education studies is taught and learned in the 2020s; they indicate just how essential it is to see education as *more than* schooling, and education studies as relevant for, *yet also important beyond,* school teaching. Contributing authors have responded to our call for chapters by providing compelling, 'on the ground' perspectives which highlight our subject community's commitment to making a difference through education in the broadest terms. Emphasising partnerships between staff and students, and with schools, placement settings and the wider world of work, these chapters offer visions of an inclusive subject which seeks to challenge and improve the educational status quo. This involves asking difficult questions, guarding against passivity, re-evaluating the past and looking to the future with hope yet not complacency. Whether concerned with the creation of citizens actively engaged in democratic, political, social and economic debate, or focused on students' wellbeing and personal development, our authors highlight the potential of education studies to help transform individual lives as well as society as a whole.

We hope you enjoy the book and feel as inspired as we do about the potential of education studies to address these critical issues and embrace its new directions.

We sincerely thank all those colleagues who have contributed chapters, and we're also very grateful to the British Education Studies Association (BESA, see educationstudies.org.uk) for funding the research which originally inspired this book and for helping us reach potential contributors. BESA exists to support our subject and you will find it useful to keep an eye on its activities and publications. We are also grateful to Stephen Ward, Series Editor for the Routledge Education Studies Series, for all of his support during the writing and publishing processes, and to Helen Purves for her unstinting dedication to manuscript accuracy.

Section 1
Positioning education studies

Ross Purves

The chapters in Section 1 help us understand how and why undergraduate education programmes in England have developed as they have, and to appreciate some of the various opportunities and challenges they have encountered. We first explore these issues from historical and international comparative perspectives. In Chapter 2, Stephen Ward traces the origins and development of education as an undergraduate university subject in the UK. He documents the complex and evolving tensions between the practical need to prepare teachers for the demands of the school classroom and efforts to offer broader, theory-based studies of education in all its forms. Ultimately, these resulted in the emergence of distinct academic undergraduate programmes with titles such as 'BA Education Studies' from the late 1990s onwards. But, as Ward notes, this has not ended debates regarding the scope, content and purpose of these programmes. In Chapter 3, David Menendez Alvarez-Hevia, Alejandro Rodriguez-Martin and Emilio Álvarez-Arregui outline a range of international comparisons with the UK which demonstrate that, whilst universities in some countries have offered academic studies of education for longer than others, similar tensions and debates to those outlined by Ward exist in many national contexts. Importantly, however, the authors also highlight that, despite the diverse nature of these programmes both in this country and internationally, all have potential to contribute to the global mission of improving education as a means of tackling the pressing challenges of our time. Chapters 2 and 3 also consider the extent to which it is appropriate and helpful for undergraduate education programmes to draw on the content of so-called 'foundational disciplines' including psychology, sociology, philosophy and the history of education. Opinions in the UK and elsewhere vary on how such content should be balanced with other contemporary topics, practical activities and vocational experiences, and also the extent to which sufficient space should be made available for the interests and reflective voice of the individual learner.

Collectively, as Jenny Elliott, Rupert Knight, Sharon Clancy and Colin Morley make clear in Chapter 4, the various questions of scope, content and purpose explored by Ward, Menéndez Alvarez-Hevia and colleagues have implications for the identities of undergraduate programmes of education – and for those who lead, teach and study them. If you are a student in this area yourself, you might have sensed some of these tensions or heard comments similar to those shared in their chapter. However, by taking the reader through some of the decision-making and motivations behind the development of one BA Education programme at an English university, Elliott and her colleagues illustrate how those of us who teach or study in this area can chart a clear course through the complexity. In doing so, they help us articulate a confident, distinctive, even imperative rationale for our studies.

DOI: 10.4324/9781003296935-2

2 Education studies as an undergraduate university subject

A short history

Stephen Ward

SUMMARY POINTS

- The Robbins Report (1963) recommended that the teaching profession should be all-graduate and BEd degrees were taught in the training colleges.
- The degree courses were judged to be over-theorised; teacher training was taken over by the government.
- In 2000, education studies grew from its role as the theory for teacher training as a popular new subject for undergraduates.
- A small-scale research project into early courses found that the academic quality was mixed and somewhat uneven.
- In recent years the subject has grown in both breadth and academic depth.
- The role of the contributory disciplines of psychology, sociology, philosophy and history is still a matter for discussion.

Introduction

Education studies is now a popular subject for undergraduates in many universities in the UK. But it has had a relatively short life, commencing mainly around the beginning of the century. This chapter traces the origins and growth of education studies from its origins as the 'theory for teaching'. It includes reference to the author's small-scale research on the first education studies programmes initiated in universities carried out in 2003–2005 (Ward, 2006). Although the data was collected at an early stage in the life of the subject, it offers some insights into the way it has since developed. The focus of the account is England, although there have been similar developments in other countries of the UK.

Theory for teachers

In 1963, the Robbins Committee on Higher Education was commissioned by the government to report on university education in the UK. Until that time only about 5 per cent of young people entered university, and Robbins duly recommended expansion with the setting up of new campus universities to match the higher education populations of other European countries. Robbins made another recommendation: that teacher-training colleges should offer four-year degree courses to enable the teaching profession in the UK to become an all-graduate one. While many secondary

DOI: 10.4324/9781003296935-3

school teachers were graduates, most primary school teachers gained qualified teacher status (QTS) from a two- or three-year practical course in a teacher-training college. Courses were relatively free of theoretical material, concentrating mainly upon providing the practical resources for teachers to function in the classroom. The new qualification for primary teachers was to be the Bachelor of Education (BEd) degree with QTS.

The training colleges, or colleges of education, in which the BEd was to be taught did not have degree-awarding powers, and so courses were to be validated and awarded by the college's local university. Crook (2002) explains that the validating universities were suspicious of teacher training, believing it not to be a proper academic subject. They insisted on a proper academic grounding for the degree; the subject disciplines were drawn in to form a theoretical basis. R.S. Peters, a philosopher at the London Institute of Education, met with C.J. Gill, Her Majesty's Inspector of Schools with responsibility for teacher training, in a closed seminar at the Department for Education and Science (DES) to agree the theoretical subjects to be included in the new degrees. The proposal was for psychology, sociology, philosophy and economics to form the theoretical basis. Economics was subsequently dropped and history of education substituted. This was a remarkably autocratic event with little open discussion, or agreement of those involved in the colleges. As Richardson (2002) points out, there was a very limited research base for the disciplines in education in the universities and little research competence in the training colleges. Any theory of pedagogy or teaching was excluded and Crook (2002) details the historical problems which educational theory encountered alongside demands for practical teacher training.

The absence of pedagogy as a core component of educational studies in the undergraduate degrees established during 1965–1968 was indicative of the general difficulties of educationists making a decisive theoretical contribution to practical problems in education.

Simon (1994) suggested that the BEd programmes which developed during the 1960s suffered from attempts by the validating universities to graft academic theory onto practical teacher training. From the start, education studies in the BEd courses had an unhappy relationship with its teacher-training parent. Crook goes on to describe the consequent neglect of the professional dimensions of teacher training as a 'wrong turn' that was corrected by 'the downgrading of educational studies in favour of longer periods of teaching practice' (2002: 70). From that time, teacher education suffered criticisms from its students and teachers as being over-theorised. This was in contrast with medical training which has generally enjoyed the loyalty of doctors, despite demonstrable weaknesses in comparison to teacher training (Booth et al., 1995).

Government controls

Such criticisms gave the government cause to take control of teacher education and led to the state regulatory frameworks imposed in the 1980s by the Council for the Accreditation of Teacher Education (CATE) and, in the 1990s, the Teacher Training Agency (later the Training and Development Agency for Schools (TDA)). The agency published the *Standards for Teaching* (DFEE/TTA, 1998), a long list of criteria to be met by teachers in practice through their training. BEd courses were compelled to be compliant with standards set by the Secretary of State (Ofsted, 1997), and Ofsted inspections were instituted to ensure such compliance.

The *Standards for Teaching* included little educational theory, and the effect was to 'de-theorise' undergraduates' studies. The curriculum for teacher education became limited to a knowledge of the National Curriculum and 'methods' for teaching it. The situation was exacerbated by a campaign to exclude universities from teacher training altogether, led by Her Majesty's former Chief Inspector of Schools in England Chris Woodhead. In the late 1990s, universities offering teacher training through BEd courses with QTS were finding themselves with staff appointed to teach from a strong academic basis but who were now unwanted or unwilling to teach to the new standards. They also found themselves with teacher education students who were engaging in courses which lacked the analysis and critique to be expected in undergraduate honours level study.

It is probably not an exaggeration to say that, in many universities, the initiation of undergraduate education studies programmes was a direct reaction to government control of teacher education. Some universities continued their BEd with QTS courses. Others introduced a new award: an education studies undergraduate degree without a teacher training element and without qualified teacher status, A third group, including Bishop Grosseteste University, Lincoln and Bath Spa University, converted the four-year BEd teacher-training degree into 'three-plus-one': an undergraduate degree in education studies with progression to a one-year Postgraduate Certificate in Education (PGCE) course with QTS. Funding came from different sources: for the BEd QTS courses, it came from the Teacher Training Agency while for the non-QTS courses, it was provided by the Higher Education Funding Council for England (HEFCE). Funding had to be negotiated, but many universities found little difficulty in securing the necessary HEFCE funding and 'the new education studies' as an undergraduate subject, free of its teacher-training encumbrances, was born.

There is just one reservation to this: Education Studies degrees had for many years been in existence as an 'exit award' granted to those students on BEd courses who had failed a final teaching practice and could not then qualify for QTS. And perhaps this is the place to note another unique exception: the University of York was founded in 1963 with its first vice-chancellor, Eric James, a former schoolteacher and High Master of Manchester Grammar School (University of York, 2013). James was a leading innovative figure in higher education and chaired the Committee of Inquiry into Teacher Training (1972) which produced the *Report on Teacher Education and Training*. James argued that in a university students should learn about education. In 1965, Professor of Education Harry Rée was appointed to introduce Education Studies as a subsidiary subject to be available with any other subject in its joint honours undergraduate degrees, for example *Mathematics with Education*. The subject was not designed to qualify students as teachers, but gave theoretical and critical insights into the nature of education, drawing on the contributory disciplines of psychology, sociology and philosophy. It included the educational aspects of another school curriculum subject and placements in schools. Graduates in the joint honours with education were given some exemptions in the university's PGCE teacher-training year which, for them, was largely school based. Rée's initiative can be seen as an interesting precursor of the growth of the subject in the 2000s.

The new education studies

From 1999, a number of education departments in universities got down to writing on blank sheets of paper their newly-fledged education studies courses for undergraduates. For the first time, education was like any other university subject with the freedom to select and define its knowledge. They were not entirely free, however, as the Quality Assurance Agency (QAA) (2000) issued its first guidance on course content, although its stipulations were broad and certainly did not limit ideas. The current author was appointed to develop the new Education Studies course at Bath Spa University and it was an exciting time, being able to draw on the knowledge and skills of colleagues in shaping a new programme. We began with the notion that the degree should equip students with the knowledge for progression to the PGCE QTS course. However, we soon saw that such limitations were unnecessary: after all most students arrive on a PGCE course with a non-educationally-related degree and no prior knowledge of education. We were able to include all sorts of diverse topics: education policy and politics, international education, radical education, education for sustainability. But there was always the lingering worry that, against these fine ideas, students would want more practical content on how to work in schools and teach, so we put in some optional modules on the school curriculum in English and mathematics. In the event we needn't have worried; students opted for the new and exciting stuff: the radical education module was consistently over-subscribed. In the first years, education studies could be offered only as a second subject in a combined awards degree because the TTA regulation was that primary school teachers should have studied a degree subject relevant to the school curriculum. In 2002, this regulation was dropped and universities were able to offer education studies in a single-honours undergraduate award.

Another feature of the growth of the new subject was the publication of a series of introductory texts: Matheson and Grosvenor (1999), Tubbs and Grimes (1999), Bartlett *et al.* (2001), Ward (2004), Kassem *et al.* (2006) and Sharp *et al.* (2006). The books were 'new' in the sense that they were targeted explicitly at students in Education Studies courses *without* teacher education, offering a broad and diverse perspective. Several of the books have gone into multiple editions and the titles in the Routledge Education Studies listed at the beginning of this volume are examples of the strong take-up of education studies programmes and the growing breadth of content.

The British Education Studies Association (BESA)

Having drafted the course with colleagues at Bath Spa University, I wondered what was going onto the blank sheets of paper in the other universities starting non-teacher training education studies programmes. We were not talking to each other. Steve Bartlett of the University of Chester and I initiated a new network of those teaching Education Studies. At a first conference of 60 delegates at the University of Chester in 2005, BESA was formed with a formal constitution. The organisation has grown, with an annual conference open to students as well as staff, and a website which includes two free-access journals (BESA, 2022). It funds small research projects, one of which formed the basis for this book.

Research into the first start-ups

As research for a doctoral thesis (Ward, 2006) I interviewed heads of department and leaders of education studies programmes in nine institutions to ask about the origins of their courses, aims and theoretical bases. Each institution had its own programme design and was not working from a national template, other than the very generalised outlines in the QAA (2000) document. There isn't space to discuss methods or to include much interview data. I simply list briefly the main findings under a series of headings together with some observations about current developments in the subject. The institutions which, of course, are anonymous were all in England and in departments which had been, or were still, running primary teacher training courses.

Not teacher training

One theme universal among all the course leaders was, "What we're doing isn't teacher training". This was expressed with an urgency and vehemence that reflected the anger and frustration which colleagues had experienced in the government-controlled teacher education courses. There were repeated expressions of relief at being away from it, and of excitement at the freedom to teach and research their academic interests. While this was invariably expressed by the course leaders, there was one case in which a leader had found it difficult to wean colleagues from the ideas and practice of teacher training to which they were so accustomed. Many tutors in the new subject had exciting new knowledge to profess, but there were those who didn't, and who were happier to continue what they had done before. In this particular case, the course included an assessed teaching practice. However, in most cases, the ambition was to be as far away from school teaching as possible. Most of the courses offered students some experiences of observing or assisting in school classrooms, but again the emphasis was on observation rather than practice.

It is interesting to note that while universities were being urged to make their courses more relevant to employment, education studies tutors were trying to shift the emphasis *away* from employment. In those early days, the mission was to create a 'purist' academic subject which was not dependent on a career in teaching. Of course, this is an attitude which has changed in recent years as education studies staff look increasingly to work placements and non-teaching employment (see Hordern and Simon, 2017, and Section 4 of this book).

Theory and content

I have to report that course leaders' responses to the question *What is the theoretical basis for the programme* were not impressive, with replies such as "Hm, I'd need to think about that one" or "Can I get back to you on that?" There was certainly an impression that 'getting away from teacher training' was the over-arching notion, with not much more. Of course, we have to remember that all were beginning with that blank sheet of paper and there was then no ready-made list of content. As noted above, the QAA (2000) had given no such form of content and there was a vast array of possibilities. Also, in many cases the courses had been constructed hurriedly in time for an early start. For another feature of the times was the rapid growth in popularity of education studies programmes. One university had quickly developed a programme based on the exit award they had given to failing QTS students. They advertised it for 25 places and received 160 applications.

In a number of cases the course content had been derived from what the available staff could offer, and there were admissions by course leaders that programmes were not ideal simply because "we have no one who can teach policy", or there was no tutor with knowledge of international education. It is a sign of the growth of the subject that the curriculum is now so wide that departments are able to select tutorial staff to teach the required content, and that new staff have learned and gained qualifications in education studies, rather than being 'converted' teacher trainers.

The disciplines

I had expected to find that the 'contributory disciplines' of psychology, sociology, philosophy and the history of education would be strongly evident as the theoretical bases of the new courses, but it was not so. A number of factors seemed to be at play. The first was a worry that the disciplines which were so maligned and discredited in the old BEd courses would similarly be rejected by the education studies students. Another was that the disciplines would be seen to be difficult. Again, we have to remember that tutors were creating courses from scratch with no experience of what students did actually think or know. In one case, the course leader was a sociologist who admitted that the course was mainly sociological. When I asked whether the students knew it was sociology he replied, "Oh no, we don't want to frighten the horses". This reflected a rather common view that education studies students were academically weak. This was especially in those universities where a BEd with QTS was still running and the education studies student population were those who hadn't the qualifications or failed to get onto the BEd. In some cases there was a sense that the subject must be academic, but not *too* academic.

Another factor was again the availability and preferences of staff. One course leader said, "We don't have much psychology in the course because we just don't have any psychologists at the moment". In another case, the course leader was a philosopher and he made it perfectly clear that it was a philosophy of education course, "… the European philosophy that I'm interested in".

We have already seen that among the course leaders there was a strong motive to create education studies as a pure university subject, and when asked about the role of the contributory disciplines some replied that they wanted to see education as 'its own discipline', not dependent on other disciplines. This is a theme which has hung over the subject for some time: the tension between the concept of education as a 'subject' or a 'discipline', with many arguing that to be a serious academic subject it needs to rely on the disciplines. Indeed, the disciplines are a strong feature of many courses these days. For example, the modules in at least one university's course are labelled 'Psychology of Education', 'Sociology of Education' and so on. Another interesting point relates to the omission of Economics from the disciplines proposed for the original BEd course in 1963. That first suggestion was prescient in that Education students now need some knowledge of economics to understand the current marketisation of schooling and higher education in England, and texts are appearing to meet that need (Bustillos Morales and Abegglen, 2020).

Conclusion

Education studies had an excited but shaky birth from its origins in teacher education. But, it is heartening to see that the ambitions of those early course leaders have come to fruition, giving us a free-standing academic subject that attracts a high standard of students and staff. It is a subject which can be studied for its own sake by those who are simply interested in education as a human activity, but it can also be the starting point for careers in a whole range of education-related fields. And, for those who progress to teacher training, it can offer us teachers who are critically informed about society, politics and the world and have a vision of education beyond the routine of government edict.

However, course leaders and tutors are still having to engage with some of the issues outlined above: how much the subject should be designed to prepare future teachers; how it can be related to careers other than teaching; the role of the contributory disciplines and whether students should study any or all of them. Such debates are addressed in this book.

Questions to consider

Why did you choose education studies as a degree subject?

Are you intending to teach, or do you see another career following your graduation in education studies?

What role do the disciplines play in your course?

What do you think of the range of knowledge content in your course?

Do you think your learning in education studies is going to assist you in a career other than teaching?

Recommended reading

Crook, D. (2002) Education Studies and Teacher Education. *British Journal of Education Studies* **50**(1), pp. 55–75. https://doi.org/10.1111/1467-8527.t01-1-00191

Crook details the origins of the BEd degree and explains how the contributory disciplines of psychology, sociology, philosophy and the history of education were selected as the theoretical basis for teacher education.

McCulloch, G. (2002) Disciplines Contributing to Education? Educational Studies and the Disciplines. *British Journal of Educational Studies* **50**(1), pp. 100–119. https://doi.org/10.1111/1467-8527.t01-1-00193

See this paper for further discussion of the roles of the disciplines.

Simon, C.A. and Ward, S. (2020) *A Student's Guide to Education Studies* (4th edition). Abingdon: Routledge.

This book is the fourth edition of one of the first texts for students of education studies. The various chapters indicate the range of topics in the current education studies curriculum.

References

Bartlett, S., Burton, D. and Peim, N. (2001) *An Introduction to Education Studies*. London: Paul Chapman.

BESA (2022) British Education Studies Association Website. Online. Available at https://educationstudies.org.uk/ (Accessed 17 February 2022).

Booth, M., Hargreaves, D.H., Bradley, H. and Southworth, G. (1995) Training of doctors in hospitals: a comparison with teacher education. *Journal of Education for Teaching* **21**(2), pp. 145–162.

Bustillos Morales, J.A. and Abegglen, S. M. (2020). *Understanding Education and Economics: Key Debates and Critical Perspectives*. Milton: Routledge.

Committee on Higher Education (Robbins) (1963) *Report*. London: HMSO.

Committee of Inquiry into Teacher Training (James Report) (1972) *Report on Teacher Education and Training*. London: Her Majesty's Stationery Office.

Crook, D. (2002) Education Studies and Teacher Education. *British Journal of Education Studies* **50**(1), pp. 55–75. https://doi.org/10.1111/1467-8527.t01-1-00191

DfEE/TTA (1998) *Teaching: High Status, High Standards. Standards for the award of Qualified Teacher Status*. London: Department for Education and Employment / Teacher Training Agency.

Hordern, J, and Simon, C.A. (Eds) (2017) *Placements and Work-based Learning in Education Studies*. Abingdon: Routledge.

Kassem, D., Mufti, E. and Robinson, J. (2006) *Education Studies: Issues and Critical Perspectives*. Buckingham: Open University.

Matheson, D. and Grosvenor, I. (1999) *An Introduction to the Study of Education*. London: David Fulton.

Ofsted (1997) *Framework for the Inspection of Initial Teacher Training*. London: Ofsted.

Quality Assurance Agency for Higher Education (2000) *Subject Benchmark Statements: Education Studies*. Gloucester: QAA.

Richardson, W. (2002) Education Studies in the United Kingdom, 1940-2002. *British Journal of Educational Studies*, **50**(1), pp. 3–56.

Sharp, J., Ward, S. and Hankin, L. (2006) *Education Studies: An Issues-Based Approach*. Exeter: Learning Matters.

Simon, B. (1994) *The State and Educational Change: Essays in the History of Education and Pedagogy.* London: Lawrence and Wishart.

Tubbs, N. and Grimes, J. (1999) *What Is Education Studies.* Winchester: King Alfred's College.

University of York (2013) *News and Events.* Available at https://www.york.ac.uk/news-and-events/events/-public-lectures/autumn-term-2013/lord-james/ (Accessed 8 April 2022).

Ward, S. (2004) *Education Studies: A Student's Guide.* London: RoutledgeFalmer.

Ward, S. (2006) *Undergraduate Education Studies as an Emerging Subject in Higher Education: The Construction and Definition of University Knowledge.* (Unpublished PhD Thesis.) Bath: Bath Spa University.

3 An international insight into education studies

David Menendez Alvarez-Hevia, Alejandro Rodríguez-Martín and Emilio Álvarez-Arregui

---

SUMMARY POINTS

- Initial teaching training and education is central to faculties of education in the UK and internationally but there is space for undergraduate and postgraduate courses that focus on other aspects of education.
- There is a wide range of understandings and possibilities when exploring education studies programmes outside the UK.
- In an international context, the study of education takes different forms that are influenced by national traditions and predispositions.
- Although with different titles, some countries outside the UK offer programmes that share multiple aspects with education studies.
- There is a global interest in the study of education. There is also an interest from the education studies community to consider global issues from an educational perspective.

Education studies: From the UK to the international context

As detailed in Chapter 2, education studies in the UK emerged as an independent subject in the late 1990s. Initially it was introduced in just few universities as an 'ideal subject as preparation for teaching and other careers' and in combination with other subjects (Simon and Ward, 2020: 2). It is now present in most universities as programmes of study in different forms (e.g. foundation, BA/BSc, single/joint honours undergraduate degrees, along with various diploma and master's programmes), with different titles (e.g. 'Education Studies', 'Education', 'Education and/with X') and is mainly associated with faculties or departments of education (Bartlett and Burton, 2016). However, it is still difficult to discuss outside the UK what 'education studies' means. In the international context, the representation of education studies is more elusive, takes multiple forms and presents distinctive epistemological trajectories associated with national settings.

Questions to consider

Think about a situation in which someone from a different country asks you to explain what you are studying. What would you say about education studies? What information would help the other person to translate your explanation to an international context?

DOI: 10.4324/9781003296935-4

Contextualising education studies outside the UK

The study of education in the European continent has a long tradition. It has its roots in ancient Greece, where fundamental questions related to education took the attention of key philosophers and thinkers (Curtis, 2011). In other parts of the world, issues about education were also a matter of concern and study since antiquity (Johnson and Stearns, 2022). The discussion has evolved and expanded globally, taking different shapes and forms that have crystallised in systematised and institutionalised approaches to studying educational matters. In our time, the study of education has been elevated to the highest academic level with in most of the university systems across the world. Many now offer programmes of study orientated to prepare practitioners, researchers, and other professionals involved in the world of education.

Table 3.1 provides some examples on the study of education in different parts of the world through the exploration of education-related university programmes.

Comparison with UK education studies

This section draws out a comparison between UK education studies programmes and what can be found in other countries.

In Portugal, the 'BA Education Sciences/Education/Education and Training' generally cover key disciplines in education (i.e., history, sociology, psychology, philosophy), curriculum studies, pedagogy, and research methods. Some courses have more practical components (e.g. through experience within different educational contexts). In general terms, the content of this undergraduate provision is very similar to UK education studies programmes. The case of Spain is very similar. The 'Bachelor's Degree in Pedagogy' and the 'Bachelor's Degree in Social Education' share some similarities with UK education studies courses. While the former Spanish programme provides a more general insight into theory and practice of education in formal and informal contexts, the latter is more focused on aspects related to informal education. Other European countries like Germany also have long traditions of undergraduate and postgraduate programmes in pedagogy and educational sciences.

In countries from the Americas like Chile, Canada, or USA, it is not easy to find programmes like UK education studies. Most provision is designed to prepare teachers. In Chile, some undergraduate courses cover different educational issues but have strong focus on learning processes and special educational needs and disabilities (SEND). In a few cases, universities from Canada offer undergraduate programmes that cover other aspects of non-formal provision such as adult education, aboriginal education, and social justice in education. However, it is more common to find these in the form of postgraduate programmes. In the USA, the flexibility to combine subjects allows students to personalise their studies. This is a form that may resemble the idea of combined or joint undergraduate honours in the UK system. UK education studies students can sometimes identify themselves as pursuing a major in education and minor in relevant subjects or areas including sociology, philosophy, psychology, and curriculum studies. In addition, some universities in the USA offer 'Bachelor's in Education Studies', and also undergraduate programmes in areas relating to childhood, youth, and learning/education, and social studies. These are non-teaching certificate programmes for individuals interested in gaining knowledge, skills, and understanding of educational theory.

Table 3.1 International education-related university programmes

International context		Information about education-related university programmes
Europe	Portugal	Faculties of education in Portugal offer a wide range of programmes. Access to pre-school and primary teaching qualifications is through the three-year 'BA Basic Education' (*Licenciatura em Educação Básica*) and a subsequent one-year master's degree in education. Like other countries, those graduated in a particular subject (e.g. chemistry, biology, literature) can obtain a secondary education teaching qualification studying a one-year 'MA Education' programme. Alternatively, faculties of education also offer programmes of study that are oriented to understand educational theory and processes in more general ways. These are non-teaching, three-year undergraduate education programmes (e.g. *Licenciatura em Ciências da Educação/Licenciatura em Educação/Licenciatura em Educação e Formação*) that provide graduates with knowledge and skills that enable them to act within and outside the formal educational system.
	Spain	Spanish universities offer a good range of undergraduate (four-years) and master's (one-year) programmes that focus on education. We can find undergraduate programmes that lead to the regulated profession of teacher of early years and primary education (*Grado en Educación Infantil/Grado en Educación Primaria*). There are also specialist routes in music education, speech and hearing, special educational needs and disabilities (SEND), foreign language and physical education. The one-year 'Master's Degree in Teacher Training in Secondary, Upper Secondary Education and Vocational Training' (*Máster Universitario en Formación del Profesorado de Educación Secundaria Obligatoria y Bachillerato, Formación Profesional y Enseñanzas de Idiomas*) is a requirement for graduate students in any discipline interested in teaching in schools of secondary and vocational education. Students can choose between different areas of specialism. Faculties of education also offer four-year undergraduate programmes that do not lead to a teaching qualification, focusing instead on a broader approach to the study of education. These courses are the 'Bachelor´s Degree in Pedagogy' (*Grado en Pedagogia*) and the 'Bachelor´s Degree in Social Education' (*Grado en Educación Social*). In addition, there is a rich portfolio of master's degrees in education that focus on particular aspects (e.g. leadership, social justice, SEND, educational psychology) designed for professional development or specialisation.
North America	Canada	A 'Bachelor of Education' programme in Canada typically lasts for four years and focuses on training teachers. If students want to study concurrent combined degrees, these generally last for five years. The education system in Canada is very decentralised and each province sets their own requirements for teachers; the training/qualification does not transfer between these provinces. A more open approach to the study of education can be found in some undergraduate and postgraduate programmes.

(*continued*)

Table 3.1 Continued

International context		Information about education-related university programmes
	USA	The USA university system is characterised by its size, heterogeneity, flexibility, and openness to combining subjects. Faculties of education allow students to graduate not only in education but also in combination with other areas of knowledge. A large majority of undergraduate programmes (four years) are intended for the training and qualification of teachers. Undergraduate education students must also take courses in a variety of the subjects taught in schools. Faculties of education offer a good number of master´s courses that mostly serve teachers. School districts incentivise the study of a 'Master's of Education', offering teachers fee waivers and pay rises. In some cases, a master's degree can be a requirement to teach.
South America	Chile	Faculties of education in Chile are mainly dedicated to teacher training. Programme titles and durations differ as the Chilean system has been immersed in a process of deregulation/marketisation. The number of master's programmes has grown in the last few years as a way of specialising teachers in aspects such as leadership, SEND, and curriculum. Faculties of psychology also offer courses that cover educational issues such as the Bachelor´s Degree in Educational Psychology (*Licenciatura en Psicopedagogia*).
Oceania	Australia	Undergraduate degrees (four years) and Master's degrees (one to two years) provide a teaching qualification and professional development for educators working in schools. Titles vary by university. Some titles include: 'Bachelor of Education (Early Childhood, Primary or Secondary)', 'Bachelor of Education Elementary', 'Bachelor of Teaching', 'Master of Education' and 'Master of Teaching'.
Asia	China	Faculties of education do not have a long tradition. It was in 1999 when the government began the transition of teacher training courses from normal schools to universities. Nowadays, these mainly offer three- to five-year 'Bachelor of Education' programmes to become an early years, primary or secondary school teacher. These programmes are highly regulated by national and regional governments. In recent years, some universities have started to offer master's programmes in pedagogy. Some also offer continuing education programmes and projects for in-service teachers or education-related professionals, such as social workers.
Africa	Nigeria	Faculties of education in Nigeria offer a 'Bachelor of Education' and a joint undergraduate degree with specialisation in teaching subjects. It is common to find within the faculties of education a department of educational foundation that focus on enriching the courses with content about traditional disciplines associated with education (sociology, philosophy, psychology, history, etc.). Some universities offer their own 'Bachelor of Educational Foundations'.

Some universities in Australia offer a three-year 'Bachelor of Education Studies' programme. This is a generalist degree that enables students to discover more about the education system and prepare them to work in many roles associated with the teaching and learning sector. The opportunities offered to graduates are very broad and such programmes look very similar to what we can find in education studies programmes in the UK. However, there are only very few universities offering this type of programme, they lack visibility, and are not very popular.

In the complex context of China, master's programmes in education have emerged in recent years. These programmes offer the students the possibility of deepening their understanding of educational issues. Most of these courses have an international orientation and in many cases are taught in English and delivered by/or in partnership with UK or Australian universities.

In the case of Nigeria, specific programmes in education studies are not very common. Nevertheless, the presence of departments of educational foundation within faculties of education plays an important role in providing a deeper and more theoretical understanding of issues.

Finally, in Middle East countries, teacher training is under strong national or regional authority control, and religious values are an important element. Initial teacher training is not always a university degree and courses like education studies can only be found in the form of master's programmes delivered by international universities.

> **Questions to consider**
>
> The Scandinavian countries have ranked continuously in the top of international assessments of education. Using the comparative foci exemplified within this chapter and conducting online research, undertake a comparison with one of these Northern European countries.

Conclusion

Education is a universal phenomenon and continues to grow as an area of study. The study of education takes different shapes and forms in distinct international contexts, with teacher training courses as the central element of faculties of education. However, as shown in this chapter, there are undergraduate and postgraduate courses that engage with more theoretical, informal and discipline-based studies of education and that are not limited to the preparation of primary or secondary teachers. These alternatives to teaching training courses share some aspects and elements with UK education studies programmes, but have developed their own characteristics and particularities. We should bear in mind that, even within the UK, education studies programmes feature different titles, content, and structures. The main challenge presented in this chapter is not the development of a common national framework for education studies programmes, but the sharing of a common approach that can help us to identify, explain, and promote education studies internationally.

To conclude, we would like to add that it is common to find units or modules on international matters and global education as part of education studies programmes. It is important to emphasise that education studies, both as a programme of study and as a discipline/field, has a strong global orientation and interest in the construction of a better world. However, this is only possible if this global approach is understood within a social justice framework that aligns education with citizenship building (Tarozzi and Torres, 2016). The education studies community shows a commitment to explore and propose educational responses to world challenges. In many cases, students are encouraged to depart from a view of the world that is volatile, uncertain, complex, and ambiguous (Stein, 2021). In a world that is becoming more globalised, it is expected that current and future professionals of education understand not only the national context but to engage with a complex educational world that is intertwined politically, culturally, and economically. As we have shown in this chapter, education studies programmes take different shapes and forms internationally. These programmes open up academic forums that nurture open, global, and critical debate. Such debate is, in many cases, more limited in initial teaching training programmes.

Acknowledgement

This work was supported by Grant *PID2020-114478RB-C22* funded by Ministerio de Ciencia e Innovación [Spanish Ministry of Science and Innovation]/Agencia Estatal de innovación [Spanish State Research Agency] 10.13039/501100011033.

Recommended reading

https://www.enic-naric.net/
This web site provides access to up-to-date information supplied by ENIC (European Network of Information Centres in the European Region) and NARIC (National Academic Recognition Information Centres in the European Union) on recognition of academic and professional qualifications for those wishing to study or work abroad.
https://www.topuniversities.com/
This web provides access to one of the most used international university rankings: the QS World University Ranking. It provides the basis for comparing universities worldwide, can be used to find out more about programmes and offers advice for studying abroad.
The UK Quality Assurance Agency for Higher Education (QAA) provides a national framework through the Subject Benchmark Statement for Education Studies. This can assist when making comparisons with other countries and is available in the following link:
https://www.qaa.ac.uk/docs/qaa/subject-benchmark-statements/subject-benchmark-statement-education-studies.pdf
Sant, E., Davies, I., Pashby, K. and Shultz, L. (2018) *Global Citizenship Education: A Critical Introduction to Key Concepts and Debates.* London: Bloomsbury.
This book is used as a textbook for different units or modules in education studies programmes. It is useful to introduce undergraduate and postgraduate students to key ideas, issues, concepts, and debates about global citizenship and education.

References

Bartlett, S., and Burton, D. (2016) *Introduction to Education Studies* (fourth edition). London: Sage.
Curtis, W. (2011) The Philosophy of Education. In B. Dufour and W. Curtis (Eds), *Studying Education: An Introduction to the Key Disciplines in Education Studies* (pp. 59–84). Buckingham: Open University Press.
Johnson, M.S. and Stearns P.N. (2022) *Education in World History.* London: Routledge.
Simon, C.A. and Ward, S. (2020) *A Student's Guide to Education Studies.* London: Routledge.
Stein, S. (2021) Reimagining global citizenship education for a volatile, uncertain, complex, and ambiguous (VUCA) world. *Globalisation, Societies and Education* **19**(4), pp. 482–495, https://doi.org/10.1080/14767724.2021.1904212
Tarozzi, M. and Torres, C.A. (2016) *Global Citizenship Education and the Crisis of Multiculturalism.* London: Routledge, https://doi.org/10.5040/9781474236003

4 Exploring the identity of an undergraduate education programme

Jenny Elliott, Rupert Knight, Sharon Clancy and Colin Morley

SUMMARY POINTS

- Undergraduate education programmes embrace multi-disciplinary academic subjects and offer pathways to a diverse range of careers. They have become very popular in English Higher Education.
- Nonetheless, there remain misconceptions about these programmes, stemming from the ways in which they developed in England.
- Using interview data, together with reflections of the authors on their professional experiences, this chapter documents the thinking that went into designing a specific undergraduate education programme at a university in England.
- In doing so, it considers some of the tensions inherent in developing the identity of such programmes.

Introduction

Questions to consider

Why are you studying education? How did you explain your studies to friends and family, some of whom perhaps thought you were going in to teaching?

It is likely that you are reading this chapter because you are an undergraduate student on a BA Education or BA Education Studies programme. It is also likely that, as you announced your plans for starting your course to friends and family, many of their responses were connected to the idea of becoming a teacher. For example:

- 'How great, you're going into teaching'.
- 'I've got a friend who's just finished their PGCE and would be good to talk to about what teaching's like'.
- 'Is it primary or secondary you want to do?'
- 'Such a great job. Challenging, but so rewarding. It's a calling, rather than a job'.
- 'Blimey, rather you than me'.
- 'So, what subject are you planning on teaching?'

DOI: 10.4324/9781003296935-5

You undoubtedly had various conversations, where you tried to explain to the well-meaning enquirer that your undergraduate education programme doesn't qualify you to become a teacher. Instead, you are studying education as a discrete, intellectual and scholarly subject as worthy of its own position on university web pages as psychology, sociology, physics, German, English, geology, etc.

It is unsurprising that undergraduate education and education studies courses are, at the time of writing in 2022 in England, still little understood, and that some 20 years after the subject entered UK universities such conversations are still common. McCulloch and Cowan (2018) discuss research that has explored the development of what is called 'Educational Sciences' that have existed in European countries since 1944, and the Baltic states and Western Australia – areas of the world, where education is already well-established as an intellectually robust, interdisciplinary subject, distinct from learning to teach (see also further international comparisons in Chapter 3). McCulloch and Cowan point out that whilst in Scotland, education as an academic and scholarly subject started emerging in the late nineteenth century, in England, until relatively recently, it was impossible to study education as an undergraduate degree without learning to become a teacher.

The interconnectedness of education as a subject and teaching is a further complication, as Furlong (2013) discusses. He argues that locating initial teacher education (ITE) courses within universities from the last quarter of the twentieth century onwards, rather than in teacher training colleges (as was done previously), has further strengthened the sense that if you are an education student at university, then you will also be learning how to be a teacher. In fact, the study of education at higher education level from 1968 was rewarded with a Bachelor of Education which was seen as being a prerequisite to teach, rather than as a summation of the subject the student had just studied (such as a Bachelor of Arts or Science). The ongoing tensions and challenges of developing a clear identity of education as a discipline, disconnected from teaching, Furlong argues, are nested within—and intricately aligned with—the tensions and challenges of the changing nature and identity of universities and university education in England. Universities, Furlong suggests, struggle with a clear idea of what they actually are, which intersects with what he refers to as education's 'lack of consensus and … coherence of some of the more established disciplines' whilst institutionally and politically functioning 'very much as a discipline in its own right, even though, for most of its existence, it has not been 'master' of its own destiny' (Furlong, 2013: 4).

The authors of this chapter work on a newly established (at the time of writing) BA Education course within a School of Education (SoE) at a university. This university also offers courses to primary and secondary PGCE students, as well as to those pursuing masters and doctoral studies related to education. The BA Education 'space', occupied by the course founders, module convenors, students, curriculum, teaching and learning, acts as a petri-dish within the wider context of the university. This enables the investigation of the contestations, difficulties and successes of articulating a clear course identity, allowing for consideration of what actually is a BA Education/Education Studies programme?

Developing an undergraduate education programme

Question to consider
When and why did the undergraduate education programme that you are on come into being?

There isn't enough space in this chapter to explore in any meaningful way the changes that have taken place since 1998, when New Labour's introduction of up-front university fees (£1,000) accelerated what has been termed the *neo-liberalisation, marketisation and commodification* of higher education. There are suggestions for further reading about neoliberalism at the end of this chapter.

What the authors of this chapter relate, however, is the lived experience of establishing a BA Education programme in 2016 within the neoliberal higher education context at the time. This serves to exemplify that university programmes do not exist in a vacuum as neutral, universally understood phenomena, but instead are shaped and formed by the economic, political, cultural and social landscape within which their institution is positioned. An interview with one of the BA Education course founders, Alex (a pseudonym), revealed a number of factors underpinning the development of the new undergraduate programme within the SoE, exemplifying this very complex interplay of historical, cultural, sociological, political and economic factors:

> *At the time, there was a general anxiety about whether we were going to have initial teacher education in the long run, and we were mindful of diversifying people's work and creating new opportunities. We had done well in (a number of) world rankings, and yet we didn't have an identity as a field or a discipline. We were quite fragmented. We had some core things that we cared about, but we didn't have a sense of being together as educationists around anything in particular.*
>
> *It transpired that (other respected universities) were all moving at the same time. There was a combination of a maturing discipline from the sixties and seventies and the public education budget was over £90 billion a year, much more than that if you include other areas of education. We found ourselves saying "Isn't it about time we said you can study education for a career in education? Let's do that! We're going to own the discipline and really define what it is that we do, who we are and what we're about".*
>
> *We wanted something that says: "We're Education and we're proud of it!" We can attract high quality undergraduate students to study education.*

Alex's comments on the reflections at the time within the SoE about developing an undergraduate Education programme indicate that these were informed by:

- Confidence in claiming education as an academic space, discrete from teacher education and worthy of its own, bespoke undergraduate degree.
- An understanding of the value of educational knowledge for graduates within a society that spends a large section of its budget on education.
- A sense that it could support a greater shared purpose, cohesion and identity within the SoE itself.
- Market (neoliberal) forces: other reputable universities offering similar programmes
- Education policy: uncertainty as to whether universities would maintain a foothold in initial teacher training provision.
- Economics: the need to diversify the SoE workforce, bring money into the school and keep jobs.

We now go on to discuss the next steps taken after these initial considerations: how the undergraduate education programme where we work was conceptualised and planned out on paper.

We juxtapose this with the eclectic, diverse nature of the programme's tutor team and discuss the ensuing shape-shifting dynamics between these two elements, and the impact this may have on the programme's emerging identity.

Developing a course identity

> **Questions to consider**
>
> What do you learn on your course and why?
> How is your course structured and why?
> Who is in your course tutor team and what are their areas of professional expertise and why?
> What does it mean to be a student of an undergraduate education programme and why?

Kelly (1996) writes about the difference between the 'planned curriculum' (what is written down to be taught) and the 'received curriculum' (what actually takes place within the learning space, in terms of what tutors teach and what is learnt by students). Returning to the conversation with Alex, he revealed the original narrative of the programme:

> *We wanted to have strands/themes that run through all three years but start with the first year rooted in the founding disciplines: psychology, sociology, philosophy, history of education. We wanted it to … (start) on those traditional disciplinary areas of education and that needed to be quite explicit in the first year. By the time you get to the third year, we wanted that to switch to much more about what Education looks and feels like **now** and what the future of education might be.*
>
> *We are very inclusive, of course. By the end of the degree, we want people who can go into publishing, or international development, or support, or teaching, and have tools that are the foundations but also the new tools of Education.*
>
> *We also wanted to bring in a strong emphasis on scholarship, method, research, a kind of self-improvement. We wanted it to be about Education as an object of study, but we also wanted it to be **educational** and to be about how to study and improve it as well.*

This serves to outline key themes that were emerging for an undergraduate education programme:

- Honouring education's underpinning disciplines: e.g., philosophy, history, sociology and psychology.
- Grounding itself in these scholarly disciplines whilst simultaneously looking forward and outwards. A tree analogy is helpful here: rooted in the earth that has given it life, yet at the same time, reaching upwards and outwards towards the skies.
- Respecting both educational knowledge and process – learning the 'what' of educational knowledge as well as the 'how' to be an educational scholar and researcher.

As well as these diverse ambitions, the new programme was also to celebrate diversity within the tutor team. The education tutor team at our university has a wide range of educational experiences and qualifications, although (for the reasons listed above) none of them holds a degree in Education. Instead, many of them come to the BA from positions of early years, primary, secondary, adult, further, higher and alternative education teaching, or have navigated their way, via their research interests, into the SoE. Other schools within the university are likely to be populated with colleagues whose research, and sometimes professional practice, has brought them to their university teaching and many of these colleagues have learnt how to convey their subject knowledge to undergraduates once in post, slotting into existing practice and with the support of developmental courses such as Post Graduate Certificates in Higher Education. In contrast, in schools of education, the research expertise of the teaching staff is education and educational practice. Staff members therefore bring with them clear, research-informed ideas of what good teaching and learning looks like. They also bring with them their own *positionality*. This comprises their personal and educational histories, political views and life experiences, in which theory and practice of education serve to illuminate one another. When this interacts with the 'planned' curriculum, a unique, dynamic process emerges.

Tutors' research-informed confidence in what comprises good teaching and learning is also added into this complex mix. This serves to contribute to the specific identity of an undergraduate education programme in that their pedagogies invariably and deliberately differ from the 'banking model' (Freire, 1970) of filling a passive learner with accepted knowledge, which is the general practice in large lecture theatres at many universities. This might also be the experience of many who have recently left the increasingly knowledge-oriented secondary school sector, influenced indirectly by the likes of E. D. Hirsch (2009). Indeed, we proudly tell students that 'our sessions are our laboratories!' and this pedagogical shift forms part of the 'knowledge how' of being an Education student rather than part of the 'knowledge that'.

Our starting point, therefore, is a *dialogic* view of education. Essentially, this is a vision of learning as a collective endeavour, grounded in the work of thinkers like Bakhtin (1986) who saw all utterances as part of a chain of communication. More recently, Mercer and Littleton (2007) have described a process of 'interthinking', whereby learners co-construct understanding in a way that surpasses any individual's capacity. Alexander (2020) suggests that deliberative, cumulative and purposeful dialogic learning like this depends on a learning environment that is collective, supportive and reciprocal. There are strong arguments for working dialogically on social, democratic and cognitive grounds. However, as Alexander himself acknowledges, this entails an often-challenging culture shift on the part of both teaching staff and students. Some of the tensions in our sessions are apparent in Table 4.1, in which we offer some commonly encountered initial student comments and our responses:

Bringing it all together

So, where does this leave us? Figure 4.1 positions education at our university at the intersection of four overlapping influences situated within a neoliberal higher education context.

The education course at our university draws on the four 'foundational' disciplines underpinning many other education programmes. However, it frequently goes beyond an interdisciplinary integration of these foundations to what we might think of as examples of a *transdisciplinary* approach, transcending boundaries and creating a coherent whole. For example, many of our modules have a disciplinary and boundary spanning function which critically examine ideas of e.g. *curriculum, equality* and *knowledge*. In doing so, we are able to explore important questions such as the nature of

Table 4.1 Student views and tutor responses from the education programme

Student comment	Tutor response (pedagogic rationale)
I want to sit at the back of a lecture theatre and not speak to anyone. That's what I was expecting when I came to university.	We don't really lecture. We work dialogically and collaboratively. We value the 'funds of knowledge' our students bring.
Why can't you just record the sessions, so I can watch them in my own time?	Recordings can be important for access and equity and assumed a new importance during the pandemic. However, they don't really capture the energy and exchange of contributions around the room that we all feed off, nor the asides of pair and group work. There are deeper philosophical reservations about perpetuating individualistic approaches to education where it is positioned as a commodity to be consumed in an atomised way. Often the best collaborations, connections, networks, conversations and thinking come from walking out of the room together after a session and going off for a coffee.
I find working with other people difficult.	Education *is* about other people. Realising that there is no one 'right' view or answer; learning to respectfully critique your own and others' opinions; learning about the value of collaborative learning as well as how to navigate the delights and difficulties experienced when working with others.
I hate doing presentations.	We know that by explaining your learning to others, you consolidate it for yourself. We respect your interpretation of the course and see you as capable of sometimes leading the learning. We know that learning to articulate your ideas publicly will stand you in good stead for your life as a graduate.
We'd prefer it if the tutor shared their expertise more, rather than us having to share with the group.	We don't set ourselves up as the sole 'experts' in the room. We position ourselves as guides a little further along the journey than our students and view knowledge as co-constructed.
I just want to be told how to pass the assessment.	This may be how you've been positioned as a learner throughout your compulsory schooling, and we'd like to challenge this. We'd often rather not assess in the ways that the university requires us to, and we want you to learn to critique assessment processes and practices. We want you to take ownership of your own progress by engaging with formative feedback and negotiating your next steps with your work. We want you to experience a variety of different assessment models, so that you can find ways that work for you to express and demonstrate your learning.
I don't like using 'I' in my assignments or presentations.	We realise this might seem unfamiliar, but we are interested in your personal, well-argued interpretations of evidence in your work. The use of the first person is fundamental to this as it embeds you within the context and acknowledges your own positionality.

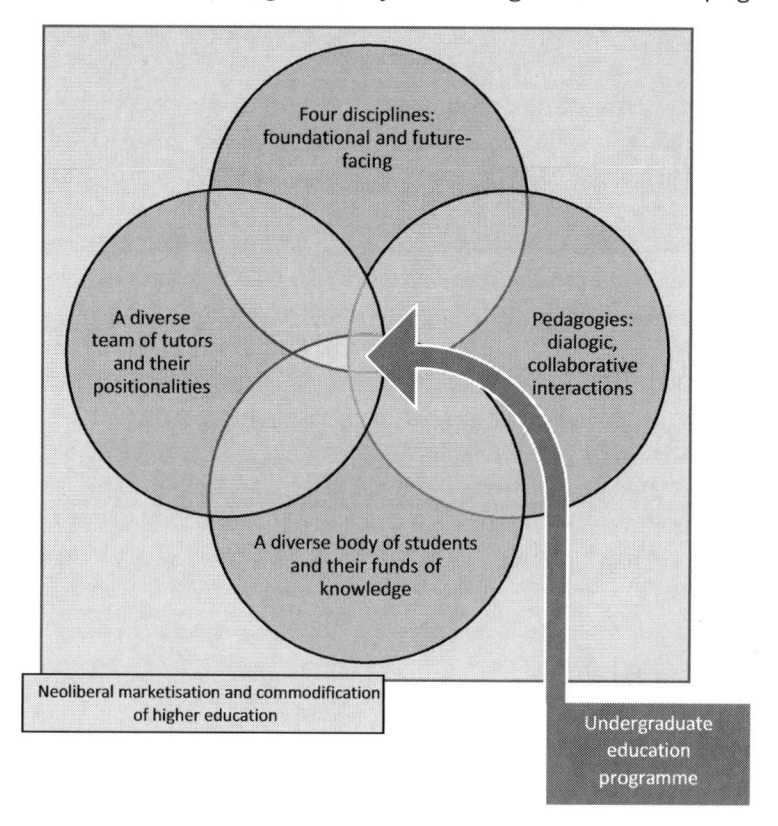

Figure 4.1 An undergraduate education programme within the neoliberal university

what is taught and learnt, why the learning of some forms of knowledge is privileged over others, and who decides.

The enactment of our course is influenced by the stories and histories of the teaching staff. Their positionality, acknowledged and shared with students, ensures a dynamic interpretation of the course content, which is brought to life with examples from their professional lives. *Reflexivity* is a term often used in relation to educational research to refer to a critical self-awareness of the impact one's biases, beliefs and experiences on a process they are involved with (e.g. Berger, 2015) and this pertains also to our teaching roles. To illustrate this, consider the contrasting perspectives of two of the authors. One is a former primary school teacher with extensive experience in teacher education and this leads to a tendency to see educational issues through the lens of the classroom and the experiences of young people in the compulsory education phase. The other is former head of public engagement at our university, with a community leadership background and a specialism in further and adult education whose lens is primarily developed through teaching adults in the further education, community and voluntary sectors.

Into this complex mix is added the unique backgrounds of our students. As implied in Table 4.1, we see students not as vessels to be filled but individuals bringing many assets and important perspectives to a conversation about education. In this, we draw on the idea of learners having 'funds of knowledge' representing 'ample cultural and cognitive resources with great potential utility for classroom instruction' (Moll et al., 1992: 134). The sharing of students' lived experiences of discrimination, for example, has informed the direction of teaching sessions, the sources included on reading lists and within module materials.

The fourth influence, and in many ways, the glue binding together the whole, is what we have termed 'dialogic collaborative interactions'. Much of Table 4.1 implies a form of pedagogy in taught sessions based on dialogue and in this we see dialogue as distinct from simply spoken interaction. For example, many university sessions feature questions, but they may not be 'authentic' questions for which the answer is not already known and there may not be genuine engagement with the response (Nystrand et al., 2003). However, dialogic education is much more about a value system than a specific form of communication. For this reason, we might more productively talk about a dialogic *stance* (Boyd and Markarian, 2011). By this we mean the creation of an environment for students and university staff alike that welcomes and takes seriously different perspectives and in which there is collaborative effort towards meaningful goals. As long as we can maintain the 'dialogic space' that appears when diverse voices and diverse pedagogies meet within the context of the modules and their content, the education course at our university will continue to be dynamic and evolving. Such dynamism and evolution rest at the very core of the identity of an undergraduate education programme.

Recommended reading

Harvey, D. (2005) *A brief history of neoliberalism*. Oxford: Oxford University Press.
This is an excellent introduction to the concept of neoliberalism more generally.
Ball, S. (2012) Performativity, commodification and commitment: An i-spy guide to the neoliberal university. *Journal of Education Studies* **60**(1), pp. 17–28.
Tomlinson, M. and Watermeyer, R. (2020) When masses meet markets: credentialism and commodification in twenty first century Higher Education. *Discourse: Studies in the Cultural Politics of Education* **43**(2), pp. 1–15.
Wilkinson, L.C. and Wilkinson, M.D. (2020) Value for money and the commodification of higher education. *Teaching in Higher Education: Critical Perspectives*. https://doi.org/10.1080/13562517.2020.1819226
These three are helpful for starting to develop your understanding of neoliberalism specifically in relation to higher education.
Furlong, J. (2013) *Education – An anatomy of the Discipline: Rescuing the university project?* Abingdon: Routledge.
Furlong's book gives an account of the history of education as a discipline and suggests how it might be repositioned for the future.
McCulloch, G. and Cowan, S. (2018) *A Social History of Educational Studies and Research*. Abingdon: Routledge.
The authors explore the development of the field of education and education studies within the UK since 1944. They argue that education is a contested interdisciplinary course, shaped by the history, politics and sociology of the higher education landscape.

References

Alexander, R. (2020) *A Dialogic Teaching Companion*. Abingdon: Routledge.
Bakhtin, M. (1986) *Speech Genres and Other Late Essays*. Austin: University of Texas Press.
Berger, R. (2015) Now I see it, now I don't: researcher's position and reflexivity in qualitative research. *Qualitative Research* **15**(2), pp. 219–234. https://doi.org/10.1177/1468794112468475
Boyd, M. and Markarian, W. (2011) Dialogic teaching: talk in service of a dialogic stance. *Language and Education* **25**(6), pp. 515–534. https://doi.org/10.1080/09500782.2011.597861
Freire, P. (1970) *Pedagogy of the Oppressed*. London: Continuum.
Furlong, J. (2013) *Education – An Anatomy of the Discipline: Rescuing the University Project?* Abingdon: Routledge.

Hirsch, E. (2009) *The Making of Americans: Democracy and Our Schools.* New Haven: Yale University Press.
Kelly, A.V. (1996) *The Curriculum: Theory and Practice.* London: Sage.
McCulloch, G. and Cowan, S. (2018) *A Social History of Educational Studies and Research.* Abingdon: Routledge.
Mercer, N. and Littleton, K. (2007) *Dialogue and the Development of Children's Thinking: A Sociocultural Approach.* Abingdon: Routledge.
Moll, L., Amanti, C., Neff, D. and Gonzalez, N. (1992) Funds of knowledge for teaching: using a qualitative approach to connect homes and classrooms. *Theory into Practice* **31**(2), pp. 132–141.
Nystrand, M., Wu, L., Gamoran, A., Zeisler, S. and Long, D. (2003) Questions in time: investigating the structure and dynamics of unfolding classroom discourse. *Discourse Processes* **35**(2), pp. 135–198. https://doi.org/10.1207/S15326950DP3502_3

Section 2
Practices and pedagogies of education studies

Rebecca Morris

This section presents a series of insightful chapters relating to the practice of education studies. By 'practice', we are referring to the myriad elements and approaches that contribute to the development and enactment of education-related courses. We hear from nine groups of authors who describe and critically engage with their own practices, sharing perspectives on issues which are central to teaching and learning in our field. These chapters draw upon many of the themes and ideas presented in the opening section, and encourage us as readers to explore and question the role of various practical approaches in the subject. Readers are invited to reflect upon the methods and perspectives presented here, and to ask themselves what it means to be an education studies student in terms of what you *do*, how you learn and the opportunities that this presents for the development of skills, knowledge and future roles.

The section begins with a chapter by Nick Pratt, Abigail O'Brien, Marlon Cole and Bethan Cillo. The authors (two tutors and two students) consider the nature of learning and the role of theory for helping us to make sense of educational issues. It provides a helpful foundation on these issues, and one which is likely to inform readers' engagement with subsequent chapters. The second chapter by Sophie Ward, Laura Mazzoli Smith and Teti Dragas prompts Education Studies students to reflect on their beliefs about, and experience of, education in order to develop their own personal philosophy. The authors ask us to consider challenging questions such as what we understand as a 'good' education and to reflect upon how these perspectives might be different to our colleagues and peers around us. They use their experience of working with digital storytelling as a method of unpacking and exploring personal stories and philosophies, and support readers to have a go at working with this approach themselves.

In Chapter 3, Tristan Middleton, Rick Millican, Sian Templeton and Lynda Kay discuss the humanist ethos and relational pedagogy approaches that they have found effective for supporting Education Studies students with the assessment and feedback elements of their courses. They present a discussion of how engaging with this ethos and practice has supported the empowerment of students in relation to their learning and has promoted resilience and academic success across the degree and into employment. The fourth chapter – by Mark Tymms – continues this theme of student learning and achievement, taking a psychological lens to introduce students to the concept of motivation and its relationship with learning and wellbeing. The chapter explores the role of educators (both students and staff) in promoting positive learner behaviours, using Self-Determination Theory as a helpful theoretical tool for thinking about these issues.

We next turn to considering global and international perspectives and participation within Education Studies courses. Leanne Cameron, Rafael Mitchell, Gurpinder Lalli and Brendan Bartram

DOI: 10.4324/9781003296935-6

present findings from a recent study exploring the role and value of comparative and international education (CIE) within education-related degree programmes. They provide a valuable introduction to the field of CIE and show, through their analysis of modules at 24 UK universities, the important debates and issues around the global and international content being taught to students and the need for further research in this area. In the following chapter, student and staff authors Yutong Liu, Rebecca Morris, Tasha Peditto, Lingxi Peng and Ross Purves present a discussion of the experiences of international students on Education Studies courses. Drawing on the personal perspectives of the three international co-authors, the opportunities and challenges associated with studying on a UK-based programme are explored. Students from both UK and international contexts, and university staff, are encouraged to think about how they can support student success and wellbeing through the development of more inclusive learning and social environments for international students.

In Chapter 7, Louise Gascoine and Laura Mazzoli Smith introduce us to some important issues relating to a commonly found element of Education Studies programmes: research methods courses. The authors focus on the pedagogy of methods modules, using their own as a case study for presenting a student-centred approach underpinned by ideas of pragmatism, and supporting students to apply their learning for the development of their own personal research interests. Following this, Dave Cudworth discusses an area of Education Studies which has grown in prominence in recent years. He persuasively argues that education for sustainability should be a key element of teaching and learning in all educational settings and provides an in-depth and insightful discussion of the power of connecting students with nature, in this case via forest schools. The section concludes with a chapter from Cheryl Cane about the role and value of arts-based learning in education studies. This chapter considers the important contributions that arts-based pedagogies and practices can make to the wider curriculum and draws our attention to some of the challenges and tensions associated with this kind of work. The author shares the potentially promising outcomes for students and staff that can come from working with arts-based approaches.

5 Knowing learning matters

Nick Pratt, Abigail O'Brien, Marlon Cole and Bethan Cillo

SUMMARY POINTS

- Learning is fundamental to education studies since in one sense or another all education is about learning.
- What learning *is* requires careful thought. It can be both a process (of learning) and a product (what has been learned). Moreover, learning can be not only in the mind but also in the body, since we learn to do things as well as to know about them.
- To make sense of learning we must theorise about it – where theorising means the process of creating a coherent and systematic understanding of something. This involves a process of theorisation and a resulting theory.
- Theorising about learning allows us to consider real-life practices in different ways to understand them as learning events.
- The theories we develop can help to make events which have become familiar, seem unfamiliar again, such that we can see and understand them in new ways.

Introducing learning and theory

In this chapter, we explore both the nature of learning and the idea of theory. Two of us (Marlon and Beth) are students and the other two (Abigail and Nick) are staff, all working on our BA Education Studies programme. Our aim is to show that these two ideas – learning and theory – are very much inseparable and are fundamental for the study of education.

To begin, let us state the obvious. Education is fundamentally *about* learning and hence education studies must involve studying the notion of learning. This may seem straightforward, but learning is a complex idea and much misunderstood. For example, it's not uncommon for the winners of TV quiz shows to be described in the media as 'the world's cleverest people', simply because they have a lot of memorised knowledge about everyday topics. Meanwhile, someone working in a home caring for the elderly might be described as quite ordinary, yet will possess great skill and experience which allows them to 'understand' their task and the people and materials with which they work. Note, though, that what they have learned may not even be expressible in words – like the quiz answers are – but might be learned 'in the body' (embodied), just as the classic 'riding a bike' example is. We are born with largely reflex actions, yet by old age, even if we do not have paper qualifications, we all have many skills, and both conceptual and emotional understanding of a great range of things.

DOI: 10.4324/9781003296935-7

Learning, then, is complex and our understanding of it is still, and perhaps always will be, only partial. One complexity is the cognitive/embodied difference outlined above; but a second is that it can also be understood as taking place at different scales. Zoom right in and neuroscientists will try to explain learning in terms of neural networks, brain signals etc. But zoom right out and sociologists will explain learning in terms of social patterns – for example the fact that the best predictors of academic success in the UK continue to be ethnicity and socio-economic status (Sammons *et al.*, 2015). The study of learning spans a disciplinary spectrum, from neuroscience, through cognitive psychology, social psychology and sociology. No wonder education libraries are so full!

But one thing ties all these ideas together. This is the notion that learning is fundamentally about *making sense*. Despite the contemporary tendency to talk about learning as an object, a noun – something I have *acquired*, as 'my learning' – it should be clear that learning must also be thought of as a process, a verb – something that I *do*, the action of making sense, or of development. Furthermore, this action of sense-making, of deliberately seeking out and organising ideas so that one can give an account of something, is what we call *theorising*.

Those relatively new to academic work might be more familiar with the word *theory* than *theorising*. Here, though, we want to make the following points: that learning involves *activity*; that the activity of learning is about *making sense of things* (sometimes consciously, sometimes implicitly); that doing this in an organised, deliberate way so that one can explain these things is called *theorising*; and that the outcome of this is a *theory* – i.e. a relatively stable, considered way to explain and make sense of something. Note how for both learning and theorising/theory there is a verb (doing) form and a resulting noun (object).

Moreover, Swedberg (2012; 2016) has a nice analogy for the *process* of theorisation comparing the role of the academic worker to that of a lawyer prosecuting a case. He points out that theorisation can be thought of as both discovery and justification. Discovering theory tends to be a convoluted and messy process of exploring, trying out and rearranging ideas, until one can 'produce something interesting and novel' (Swedberg 2012: 6). At this point, the theorisation starts to become more organised and the academic can justify her ideas clearly and concisely. Metaphorically, Swedberg argues, this is like the lawyer preparing and presenting a case; 'the context of discovery is where you have to figure out who the murderer is, while the context of justification is where you have to prove your case in court' (Swedberg 2012: 6). Relating this to our previous point about action and outcome, the resulting case/theorisation, recorded in the court proceedings for posterity, becomes 'the theory'. Of course, in social sciences, including education, such cases are often open to review; as people think about the ideas in new ways and as new research provides further evidence, academics are re-discovering theory and we all must return to court for a retrial.

We hope that the foregoing discussion offers you an insight into the idea that learning is complex, so complex that it needs different ways of theorising it to offer different kinds of insights – like spotlights which illuminate it from different angles, allowing different ideas about it to emerge. Meanwhile, this is what we mean by theorising: the attempt to organise these approaches to understanding learning into arguments which then can stand as theories and offer access to the idea for others. In that sense theories are said to 'frame' the topic (of learning) because they offer an organised way to think about it.

On the education studies programme on which we all study and work, this process of theorising learning and using such theory to explain experiences is explicitly addressed in one of the modules, entitled Learning Matters. As part of the assessment for this module the staff challenge students to create a five minute 'Talking Heads' video in which they (students) record themselves speaking to camera about a learning event from their own lives and how they can reconceptualise and explain it in relation to one or more established learning theories. The task therefore asks them to theorise learning taking place in a particular context, working with both the already established theory in the literature and their own novel theorising. In the rest of this chapter Beth and Marlon summarise their experiences of doing this task, before Nick and Abigail then pick up their accounts in illustrating some of the general points above, in practice.

Marlon:

The five minute 'Talking head' video involved applying an aspect of learning theory to a non-traditional educational context. Instantly, I felt challenged (not least in being camera shy!) as this method of assessment was new to me, requiring some initial reading in the area to feel comfortable making a start with how I was going to make sense of learning. During lectures, I began to think about classic learning theories mainly through a sociocultural lens as I began to understand how to apply these concepts situated in practice and educational contexts, needed for the analysis in the assessment. It wasn't until reading "Learning theory: Beyond the Three Wise (White) Men", a blog piece [https://plymthinked.wordpress.com/2020/11/16/learning-theory-beyond-the-three-wise-white-men/], that I was inspired to think outside the box, deciding to steer away from focussing on an already well covered learning aspect, in the search for something more original. I ultimately landed on the Kaizen philosophy, which I had learnt a little about through media in the midst of this process by chance. Although a Japanese business model, I saw an interesting opportunity to apply it as a learning theory for team sports, namely football. My thought process was that already being apprehensive about the method of assessment and arriving at this slightly unfamiliar learning theory, I would choose a context I was familiar with, to help best make sense of learning.

Through reading it became clear that Kaizen is comprised of five key tenets, whilst centred around continual improvement, which is made possible through the use of a reflective-based cycle. Drawing on my experiences of football training allowed me to think about how to apply various aspects of this philosophy in the situated learning context. For example, in Kaizen philosophy perfection is not possible; that is, no area of learning can be 'completed' – I recognised that there is also no way to 'complete' skills in football and always room for improvement through training. In doing so I was challenged to think about my preconceived perception of knowing and learning, questioning whether this new concept contrasted with my previous thoughts. I developed my understanding of learning to be rather social constructivist orientated, seeing knowledge as embodied, which can be measured in practice via continuous development of small, manageable goals. Regular reflection is important to avoid confirming bias of what we think we 'know' and keeps us questioning ourselves which aids progression. Through choosing to focus on a learning philosophy that was less known to me and usually applied in a different context, I was forced to really dive into what it was all about and explore implications for learning from a completely new place which I found to be very motivating and exciting. This ultimately led to me gaining more out of the task than if I had chosen a familiar classic learning theory, an approach I decided to take in subsequent assignments for other modules and will continue to use in the future when learning about learning.

> **Beth:**
>
> Taking part in the talking heads assignment allowed me to make sense of a variety of learning theories in greater depth. Prior to completing the talking heads assignment, I viewed learning as a process as greatly complicated and a broad subject that I would never gain a solid understanding of. However, I found that being able to relate it to a personal experience which I have a greater understanding of allowed me to grasp the subject with a deeper understanding.
>
> During my talking heads assignment, I focused on three learning theories which included Situated Learning by Lave and Wenger, Zone of Proximal Development (ZPD) by Vygotsky and Scaffolding by Wood, Burner and Ross. My personal topic that I chose to relate these learning theories to was starting a new job working behind a bar, learning skills such as working the till, pouring the pints and serving customers. I chose this topic as I have previously worked behind a bar for many years; from being a new member of staff and being trained, to progressing to training the new members of staff myself.
>
> Situated learning theory by Lave and Wegner is a process that suggests that learning is situated in a specific context and embedded within a particular social and physical environment. My learning context linked to this as the new member of staff would be learning the necessary knowledge in the authentic setting of the bar. Additionally, I used the ZPD by Vygotsky. This theory focuses on what an individual can complete without assistance and what they can achieve with guidance from a more knowledgeable other, which works alongside my learning context as a new member of staff would have to be taught the required skills needed for the job from a more knowledgeable other, in this case the bar manager or a well-trained member of staff. The last learning theory that I linked to my learning context was Scaffolding by Wood, Bruner and Ross. Scaffolding is a process that enables someone to achieve a task or goal that would not be possible unassisted, in my learning context, scaffolding would be carried out by the manager or other staff member modelling the skills required to carry out the job.
>
> Before completing my talking heads assignment, I viewed learning as a process as a subject that I was not yet, or may never be, knowledgeable enough to gain an understanding on or explain to others. I would look at a task and immediately decide whether it was achievable or not in that current moment; if I felt I was going to struggle with the task I would automatically assume it was not worth attempting. However, from completing my talking heads assignment I am now able to look at a task, regardless of the difficulty and find a solution to attempt to complete it. I still believe that learning as a process is complex but I now do not believe that it is unattainable for me, and many others, to understand.

In many ways, we hope that these accounts from Beth and Marlon speak for themselves. There are many things all four of us could comment on but with limited space to write, here we have picked up just two: the process of theorising; and the complexity of learning.

The process of theorising

Marlon describes his feelings towards tackling the task ahead in terms of being 'apprehensive' due to the unfamiliarity with learning theory. The process of theorising is, itself, in part what learning theory entails. Because it is a journey of discovery into the unknown, all who theorise will encounter these feelings; beginning, and experienced, academics alike. Marlon describes it as something 'new' that requires 'some initial reading in the area to feel comfortable making a start on getting to grips with how ... to make sense of learning'. This 'making sense of learning' can be daunting. In our discussions we noted a cyclical process here, of struggling to make the unfamiliar, the confusing new ground, become familiar. Good idea, therefore, to begin with 'some classic learning theories', a place of familiarity before being 'forced to really dive into what it was all about and explore implications for learning from a completely new place' as one realises the implications of considering established theories in new contexts. Discovery is creative and exciting; but trying to *justify* one's new thinking can end up pointing to the holes in the argument that still need patching up, holes that get deeper and wider as you explore them further. Like an ever-expanding game of minesweeper, when the process is begun you cannot yet see what hides below the unturned squares. The more you explore the more there is to see, be wary of, and learn about the field.

Like Marlon, Beth also felt she 'was going to struggle' and that this learning about learning as a process and a subject was something she 'was not yet' and 'may never be, knowledgeable enough to gain an understanding of'. She found three different perspectives (Lave and Wenger, 1991; Vygotsky, 1978; Wood et al., 1976) to work with and this breadth helped in allowing her to theorise learning her job as involving three different elements. Marlon, on the other hand, focuses on just one idea, but explores it more deeply. Again, this illustrates the challenge of trying to deal with something as complex as learning. One can always find a different way to make sense of it or can theorise more deeply. Breadth inevitably comes at the expensive of depth; a choice we all must make in academic work. Just when should I stop reading?

The complexity of learning

The complexity of learning can leave us all with some discomfort, which is natural for the process of theorising since, as Swedberg notes, 'what you are after ... is something *new*, something that does not yet exist' (Swedberg, 2016: 14, emphasis in original); to 'think outside the box' and ultimately take up the 'interesting opportunity to apply it' as Marlon so clearly describes it. Moreover, as Marlon notes, 'no area of learning can be "completed"' – what starts off as familiar soon becomes unfamiliar as a new perspective is opened up on it and learning grows. And although Beth feels more confident to be 'able to look at a task, regardless of the difficulty and find a solution to attempt to complete it' we would all argue that understanding, and therefore, learning, is never 'finished'. But note how this gets mixed up with the need to demonstrate that you *do* 'understand it', that you *have* 'learnt it', particularly when an assessment of some kind demands that you demonstrate 'your learning' (individually, and as a noun again!). Summative assessments have the effect of freezing learning, of focusing on the object, not the process, so that sometimes the justification becomes a game of pretence.

For Nick and Abigail too, with far more experience of academic theorising and writing, this fear and excitement still exists, though we have learnt to keep it well guarded. Important then that we share it with those who (perhaps like you?) are less experienced. Proposing and jointly writing this chapter as a group, was not for the faint-hearted. Would we find something interesting and new to say? Could we make sense of our experiences? Would we fail? As ever, you, the reader, becomes the judge!

So learning is complex, but nonetheless, progress can be made; theorising can both happen and help. One important step for us has been to come to understand that learning does not have to be thought of only as cognitive – in the head. Rather, 'I developed my understanding of learning to be rather social constructivist orientated, seeing knowledge as embodied, which can be measured in [terms of] practice' (Marlon). Similarly, another new perspective is to see learning as 'situated in a specific context and embedded within a particular social and physical environment' (Beth), so that learning in one context may not be the same as learning in another. Again, this points to learning as being more than just the development of individual minds as well as to the importance of the context, not just the content.

Knowing learning matters

In this short chapter we have tried, as four people working together, to show that learning involves 'matter' (the ideas about it that one develops) but more importantly that it matters how we go about it too. One can pick theory from a shelf, but to understand it in any depth one must be more active: starting with something that will feel unfamiliar; working on it and playing with it alongside one's initial thoughts to discover new ideas; and then working on organising these into new theories in a process of justification. Making the unfamiliar, familiar … and expecting new unfamiliar territory to then open up again.

Questions to consider

- What might 'know' mean in: 'know my times tables'; 'know how to play the trumpet'; 'know what love is'; 'know my A-level revision'?
- We 'know about …' and 'know how to …' but what other words or phrases can go after 'know' and what do they imply?
- As you go about life, and particularly if you are an education student, listen out for how the word 'learning' is used. Is it used as a noun (a product or object), or as a verb (something one is doing)? What effect does each of these have?
- What sort of feelings do you get when you face something you have to learn? Where do these come from and why are you feeling this way?
- Do you think the education system that you have been part of (as school/university/professional courses etc.) reflects what we have said above? How does this system tend to represent 'learning'?

Finally, you might like to try creating your own Talking Head video. Think about a context in which you have learnt something, or to do something, and try talking to camera (on your phone, tablet or PC) for five minutes about it. Even if you never show it to anyone else, it will help you to think about how you are beginning to theorise learning.

Either way, we hope you enjoy the challenge, just as we have done, of knowing learning matters.

Recommended reading

Waite, S. and Pratt, N. (2015) Situated learning (Learning In Situ), pp. 5012–5032, In J. D. Wright, (Ed) *International Encyclopedia of the Social and Behavioral Sciences*. Oxford: Elsevier.
This encyclopaedia entry explains how learning can be understood as both the product of social activity and as fundamentally rooted in social contexts. 'Situated learning' is the idea that we can only know things in terms of, and through, the materials and surrounding context in which we are operating.

Biesta, G. (2005) Against learning: reclaiming a language for education in an age of learning. *Nordisk Pedagogik*, **25**(1), pp. 54–66. https://doi.org/10.18261/ISSN1891-5949-2005-01-06

A paper that explores the idea that learning is becoming an object, rather than a process, and is being 'commodified' – i.e. turned into something that can be packaged and delivered – rather than being a process of personal development.

Holt, J. (1964) *How Children Fail*. London: Pitman Publishing Company.

A classic. First published in 1964 (but with subsequent editions which are easier to access), John Holt demonstrated how the school system set up some children to succeed and others to fail. It explores the way in which children learn and contrasts this with the demands of schooling – classes, testing etc. – and though 60 years old it still has lots to say about the modern system.

References

Lave, J. and Wenger, E. (1991) *Situated Learning: Legitimate Peripheral Participation*. Cambridge: Cambridge University Press.

Sammons, P., Toth, K. and Sylva, K. (2015) *Background to Success: Differences in A-Level Entries by Ethnicity, Neighbourhood and Gender*. University of Oxford and The Sutton Trust. Available at: https://www.suttontrust.com/wp-content/uploads/2019/12/Background-to-Success-Final-1.pdf (Accessed 12 May 2022).

Swedberg, R. (2012) Theorizing in sociology and social science: turning to the context of discovery. *Theory and Society*, **41**(1), pp. 1–40. https://doi.org/10.1007/s11186-011-9161-5

Swedberg, R. (2016) Before theory comes theorizing or how to make social science more interesting. *The British Journal of Sociology*, **67**(1), pp. 5–22. https://doi.org/10.1111/1468-4446.12184

Vygotsky, L. S. (1978) *Mind in Society: The Development of Higher Psychological Processes*. Cambridge, MA: Harvard University Press.

Wood, D., Bruner, J. S. and Ross, G. (1976) The role of tutoring in problem solving. *Journal of Child Psychology and Psychiatry*, **17**(2), pp. 89–100. https://doi.org/10.1111/j.1469-7610.1976.tb00381.x

6 Discovering your philosophy of education through digital storytelling

Sophie Ward, Laura Mazzoli Smith and Teti Dragas

SUMMARY POINTS

- Everyone has their own experience of education and beliefs about education that are shaped by that experience.
- By comparing our beliefs and personal experience of education with philosophies of education that have developed over many centuries, we are able to develop our own philosophy of education.
- There is no right or wrong answer to the question, 'What is a good education?' This chapter introduces Digital Storytelling as a method to help you answer this question for yourself.

Introduction

This chapter is inspired by John Dewey's (1897) *My Pedagogic Creed*. Dewey begins this creed by boldly asserting his answer to the question, 'What is education?' How many students, after embarking on education studies, are able to answer this same question? It was with this latter question in mind that we developed a new level one undergraduate module, Historical and Philosophical Ideas of Education. In this module, we employ Digital Storytelling as a constructivist method of assessment to help students situate the theoretical and conceptual content in what we might call their own philosophy of education – their pedagogic creed – as they undertake a broad engagement with educational philosophy and practice from Ancient Greece and China to the present day.

In this chapter, we aim to help you discover *your* philosophy of education by asking:

- What is a 'good' education?
- What is your own education story?

We introduce Digital Storytelling as a method to help you to reflect on and develop your own beliefs about the value and purpose of education and education studies.

What is a 'good' education?

Internationally, students are encouraged to 'invest' in higher education (HE) to enhance their employment prospects, and to 'measure the value of this commodity in terms of the subsequent market

DOI: 10.4324/9781003296935-8

value it confers upon them' (Connolly, 2013: 229). Graduate employability rankings are published annually in order to help applicants understand 'which universities are producing the most employable graduates' (QS, 2022). Is this the best way to determine what is, and is not, a 'good' education? According to the Roman philosopher, Seneca, it is not possible to admire education if 'its end is the making of money' (Seneca, 1969: 151). For Seneca, it is wisdom that makes a life worthwhile. The Ancient Greek philosopher, Aristotle, argued that we should study for the sake of knowledge itself, because it is *knowledge*, rather than money, that helps us obtain the final unchanging goal of spiritual nobility (Ward, 2017). Aristotle pitied those who have no ultimate goal: choosing things for the sake of something else, he says, they constantly ask 'What *use* is this?' (Heath, 2008: 251). For example, at school we may decide that it is not worth trying to understand complicated ideas when our exam system rewards our recollection of formulaic responses, rather than our creativity. We may decide that it is not worth studying for a degree with low employability prospects, even if it means that we choose a degree programme that we do not find interesting. We may decide to pursue a lucrative career, rather than a fulfilling career, in order to provide the best material goods for ourselves and our families and earn money for our retirement… and then what? Have we found value in the various stages of our lives, or has each moment been spent thinking about what is coming next?

When thinking about the value and purpose of education, it is commonplace to invoke the educational philosophy of Ancient Greece and Rome (see, for example, the work of the Jubilee Centre https://www.jubileecentre.ac.uk/). Less well-known today are the beliefs about education that bridge the gap between the ancient world and the present day. In medieval Europe, the belief that a 'good' education cultivates the soul formed the basis of the curriculum established by St Augustine (354–430 AD). By today's standards, this curriculum was both narrow and grim: underpinned by the belief that God communicates truth directly to the human mind, it involved corporal punishment and the memorisation of rules to discipline both the body and the mind for maximum receptivity. By the thirteenth century, faith in Divine revelation was beginning to be challenged by the idea that truth is secured by reason acting on sensory data (Bowen, 1975). The Renaissance artist, Leonardo da Vinci, argued that good art is born of the artist's sensory experience of the natural world, rather than their memorisation of artistic convention, and his prodigious talent secured a wide audience for his debunking of medieval scholasticism. Now, obedience to rules as a precondition for the gift of truth no longer seemed to be a 'good' education. Instead, a 'good' education meant the development of 'the whole man, mind and body, taste and knowledge, heart and soul' (Payne, 1900: 84) through the study of scholarly texts handed down from Ancient Greece and Rome. It was during the Renaissance that some of England's most famous schools were established to cultivate the 'whole man'; examples include Eton College in 1440, Rugby School in 1567 and Harrow School in 1572.

Some notable critics of the theory that the Renaissance curriculum provided a 'good' education helped, in their different ways, to deliver the kind of education we are familiar with today. In 1762, the French philosopher and father of Romanticism, Jean-Jacques Rousseau (1712–1778), published his treatise on education, *Émile*. In this book, Rousseau (1762) rejects the constraints of the classroom, arguing that *nature* awakens the senses and the imagination, enabling children to learn through their sensory experience to become their natural, authentic self. The idea that a 'good' education might involve learning through play, or through talking with, rather than listening to, the teacher inspired the movement known as child-centred education, in which the child's learning needs are placed at the centre of the education process. The Pestalozzi Method was founded in

1805; Fröebel's Kindergarten was founded in 1837; Dewey's Laboratory School at the University of Chicago was founded in 1896; the Montessori approach was founded in 1907; the first Steiner school was founded in 1919. These are just some of the many child-centred approaches to teaching and learning grounded in Rousseau's conception of the natural development of the child, many of which are still available to children today. It should be noted that the majority of child-centred schools in the UK are fee-paying, meaning that parents sympathetic to Rousseau's philosophy must pay for a 'good' education for their child.

The English philosopher and father of Utilitarianism, Jeremy Bentham (1748–1832), proposed a model of education that was radically different from Rousseau's, yet his ideas also inform education today. Bentham argued that the curriculum in England's finest schools was useless, and in 1816 he unveiled his plan to instruct middle class pupils in the Chrestomathic School, named after the Greek word for useful knowledge (Itzkin, 1978). In this school (which was never built), religion and the arts would be excluded, and learners would be taught science and technology using innovative methods, such as wall charts, ability grouping and peer competition. Notoriously, Bentham based his design for the Chrestomathic School on his previously published plans for a circular prison – the Panopticon (from the Greek for 'all seeing') – that enables one person to observe a multitude. In Bentham's model school, nobody knows who is being watched, and thus everyone self-regulates their behaviour: a phenomenon familiar today to anyone who has visited a shop and seen their image displayed on CCTV.

In keeping with Bentham's wishes, schools around the world today prioritise the teaching of science and technology over the arts (Lilliedahl, 2021), encouraged in no small part by the OECD's Programme for International Student Assessment (PISA). According to the OECD (2000: 11), PISA examines 'the degree of preparedness of young people for adult life and, to some extent, the effectiveness of education systems around the world'. No mention is made of the arts in this preparation for adult life. Instead, PISA 'measures 15-year-olds' ability to use their reading, mathematics and science knowledge and skills to meet real-life challenges' (OECD, 2022). Recently, creative thinking has been added to PISA's tests (OECD, 2019). The OECD (ibid; 5) defines creative thinking as 'a tangible competence, grounded in knowledge and practice, that supports individuals in achieving better outcomes, oftentimes in constrained and challenging environments'. Creative thinking is thus positioned as utilitarian, in keeping with Bentham's model of education.

Today, the marginalisation of the arts in education is of concern to educators, artists and the general public alike. For example, the Durham Commission on Creativity and Education (2019: 5) states that our current education system only partly equips learners with necessary skills, and that we 'need to make the most of our human capacity for imagination and critical judgment'. In 2006, the World Alliance for Arts Education (WAAE, 2006: 1) was formed to champion arts education as a means to develop citizens' capacity for critical thought, communication, intercultural understanding and 'an empathetic commitment to cultural diversity'. In its campaign for outdoor education, the English Outdoor Council (2018) echoes Rousseau saying, 'life is best approached in a spirit of exploration, adventure and enterprise'. UNESCO (2022) has declared the 4th week in May to be 'International Arts Education Week', stating that the arts enable us 'to feel and to understand what unites humanity'. All this would, of course, be dismissed as bunkum by Bentham and his admirers.

Despite the concerted efforts of arts education campaigners, the esteem accorded to PISA continues to result in national funding decisions about education that favour maths, science and technology (STEM) over the arts (Volante, 2015). Around the world, students are being encouraged to study STEM subjects at university through targeted interventions, such as the OECD's HP Catalyst Initiative (Kärkkäinen and Vincent-Lancrin, 2013). In some countries, government funding for arts degrees in HE is being withdrawn to discourage such study altogether (Musicians' Union, 2021). Is this a 'good' education?

For many people today, a 'good' education conforms to the Brazilian educator and philosopher, Paulo Freire's (1921–1997), theory of *praxis*, which he defines as 'reflection and action upon the world in order to transform it' (Freire, 2005: 51). Freire developed his critical pedagogy during the 1960s in response to social and economic oppression in Brazil. Freire objected to the idea that individuals might be reconciled to their bleak living conditions through therapy, and instead aimed to raise learners' consciousness of structures that dehumanise both the oppressor and the oppressed, so that they might achieve liberation. For Freire, a 'good' education inspires class solidarity and creates a space for community members to celebrate and share 'community-based knowledges and ways of being in and with the world' (Walsh, 2021: 470). In the face of adversity, Freire encourages us to 'Reconstruct hope' (Freire in Walsh, 2021: 469). This mission is evident in other forms of critical theory, first expounded by the German philosopher and sociologist, Max Horkheimer (1895–1973). The aim of critical theory is to explain the domination of some groups over others and to provide goals for the transformation of society. Examples include critical gender theory, critical race theory, critical disability theory and critical sexuality theory. For exponents of critical theory, a 'good' education brings to light the sometimes unconscious privileging of the status of one social group over another, and cultivates dialogue and action for liberation.

Unlike Rousseau's child-centred education and Bentham's utilitarian education, Freire's *praxis* does not currently enjoy widespread support. At the time of writing, at least 15 states in the USA are seeking to ban the teaching of critical race theory (Wong, 2021), and English schools have been told that they cannot teach 'contested theories and opinions' such as 'white privilege' (Hall, 2021).

Questions to consider

How do *you* define a 'good' education?

Thinking about your own experience at school, to what extent were you encouraged to use your imagination, and to what extent were you encouraged to memorise information for tests?

What is your own education story?

Nelson Mandela famously said, 'Education is the most powerful weapon which you can use to change the world'. Evidence to confirm Mandela's theory is all around us. Internationally, efforts are underway to rediscover and reinstate indigenous knowledge by decolonising the curriculum; raise awareness of environmental issues and empower learners to take action to improve the environment, and cultivate learning spaces that liberate learners from sexism, racism, classism, homophobia and religious intolerance. These are just some of the many ways that education is changing the world. But how has education changed *you*?

Many of us have been involved with education our whole lives, so it is difficult to assess its impact on us. Digital Storytelling enables us to bring to our consciousness the dynamic forces that shape our values, behaviours and motivations in educational contexts and beyond. By expressing ourselves in narrative form (i.e. telling stories about our lives) we are able to 'reshape, reassess and reconstruct particular events' (Alterio, 2002: 3). We are able to learn from discussing our educational experiences with others, who 'may raise alternate views, suggest imaginative possibilities and ask stimulating questions' (ibid). Digital Storytelling allows learners to combine their narrative with computer-based graphics, voice recording, text and music to create a recording that can be played on a computer and uploaded to the internet.

Digital Storytelling can be considered to be a constructivist approach to learning, drawing in particular on the educational theory of the American philosopher John Dewey (1859–1952), who espoused education as an active and experiential process. Dewey's (1938/1997) philosophy claims that students learn best when they interact and engage with their learning, and where the content is relatable, particularly to prior experiences. This deepens the connection to new knowledge in a constructivist process of personal knowledge generation. So, we use Digital Storytelling in our module to explicitly link the theories discussed above with students' own learning biographies. Linking their own personal story to an aspect of the module – a theoretical idea or key thinker – encourages our students to engage more meaningfully with such ideas, linking theory to lived experience and actively engaging with this material through their present lives. It is this constructivist approach to learning which underpins Digital Storytelling and makes it such a sophisticated and effective tool for promoting personal knowledge development in students. This statement of Dewey's on his educational philosophy is at the heart of the potential inherent in the digital storytelling process:

> I take it that the fundamental unity of the newer philosophy is found in the idea that there is an intimate and necessary relation between the processes of actual experience and education.
> (Dewey, 1938/1997: 20)

Questions to consider

What is *your* education story?
   Was there a friend, family member or teacher who transformed how you think about yourself as a learner?
   Can you recall a moment of inspiration, or a time when you overcame an obstacle to your learning?
   Do you have an education 'hero'?

How do you create a digital story?

Digital Storytelling is a facilitated process that often follows a number of key steps whereby you are guided to discover, script, record and build a short digital story from your own experience. The infographic below, created by Samantha Morra (see https://samanthamorra.com/digital-storytelling/), encapsulates the key steps in the process of creating a Digital Story that most Digital Storytelling workshops employ.

The process above shows what you do as a basic starting point, but it does not tell you how to work through this process. This necessitates support in both a practical and conceptual sense. For example, you will need to learn how to use tools and technology; work with story, image and

Discovering your philosophy of education 45

Figure 6.1 Key steps in creating a digital story

sound/music; write, script and revise; audio-record your voice; source and select images and short video clips, and build your story using video-editing tools. Some of this you may already know as you may have experimented with some of these tools before. As you do this, you will also be working through a reflective process, drawing on your experiences to craft the story. The process is facilitated in a group as, much like traditional storytellers, it is important to tell your story to an audience of listeners and to 'hear' your story and get feedback. At all stages, this collaborative, reflective approach is important. It is also useful to reflect on what this all means and how it links to ideas about a 'good' education once you are done. You can do this by writing a short reflective account or a blog post, for example. (To view some examples of digital stories and some blog posts: https://digital-storytelling.webspace.durham.ac.uk/.)

Below is a list of some of the key steps and questions you can ask yourself as you go:

Step 1, 2 and 3: Begin by reflecting on yourself as a learner. What is the 'transformational' story that only you can tell? What was the event or problem? How did it make you feel? What was the outcome? If it was a problem, how was it resolved? Share with someone. Your listener will help you to hear your story and redraft it, so you will be ready to record.

Step 4 and 5: Begin to gather images and clips that will illustrate your story and add other layers of meaning. These may be pictures you have found online, or your own photographs or drawings. Ask yourself, how well do the images help convey the ideas/themes in the story? Do your images hold explicit meaning (a time, a place, a person)? Do they hold emotion? How many different images are used in the story? How fast do they change? Think about the effect of this.

Step 6: Next, select a video editing tool to create your Digital Story. This can be simple or more complicated. You can experiment and get feedback on this.

Step 7 and 8: Share your story and reflect on what you have learnt. How does this link to key thinkers or theories of education? How does it help you to understand these from another point of view?

> **Questions to consider**
>
> Create and share your Digital Story about education. What links, if any, are you able to observe between your story and some of the beliefs about a 'good' education outlined in this chapter?

For more information about Digital Storytelling, and to view some examples, you might like to visit StoryCenter's website: https://www.storycenter.org/

Conclusion

The history of education is an ever-changing story in which the characters question the nature of knowledge, the source of knowledge and who controls access to knowledge. Our module attempts not only to convey this story but also to *add* to it through our students' creation of Digital Stories about their own learning. There is no right or wrong answer to the question, 'What is a good education?' Each of us has our own experience of education and beliefs about education that are shaped by that experience. By exploring some of the 'big' ideas about the purpose and value of education, and by creating your Digital Story, we hope that you will begin to formulate your own philosophy of education: your personal 'pedagogic creed' (Dewey, 1897).

Recommended reading

Shuffleton, A. (2017) Jean-Jacques Rousseau, the Mechanised Clock and Children's Time. *Journal of Philosophy of Education*, 51, (4), pp. 837–849.
In this paper, Amy Shuffelton uses Rousseau's critique of 'clock time' to challenge our current belief that homework, standardized testing and extra-curricular activities provide a 'good' education.
Giroux, H. (2010) Rethinking Education as the Practice of Freedom: Paulo Freire and the promise of critical pedagogy. *Policy Futures in Education*, 8 (6), pp. 715–721. https://doi.org/10.2304%2Fpfie.2010.8.6.715
In this paper, Henry Giroux uses Freire's critical pedagogy to challenge our belief that education for employability constitutes a 'good' education.
Hyslop-Margison, E. J. and Strobel, J. (2007) Constructivism and education: Misunderstandings and pedagogical implications. *The Teacher Educator*, 43 (1), pp. 72–86.
This paper sets out the implications of constructivism for education.

References

Alterio, M. (2002) Using Storytelling to Enhance Student Learning. Available online at: https://desarrollodocente.uc.cl/wp-content/uploads/2020/03/Alterio_M._2003.pdf [Accessed 13/01/22].
Bowen, J. (1975) *A History of Western Education. Volume 2: Civilization of Europe*. London: Methuen and Co. Ltd.
Connolly, R. (2013) Have You Ever Considered a Career in Total Revolution? Drama and the Corporate Reform of UK Higher Education. *Studies in Theatre and Performance*, 33 (2), pp. 225–243. http://dx.doi.org/10.1386/stap.33.2.225_1
Dewey, J. (1897) *My Pedagogic Creed*. Available online at: http://dewey.pragmatism.org/creed.htm [Accessed 12/01/22].
Dewey, J. (1938/1997) *Experience and Education*. New York: Touchstone.
Durham Commission on Creativity and Education (2019). *First Report*. Available online at: https://www.dur.ac.uk/resources/creativitycommission/DurhamReport.pdf [Accessed 07/01/22].
Freire, P. (2005) *Pedagogy of the Oppressed. 30th Anniversary Edition*. New York: The Continuum International Publishing Group Inc.

Hall, R. (2021) English Schools Must Not Teach 'White Privilege' as Fact, Government Warns. *The Guardian*. Available online at: https://www.theguardian.com/education/2021/oct/21/english-schools-must-not-teach-white-privilege-as-fact-government-warns [Accessed 19/01/22].

Heath, M. (2008) Aristotle on Natural Slavery. *Phronesis*, 53, pp. 243–270.

Itzkin, E.S. (1978) Bentham's *Chrestomathia*: Utilitarian Legacy to English Education. *Journal of the History of Ideas*, 39 (2), pp. 303–316.

Kärkkäinen, K. and Vincent-Lancrin, S. (2013) Sparking Innovation in STEM Education with Technology and Collaboration: A Case Study of the HP Catalyst Initiative, *OECD Education Working Papers*, 91. Paris: OECD Publishing. https://doi.org/10.1787/5k480sj9k442-en.

Lilliedahl, J. (2021) Is There a Transnational Trend of "Nudging" Away from the Arts? How the Selection Device Works in the European–Swedish Context. *Arts Education Policy Review*. http://dx.doi.org/10.1080/10632913.2021.1903639.

Musicians' Union (2021) MU Outraged as Planned Cuts to Government Funding for Higher Education Arts and Music Confirmed. Available online at: https://musiciansunion.org.uk/news/mu-outrage-as-planned-cuts-to-government-funding-for-higher-education-arts-and-music-confirmed [Accessed 8/01/22].

OECD (2000) *Measuring Student Knowledge and Skills: A New Framework for Assessment*. Paris: OECD.

OECD (2019) *PISA 2021 Creative Thinking Framework. (Third Draft)*. Available online at: https://www.oecd.org/pisa/publications/PISA-2021-creative-thinking-framework.pdf [Accessed 06/01/22].

OECD (2022) *Programme for International Student Assessment*. Available online at: https://www.oecd.org/pisa/ [Accessed 05/01/22].

Payne, W.H. (Trans. and Intro.) (1900) *The History of Pedagogy by Gabriel Compayré*. Fourth Edition. London: Swan Sonnenschein and Co., Ltd.

QS (2022) QS Graduate Employability Rankings 2022. Available online at: https://www.topuniversities.com/university-rankings/employability-rankings/2022 [Accessed 5/01/22].

Rousseau, J.-J. (1762) *Emile*. Available online at: https://www.gutenberg.org/ebooks/5427 [Accessed 07/05/22].

Seneca (1969) Letter LXXXVIII. In R. Campbell (trans. and intro.) *Letters from a Stoic*. London: Penguin Books Ltd.

The English Outdoor Council (2018) *Campaigns*. Available online at: https://www.englishoutdoorcouncil.org/campaigns-initiatives [Accessed 7/02/22].

UNESCO (2022) *International Arts Education Week*. Available online at: http://www.unesco.org/new/en/culture/themes/creativity/arts-education/ [Accessed 8/01/22].

Volante, L. (2015) The Impact of PISA on Education Governance: Some Insights from Highly Reactive Policy Contexts. *International Studies in Educational Administration (Commonwealth Council for Educational Administration and Management (CCEAM))*, 43 (2), pp. 103–117.

WAAE (2006) The World Alliance for Arts Education. Joint Declaration. Available online at: https://www.waae.online/uploads/1/2/9/2/129270960/history-of-waae.pdf [Accessed 8/01/22].

Walsh, C.E. (2021) (Re)existence in Times of De-existence: Political–Pedagogical Notes to Paulo Freire. *Language and Intercultural Communication*, 21 (4), pp. 468–478. http://dx.doi.org/10.1080/14708477.2021.1916025.

Ward, S. (2017) *The Tempest. Using Shakespeare's Plays to Explore Education Policy Today: Neoliberalism through the Lens of Renaissance Humanism*. Abingdon: Routledge.

Wong, J.S. (2021) The Fight to Whitewash US History: 'A Drop of Poison Is All You Need', *The Guardian*. Available online at: https://www.theguardian.com/world/2021/may/25/critical-race-theory-us-history-1619-project [Accessed 19/01/2022].

7 Assessment for transformation

Adopting a humanist approach to assessment and feedback on a BA Education course

Tristan Middleton, Rick Millican, Sian Templeton and Lynda Kay

---

SUMMARY POINTS

- A relational pedagogy helps to ease the stresses and disappointments that assessments and feedback can cause.
- A humanist approach to education cares about the student as an individual and considers their health and wellbeing needs as well as their academic needs.
- This, alongside a developmental approach to assessments, helps develop self-efficacy, autonomy and resilience.
- Key indicators of academic buoyancy are an internal locus of control, assessment literacy, being forward looking, being improvement focused and being action orientated.

Introduction and Context

Research indicates that students, alongside individuals in general, are showing an increase in levels of poor mental health. While the Department for Education (DfE 2019, 2020) identifies a mixed picture of positive and negative experiences, other surveys report a trend of lowering rates of life satisfaction during the last decade (Children's Society, 2021; Prince's Trust, 2021). Indeed, the Office for Students reports an increase in the percentage of the undergraduate student population who have disclosed a mental health condition from 0.7 per cent in 2010/2011 to 4.2 per cent in 2019/2020, a greater increase than for any other disability (OfS, 2021). This could partly be caused by concerns young people have about societal injustices and worries about their future in a rapidly changing and potentially vulnerable world. One example of this is the Coronavirus pandemic that impacted upon individuals across the planet (Children's Society, 2020); other research highlighted young people's heightening concerns about employment opportunities and identified raised levels of anxiety (Children's Society, 2021; Prince's Trust, 2021).

In amongst this, assessment and feedback form part of the academic experience of all students and are highly influential in shaping the learning behaviours and activities of students (Hattie and Timperley, 2007). Within Higher Education (HE) assessment is an activity which is frequently reported negatively in surveys, such as the National Student Survey (NSS) (MacKay *et al.*, 2019), and may be a factor within the learning environment that impacts on stress (Tharani et al., 2017) owing to issues such as worrying about the risk of failure or a disappointing grade (Hull et al., 2019). For tutors and students, this is concerning because of the potential additional negative influence this anxiety has on learning and wellbeing (Hull et al., 2019).

Key principles underpinning the course

Given this context, one might reflect on the role of Higher Education and take one of three responses:

1. That it is not the responsibility of HE to attempt to address mental health and wellbeing concerns, as the domain of HE is simply that of academic study
2. That HE should endeavour to do no harm and as such should check that practices and expectations are not causing unreasonable stress and exacerbating the mental health of students
3. That HE should actively seek to support student health and wellbeing and look to structure practices to help optimise student resilience

> **Question to consider**
> Which of the above would be your perspective and why?

As a course team of education practitioners, we firmly believe that education and health are inexorably linked and that to optimise learning students need to feel comfortable, relaxed, healthy and happy. Theories such as Maslow's Hierarchy (1943) show us that it is likely to be hard to concentrate and focus on learning if there are challenges to physical and/or mental health which are distracting. Studies into resilience (see ahmed Shafi et al., 2020) indicate that a student's ability to cope can be reduced if the systems around them (i.e. the university, tutors, assessment practices) are causing too many risks (stresses) and are threatening the systems that protect them. As a consequence, the course team feels a responsibility to take perspective 3 above and actively look at course practices to explore approaches to supporting student wellbeing and optimising resilience.

In response to this, we have adopted a humanist approach to our work. By this, we mean one that follows a Rogerian approach (see Rogers, 1979) that aims to view and treat students as individuals with their own unique stories, feelings and sets of challenges. As Rogers suggests, to achieve this it is important to develop a 'growth-promoting climate' based on relationships that are genuine and real and that adopt a stance of unconditional positive regard and empathic understanding (ibid). Rogers argues that this helps learners 'develop more self-understanding, more self- confidence, more ability to choose ... behaviours. They learn more significantly, they have more freedom to be and become' (Rogers, 1979: 7).

For us, this means analysing behaviours and processes at an individual and course level to see if they could be aligned more closely with this ethos. An example of this is, as mentioned above, the assessment process. While assessment is an integral part of the HE experience, as both a formative and summative evaluation of progress and performance, studies of student anxiety show that it is stressful and that the grade and feedback received can add disappointment which can threaten academic buoyancy and ability to cope and move forward (ahmed Shafi et al., 2018). Middleton et al. (2020) revealed five factors (the Key 5) that could add protection for students and help them recover from such disappointments:

    i.   an internal locus of control;
    ii. assessment literacy;
    iii. being forward looking;
    iv. being improvement focused, and
    v.   being action orientated.

So, whilst we are not in a position to abandon assessments, we can actively consider their design and the feedback method and explore ways to make the process more supportive. We can also consider how we prepare students and help them help themselves to be better equipped in managing them.

A further example of action that can be taken to mitigate against stresses that might threaten student mental health is illustrated by ahmed Shafi et al. (forthcoming) which argues that at times of challenge students found relationships with course teams and tutors a major source of support and protection. This highlights the need for a course approach that provides a sense of belonging and offers meaningful relationships and pathways of support.

This underpinning course ethos and the research findings have led us to make changes to our practice which we believe contribute to the health and wellbeing of our students, better enable them to actualise (see Maslow, 1943; Rogers, 1979) and hopefully lead to a stronger, richer and transformative learning experience (see Mezirow, 1997).

> **Questions to consider**
>
> How stressful do you find assessments and what do you find helps you manage any stress?
> How important do you feel it is to have a close relationship with your tutors and fellow students?
> How aware are you of the underpinning values and ethos of your course/course team and are they important to you?

The practice of our BA Education course

This section discusses some of the ways our BA Education course has developed its approach with this in mind and outlines some key areas of practice.

Course ethos

Underpinning our humanist approach to practice on the course is an ethos of relational pedagogy, with Hickey and Riddle (2021) emphasising that informal relationships between learner and educator can serve as pedagogical activators. As a team we have explicitly talked about this and an action-research approach to developing practice within the course has both prompted and enabled in-depth discussions and research-informed practice.

This ethos begins with induction; a significant amount of time and focus is spent on building relationships between students and the teaching team including a residential trip in the early part of the first year of study. Lecturers operate an open-door policy and learn all the students' names early in the term, knowing them and treating them as individuals. These core foundations, supported by a Personal Tutor system, help to maintain positive informal relationships.

Pedagogical approach

The skills, preferences, interests and contexts of our students are diverse and continue to develop both with the arrival of new students and as continuing students widen their experiences. We believe that this diversity not only enhances the learning opportunities within the course but that it should be positively developed within the curriculum. This reflects an affirmative approach which links closely with the empathic nature of our humanist ethos (Watson, 2002).

As such our course teaching has moved away from a model of knowledge and content delivery, via a format of lectures, to all sessions being run as 'seminars' with individual and group activities spread throughout the sessions and student contributions and questions encouraged and facilitated. This approach enables students to explore and develop their own interests, thereby co-constructing the learning process and learning from the interests of peers. This affirmative, active learning approach supports students' development as critical participants. For example, in a recent session on the topic of creating inclusive learning environments, a student discussed their experience of discussing staff development with the head of their setting, whilst another student brought their experience of working with families of children at risk of exclusion. These opportunities for the sharing of diverse experiences broaden students', and lecturers', perspectives relating to how education could work and contribute to an improving educational experience. Furthermore, the affirmative nature of the co-creation of learning experiences within safe learning spaces helps our students to develop confidence to communicate their own views and experiences. Therefore, in their assessment tasks they are more confident to express their own views, explore and share their ideas and develop original ideas within the pieces they submit, without feeling constrained to include pre-determined ideas in order to meet assessment criteria.

Design of assessment

In line with the ethos and teaching approach outlined, our design of assessment tasks does not follow a standard model. In recognition of the diverse skills and experiences of our students, and more specifically the range of skills which could be used to communicate understanding of theories and the development of new ideas, we offer a range of assessment modes within the course.

Example assessment modes used include:

- Standard essays
- Timed essays
- Reflective pieces
- Discussion fora
- Presentations
- Web-site creation

- Recorded discussions
- Portfolio
- Posters
- Micro-teaching
- Expanded bibliography
- Dissertation

This range of assessments provides the opportunity for our diverse student group to experience success in their assessments whilst developing future employability skills. Group work is included across assessments and offers the opportunity for students to learn from, and support, each other.

Across all of the assessment formats, choice is an important element with open questions and titles enabling students to pursue and develop their own particular interests making links to their experiences and knowledge.

> **Questions to consider**
>
> What are your thoughts about the range of assessments you have experienced?
> Are there some that you feel are more supportive/helpful for your learning?

Design of assessment feedback

Action research helped us identify a number of factors which could support students' emotional responses to assessment feedback, which led to changes in our approach. For example, as a way of leading students towards a position of metacognitive strength in relation to managing the impact of assessment feedback, we include direct teaching about the Key 5 (ahmed Shafi et al., 2018) supporting their development.

The feedback process has also been redesigned to incorporate the Key 5. The feedback sheet has been reorganised to provide clear grading descriptors against each criterion identifying 'Strengths' as the first comments, followed by 'Recommendations'. In order to promote an internal locus of control and to be improvement focused, the feedback sheet prompts students to record 'Student devised action points'. Assessments are followed up in Personal Tutor meetings where students are asked to summarise their chosen feedforward actions in response to comments provided, thereby providing important relational interactions within the process (Middleton et al., 2020).

Student experience

The value of a holistic approach focusing on student wellbeing alongside their academic selves, underpinned by the active development of relationships, appears to have had impact on the trajectory of the journey that students take whilst studying with us. The testimony of Student A below is an illustrative case study exploring the potentially transformative experience for some of our students resulting from the course ethos, pedagogy and assessment structure. Student A arrived unable to deliver an assessed presentation in front of her peers. On graduating and moving on to employment, she now leads training with large groups of staff within a secondary school, organising events alongside providing individual support for vulnerable learners within her setting. She attributes this transformation to her experiences throughout the course and the interpersonal support and flexible approach of the course team. The importance of 'being known' and an ongoing informal person-centred approach to interaction and feedback with our students, not just as a member of a wider group but on an individual level, appears key in this particular circumstance. On the basis of these informal, implicit processes, the links to Vygotsky's zone of proximal development (ZPD) and the idea that collaboration supports learning which in turn leads to an internalisation of skills and psychological tools (Shabani et al., 2010) is apparent. In her previous educational experience Student A frequently shut down, entering into the freeze response as a result of challenge from outside of her ZPD which, in turn, had a detrimental impact on both self-efficacy and skill development. Instead, a combination of an awareness of Student A's history, alongside an explicit consideration of her future (Shabani et al., 2010), allowed us to work with her to gradually re-define her self-concept to optimise opportunities for success and development. Our assessment design process was integral to supporting this process through the utilisation of the Key 5 skills in order to support both personal development and academic development.

Student A

> I started my university journey as a mature student with very little traditional education and I was filled with extreme anxiety, I wasn't particularly academic at the time and was unsure how I would cope with the assessments. Hearing that there would be group projects, presentations, exams and essays completely filled me with dread. The thought of having so many different forms of assessment was nerve wracking, mainly because I hadn't experienced it before.
>
> While at first, I found this all very daunting, in the end it was the best way in supporting me to develop not only academically but also personally. My lecturers were incredibly supportive from day one. The day I found out the date of my first presentation I had a major panic attack and couldn't imagine standing in front of a group of people talking. I spoke with my lecturers and came up with a plan of action to support me with my anxiety. Over the course of three years, with the support of my lecturers, I slowly built up from presenting in front of two lecturers, to a room full of peers and lecturers. The feedback process was also incredibly helpful, especially for someone with anxiety. They provided brilliant running feedback, areas of strength and areas in which you could improve on next time. They also allowed the time and space to discuss any points that you might have been unsure of. Five years later I can speak to secondary school pupils in assemblies about the journey I have been on.
>
> It was the ethos of the team and the approach to assessments that supported me in this achievement. If the course hadn't offered a variety of assessments, I wouldn't have tackled my fear of presentations. This is only one example of how the ethos of the course and the approach to assessments helped me beyond measure both academically and personally.

Student toolkit

Within our assessment design process, our aim is not only to provide summative evidence towards a final degree classification, but also to empower our students with a varied 'toolkit' which can support them entering employment. As discussed previously, the course pedagogical practice has been developed in line with the belief that in order to be able to access learning students need to feel emotionally safe and secure (Beard *et al.*, 2007). Although more traditional approaches to assessment within an HE environment (such as essay writing) are included within module assessments our other modes of assessment (detailed above) have an equal contribution to make to the final awards that students achieve. A number of these assessment modes raise the anxiety levels of the students due to the novel experience for the student and/or falling outside of their comfort zone. This anxiety is often linked to concerns about expectations and student self-efficacy linked to their ability to meet these expectations. However, Pajares (1996) advocates that to promote self-efficacy challenging and meaningful tasks need to be provided for students thus creating a cycle which can be efficacy enhancing, but can also result in students feeling more vulnerable due to being taken outside of their comfort zone. Optimistically there is evidence that students are more likely to have a positive view on their future performance based on feedback which includes clear actions for future work (Hull *et al.*, 2019), thus reinforcing the Key 5 approach. In addition to this, assessments such as presentations which have a group-work focus and opportunities to work in collaboration with others have been shown to promote academic self-efficacy (ibid).

The assessment design process discussed earlier in this chapter therefore aims to create a 'toolkit' for the students whereby they develop a range of skills (such as website design and the ability to present either individually or as a team), alongside agency and a belief in their ability to make a positive difference. These assessments are challenging for a number of students, but the impact on their self-concept, self-esteem and self-efficacy in overcoming these challenges enables them to develop a sense of agency and control over future capabilities. Our aim through this process is to empower our students to develop a more critical perspective of the world, and in particular, education. We then encourage them to use their 'toolkit' which includes a range of skills enhanced by knowledge and understanding of empirical evidence-based practice as a backdrop to becoming effective future educators.

Question to consider

How might you respond to feedback to support you positively with developing your own toolkit?

Conclusion

The planning of assessments needs to consider the socio-cultural context (MacKay *et al.*, 2019) as well as the purpose of the assessment activity. The importance of considering both of these dimensions is highlighted by the context of increased prevalence of poor mental health together with concerns about how the learning environment within HE may affect student wellbeing. Our varied assessments and assessment design have the potential to have a positive impact on student self-efficacy in line with the humanistic course ethos; however, in addition to this they also provide additional skills and experience which can be drawn upon within the workplace in educational practice. The pedagogical approach of the course team aims to support students in their development into future skilled and flexible educators who will work within a variety of settings and contexts linked to education. We are therefore mindful of the varied skills that would be of benefit to our students to enhance their employability. However, in an increasingly competitive market, skills alone do not suffice; personal attributes alongside a belief in themselves and their ability to communicate both skills and attributes to future employers is key. In this way, the elements of relationships between students and course teams and humanist practices developed provide protections for students to mitigate the stresses associated with assessment and aim to transform the quality of the assessment experience for students, the richness of the learning opportunity and support the students in developing autonomy and criticality and the ability to deal with the challenges of the course, and of life and employment more generally.

Recommended reading

ahmed Shafi, A., Middleton, T., Millican, R. and Templeton., S. (2020) *Reconsidering Resilience in Education: An Exploration Using the Dynamic Interactive Model of Resilience.* Switzerland: Springer Nature.

This book explores current understandings of the concept of resilience and the movement from ideas around resilience being a 'fixed character trait' to something that is much more dynamic and influenced by context. It goes on to explore resilience in a range of educational fields and settings including how assessment and feedback can be used to enhance student resilience.

Barrow, C. and Westrup, R. (2019) *Writing Skills for Education Students.* London: Bloomsbury Academic

This book provides a useful overview to support your development as a writer within the field of Education. It gives you a step-by-step approach to planning and structuring your writing alongside tips for the variety of written assessments you might come across during your studies.

Middleton, T., ahmed Shafi, A., Millican, R. and Templeton, S. (2020) Developing effective assessment feedback: Academic buoyancy and the relational dimensions of feedback. *Teaching in Higher Education.* https://doi.org/10.1080/13562517.2020.1777397

This paper presents research into developing effective feedback drawing on the notion of academic buoyancy, the key 5 and the role of relationships and dialogue. It provides further insight into concepts and ideas discussed in this paper.

Quinlan, K. M. (2016) How emotion matters in four key relationships in teaching and learning in higher education. *College Teaching*, 64(3), pp. 101–111.

This paper examines the role of emotions and relationships with teaching and learning. It argues that consideration of these elements are enriching to student development. It explores four key relationships; students' relationship with the subject, with their teacher, with their peers and with their developing self.

References

ahmed Shafi, A., Hatley, J., Middleton, T., Millican, R. and Templeton, S. (2018) The role of assessment feedback in developing academic buoyancy. *Assessment and Evaluation in Higher Education*, 43(3), pp. 415–427. https://doi.org/10.1080/02602938.2017.1356265

ahmed Shafi, A., Templeton, S., Middleton, T., Millican, R., Vare, Pritchard, R., and Hatley, J. (2020) Towards a dynamic interactive model of resilience (DIMoR) for education and learning contexts. *Emotional and Behavioural Difficulties*, 25(2), pp. 183–198. https://doi.org/10.1080/13632752.2020.1771923

Ahmed Shafi, A., Millican, R., Middleton, T., Templeton, S. and Hill, J. (forthcoming) 'Learning in a Disrupted Environment: Exploring Higher Education Student Resilience using the Dynamic Interactive Model of Resilience'.

Beard, C., Clegg, S., and Smith, K. (2007) Acknowledging the affective in higher education. *British Educational Research Journal*, 33(2), pp. 235–252. https://doi.org/10.1080/01411920701208415

Children's Society (2020) *Life on Hold: Children's Well-Being and COVID-19.* Available at: https://www.childrenssociety.org.uk/sites/default/files/2020-10/life-on-hold-childrens-well-being-and-covid-19.pdf (Accessed 8 April 2022).

Children's Society (2021) The good childhood report 2021. Available at: https://www.childrenssociety.org.uk/information/professionals/resources/good-childhood-report-2021 (Accessed 4 December 2021).

DfE (2019) State of the Nation 2019: Children and young people's wellbeing research report. Available at: https://assets.publishing.service.gov.uk/government/uploads/system/uploads/attachment_data/file/925329/State_of_the_nation_2020_children_and_young_people_s_wellbeing.pdf (Accessed 8 April 2022).

DfE (2020) State of the Nation 2020: Children and Young People's Wellbeing – A report on wellbeing in children and young people in 2020. Available at: https://www.gov.uk/government/publications/state-of-the-nation-2020-children-and-young-peoples-wellbeing (Accessed 8 April 2022).

Hattie, J. and Timperley, H. (2007) The power of feedback. *Review of Educational Research*, 77(1), pp. 81–112. https://doi.org/10.3102/003465430298487

Hickey, A. and Riddle, S. (2021) Relational pedagogy and the role of informality in renegotiating learning and teaching encounters. *Pedagogy, Culture and Society*, pp.1–13. https://doi.org/10.1080/14681366.2021.1875261

Hull, K., Lawford, H., Hood, S., Oliveira, V., Murray, M., Trempe, M., Crooks, J., Richardson, M., and Jensen, M. (2019) Student anxiety and evaluation. *Collected Essays on Teaching and Learning*, 12, pp. 23–35 Available at: https://celt.uwindsor.ca/index.php/CELT/article/view/5409 (Accessed 4 December 2021).

MacKay, J.R.D., Hughes, K., Marzetti H., Lent, N., and Rhind, S.M. (2019) Using National Student Survey (NSS) qualitative data and social identity theory to explore students' experiences of assessment and feedback. *Higher Education Pedagogies*, 4(1), pp. 315–330. https://doi.org/10.1080/23752696.2019.1601500

Maslow, A.H. (1943) A theory of human motivation. *Psychological Review*, 50(4), pp. 370–396. https://doi.org/10.1037/h0054346

Mezirow, J. (1997) Transformative learning: Theory to practice. *New Directions for Adult and Continuing Education*, 74, pp. 5–12. https://doi.org/10.1002/ace.7401

Middleton, T., ahmed Shafi, A., Millican, R., and Templeton, S. (2020) Developing effective assessment feedback: Academic buoyancy and the relational dimensions of feedback. *Teaching in Higher Education*. Available at: https://doi.org/10.1080/13562517.2020.1777397 (Accessed 8 April 2022).

Office for Students (2021) *Equality, Diversity and Student Characteristics Data. Students at English Higher Education Providers between 2010–11 and 2019–20*. Available at: https://www.officeforstudents.org.uk/media/0e05ebc4-dbd8-40ae-8bdf-9d9aa7f338b4/equality-diversity-and-student-characteristics-data-june-2021.pdf (Accessed 23 September 2022).

Pajares, F. (1996) Self-efficacy beliefs in academic settings, *Review of Educational Research*, 66(4), pp. 543–578. https://doi.org/10.2307/1170653

Prince's Trust (2021) *The Prince's Trust Tesco Youth Index 2021*. Available at: https://www.princes-trust.org.uk/about-the-trust/news-views/tesco-youth-index-2021 (Accessed 4 December 2021).

Rogers, C. (1979) The foundations of the person-centred Approach. Available at: http://www.unifiedcommunities.com/ucs/Rogers_Person-Centered-Approach_1979.pdf (Accessed 28 September 2022).

Shabani, K., Khatib, M., and Ebadi, S. (2010) Vygotsky's zone of proximal development: Instructional implications and teachers' professional development. *English Language Teaching*, 3(4), pp. 237–248.

Tharani, A., Husain, Y., and Warwick, I. (2017) Learning environment and emotional well-being: A qualitative study of undergraduate nursing students. *Nurse Education Today*, 59, pp. 82–87. https://doi.org/10.1016/j.nedt.2017.09.008

Watson, J.C. (2002) The role of empathy in psychotherapy: Theory, research, and practice. In D.J. Cain and J. Seeman (Eds) *Humanistic Psychotherapies: Handbook of Research and Practice*. Washington, DC: American Psychological Association. Available at: https://doi.org/10.1037/14775-005 (Accessed 4 December 2021).

8 Student achievement and wellbeing

Understanding motivation through self-determination theory

Mark Tymms

SUMMARY POINTS

- Motivation refers to our willingness to engage, and the quality of that engagement, with any behaviour over time;
- Motivation is a key driver of learner performance and wellbeing;
- Motivation can be influenced by the intrinsic or extrinsic focus of learning;
- Motivation can be raised and maintained by meeting the 'psychological needs' of learners; Self-Determination Theory defines these needs as autonomy, competence and relatedness;
- Learner motivation, performance and wellbeing may require the prioritization of 'need satisfaction' above the focus on single educational goals.

Introduction

Questions to consider

Think of two tasks, one in which you were successful and one in which you weren't. Reflect on the reasons why your achievements varied. What was it about those tasks that helped or hindered your efforts to succeed?

As you will discover through the course of your educational career, success and failure are not simply products of your perceived levels of ability, but are dependent on a wide range of psychological and environmental factors. These influence the ways in which you engage with tasks and how you maintain your levels of engagement during their completion. In addition, these factors will not only impact on the outcomes that you achieve, but how you feel during the task and how you feel as an individual post-completion. It is this perception that enables us to build a relationship between motivation and wellbeing.

The aim of this chapter is to inform your understanding of the factors underpinning the academic performance of learners, specifically drawing on psychological theory to highlight the role of motivation. It is not straightforward.

> **Questions to consider**
>
> As you work through this chapter, you will find that different forms and levels of motivation will have very different psychological consequences. For example, the strength of your desire to be a teacher may help you decide which course to take, but it will also influence your potential levels of engagement, performance and wellbeing whilst studying.
>
> To better understand this complexity, think about why you are studying education. What is motivating you to do this? It is likely that you are doing so because you want to be a teacher, but try thinking more deeply about your motivations. Ask yourself, what you will be or are gaining from the process and why that is so valuable to you?

From a psychological perspective there are many different interpretations and conceptualizations of motivation, but in this chapter we will be focusing specifically on Self-Determination Theory (SDT). As such, there will not be room to offer a complete explanation of motivation as a psychological construct, but the chapter will include sufficient detail to help you understand the potential relationship between learner motivation and the teaching environment, as well as links to other significant areas such as psychological wellbeing. It should act to start your journey into learner motivation and help you to better understand learner performance, including your own performance, at a more holistic level.

Understanding motivation

> Human beings can be proactive and engaged or, alternatively, passive and alienated, largely as a function of the social conditions in which they develop and function... our education systems, including tutoring, as a significant factor within students' social environment, can drive student introjection of non-optimum psychological behaviours through the promotion of apathy, passivity, alienation and the rejection of personal responsibility'
>
> (Deci and Ryan, 2000: 67)

We have started with a quotation from Deci and Ryan on the ways in which contexts, such as education, have the potential to both support and constrain personal motivation. Academic writing can sometimes be difficult to follow and understand, but if we look to the key themes in the quotation, we are being presented with two often competing perspectives built around the concepts of passive/active and engaged/alienated. For Deci and Ryan, the ways in which these are combined within the learning environment, including the actions of teachers and educators, help to shape the student's ability to acquire and apply optimal psychological behaviours, which raise motivation, or non-optimal psychological behaviours, which reduce motivation.

But what do those themes mean?

Go back to the first task from the box above and analyse the examples that you worked with. First, in those examples, were you working with ideas, skills or knowledge that had been given to you and merely required replication? When you used them, did you use them in exactly the same way that they were originally given to you? Wohlwill called this a 'hospital bed model of experience'

(1973: 100) in which your knowledge and behaviours are chosen for you by others within your environment, and shape your thoughts and behaviours as a reflection of them. In hospital, you are less knowledgeable about your condition than the people taking care of you, and as such you are likely to give over your personal power to them as experts. Tests can sometimes be experienced in this way if you feel that you are being asked to give back information in the same way that it was originally given to you, and that you are doing that at a time and in a style that you haven't chosen. In this instance, you would consider yourself a 'passive' learner because you aren't personally adding anything to that knowledge, merely repeating it. The learning, and indeed the learner, is defined and controlled externally, and it is for this reason that such a process commonly promotes extrinsic motivation, where your reasons for participating in the learning process aren't your own.

Alternatively, did your task allow you to be creative with your knowledge or allow you to adapt and apply it to new spaces and for new purposes? In the first task you were perhaps controlled by your environment as a 'passive learner', but here you were instead free to act as you wish and create new or novel learning as the result of your own preferences, experiences and intentions. Wohlwill called this the 'swim-meet model of experience' (1973: 101), and in this instance you are being an 'active' learner and free to work as you wish within the opportunities presented to you by the environment, in this case the swimming pool. Here, you are adding something to the learning process, and you are a fundamental part of that process. As such, you are also more likely to be intrinsically motivated, because you lie at the heart of the learning processes of which you are a part and your growth isn't being defined by others. We will return to the concepts of extrinsic and intrinsic motivation in the next section.

Second, think about the reasons why you were completing the task under consideration. In the same way that passive learners are sometimes seen as controlled by the environment (such as in a school or classroom), were you completing the task because you wanted to, because of environmental pressure, or to obtain some kind of reward that was being provided by the environment? Here, we are no longer thinking about the 'what' of the task, but the 'why'. The more personally motivated you are to complete a particular task, the more you are considered an 'engaged' learner, whilst the more your reasons for task completion stem from factors outside of yourself, then the more you are considered an 'alienated' learner because the task will potentially lack personal meaning or significance for you.

In reality, very few tasks can be seen as a simple choice between two clearly distinct options, such as passive or active. Most tasks instead sit on a continuum between the two, some more passive/alienated and some more active/engaged (Lemos and Verissimo, 2014). The key point, however, is that for Deci and Ryan, each can produce different psychological behaviours; passive/alienated contexts being more likely to constrain learner motivation and wellbeing, and engaged/active contexts more likely to promote learner motivation and wellbeing.

Introducing self-determination theory

SDT is a motivational model that has been used in a diverse range of psychological areas, including education, wellbeing and business. As a theory it shifts the focus from motivation as a single, quantifiable psychological dimension of an individual to an understanding of motivation as a range of attitudes which can act fluidly and dynamically according to time and context. Here, Deci and Ryan (2008), have drawn on the previous discussion about passive/active, engaged/alienated, to

Table 8.1 Types of regulation and motivation in self-determination theory

Form	Focus	Characterization
Autonomous	Internal/Intrinsic, Active/Engaged	Priority given to individual goals, needs and processes. Highest level of self-determination leading to intrinsic motivation and regulation, because the learner is in charge of their own learning and can directly understand what they are doing, why they are doing it and what they want to achieve through it.
Controlled	External/Extrinsic or internal/intrinsic, Engaged or Alienated	Priority given to the wishes and needs of those defining, presenting and measuring the learning. This can lead to extrinsic motivation where the needs, wishes and intentions of the learner do not match those of the provider. Where the needs, wishes and intentions of the learner do match those of the provider (internal = external) then controlled learning forms can promote intrinsic and engaged motivation.
Amotive	Lacking directive, Alienated	No individual or contextual priority is present Lowest level of self-determination Leading to non-regulated behaviours

construct three motivational types which can be characterised by different and distinct motivational behaviours. These can be seen in Table 8.1, with Deci and Ryan (2008) highlighting the different characteristics and influences of autonomous motivation (intrinsic/active/engaged), controlled motivation (extrinsic/passive/alienated), and amotivation (disengaged/alienated).

Educationally, the significance of these types is that each can be used to promote the acquisition and application of particular psychological behaviours. For instance, both autonomous and controlled motivation have been shown to produce improved academic performance, although the promotion of autonomous motivation offers greater potential gains for the student in terms of conceptual learning, engagement, performance, persistence and resilience (Jang, Reeves and Halusic, 2016). Only amotivation was shown to be universally negative in all conditions (Ratelle *et al.*, 2007).

> **Questions to consider**
>
> As someone that is interested in learner motivation, and in particular the study of learner motivation, it is important that you persistently seek an understanding of why events or relationships occur. Therefore, ask yourself why does autonomous motivation lead to improved academic performance and resilience, and why does controlled motivation potentially hinder student performance and resilience?

SDT as psychological need satisfaction

For Deci and Ryan (2008), motivational forms are important because each relates differently to the satisfaction of particular psychological needs that we all have. These 'needs' can be seen as underpinning our reasons to act, and the potential levels at which we function when we do so. The

Table 8.2 Psychological needs in self-determination theory

Need	Focus	Benefit
Autonomy	• Intrinsic motivation • Personal responsibility • Personal meaning	• Increased ownership and responsibility for the learning process. • The recognition of personal effort as central to goal achievement • Increased relevance strengthens the connection between action and identity
Competence	• Autonomy acceptance • Performance beliefs	• Individuals feel capable of acting autonomously • Increased levels of optimism when acting autonomously. • Individuals feel more capable of taking greater levels of risk when approaching new styles of learning
Relatedness	• Perceived belonging • Autonomy acceptance • Self-esteem • Positive affects	• Strengthening positive group Identities • Freedom to act separately from the group without punishment • Higher levels of self-worth and self-compassion • Experiencing positive emotional expressions during group interaction

levels to which individual actions satisfy those needs determine the levels of effort and engagement that individuals are willing to apply when carrying out those actions. For instance, our choice to go to university may be based on the need for independence, to meet new people, or simply because we love learning about the subject that we have chosen to study. The extent to which those needs are met by life at university will impact on our motivation to be there, the levels at which we work, and how positively we feel about ourselves and the university context.

Table 8.2 highlights the three central themes on which SDT is built: autonomy, competence and relatedness. The table offers you more detail on the nature of each need, but in essence we can understand them as:

1. **Autonomy** is the perception of freedom when thinking and acting, and the acceptance of personal responsibility when doing so.
2. **Competence** is the confidence in one's ability to act autonomously.
3. **Relatedness** is the experience of social support for autonomous action, and the perceived freedom from negative personal judgement and social rejection when acting autonomously.

What should be noted from the table is that whilst these are offered as distinct needs they exist in a very integrative space. Perceptions of personal autonomy influence our perceptions of competence, which, in turn, are influenced by our perceptions of relatedness, which again influence our sense of autonomy. None sits in isolation from the others. For instance, if you don't feel positive about yourself as a student because of poor grades, then you may deny responsibility for your studies and withdraw from making academic choices. Here, a loss of perceived university competence is also leading to a loss of autonomy, and quite possibly a loss of relatedness if those worries result in a withdrawal from university attendance. As such, it is all three working in harmony that possesses the greatest potential for improved motivation and performance through their separate and combined promotion of intrinsic motivation (Tabenero and Hernandez, 2011).

As noted earlier, whilst controlled motivation, which commonly works extrinsically, has often been shown to offer academic benefit, it has not been found to offer the psychologically holistic benefits, including performance, associated with intrinsic motivation (Tymms, Peters and Scott, 2013). These additional benefits are many, and include creativity (Deci and Ryan, 1991), improved levels of self-esteem (Deci and Ryan, 1995), resilience (Jang, Reeves and Halusic, 2016) and psychological wellbeing (Ryan, Deci and Grolnick, 1995). At a time of increasing focus on the issue of learner wellbeing, the proposed relationship between intrinsic motivation and wellbeing is of particular significance. Research has shown that, in spite of extrinsic and intrinsic motivations both supporting academic performance, albeit at different levels, only intrinsic motivation has been significantly related to positive wellbeing (Niemiec, Ryan and Deci, 2009). Indeed, similar research has generally supported a negative relationship between extrinsic motivation and both psychological wellbeing and learner resilience (Burton et al., 2006). As such, SDT as a developmental tool, prioritises the need to reject external, or extrinsic, behavioural goals and drivers in favour of internal, or intrinsic goals and motivations (Ryan, 1995).

In short, this means that learners need to be motivated intrinsically (where we feel autonomous and in control of our learning) in order to benefit from the wider psychological needs and benefits accessible to us from learning; extrinsic motivation (the hospital bed model, doing things because the environment tells us we should) is not sufficient in this respect. SDT, therefore, promotes the need to unify social and educational processes around the prioritisation of intrinsic motivators in order to help learners to be both more effective in their learning journeys but also to be more holistically effective members of a successful democracy. Where learner responsibility is lost within teacher-led practices so the potential exists for those learners to be unable to accept their individual and social responsibilities post-education (Dickinson, 1995).

Questions to consider

Think of a time when you have felt intrinsically motivated to learn and achieve something, when you have felt autonomous and in control of your learning. Using the ideas in the section above to prompt you, reflect on the range of psychological benefits that the learning offered and the personal needs it met.

SDT and the role of environmental influence

As previously discussed, SDT offers an unusual perspective on motivation and wellbeing because it not only focuses on an individual's perceptions of 'self' as a key driver of their own actions, but also the ability of the environment to support or change those perceptions. When considering the educational environment and the ways in which it influences learner behaviours, teachers must therefore be considered a fundamental driver of learner motivation and wellbeing, and if the tenets of SDT are to be accepted so teacher behaviours should be seen to be built around the promotion of intrinsic motivation and psychological need satisfaction. Teaching methods that support learner autonomy increase need satisfaction and through that increased engagement. Alternatively, teaching methods that control learner behaviours increase need frustration and with that the potential for learner amotivation. Cheon, Reeve and Song (2016) have referred to this as the working to the light or dark side of student motivation. In this vein, Nolan, Horn and Ward (2015) have highlighted the need for teachers to engage with students through interventions that acknowledge the fluidity and dynamism of individual patterns of meaning, identity and motivation, while Núñez and León (2015) found that this was best promoted through teacher behaviours that offered students clear and meaningful study rationales, choices, non-controlling language, and a balanced attitude towards the expressions of both positive and negative emotions. Where this was provided, students were found to experience improved academic performance, enhanced creativity and higher levels of wellbeing.

To achieve this doesn't need to be taxing for the educator in terms of practice, but should be reflected in the relationship between the teacher/lecturer and learner and the levels of engagement that the learner has in their own learning processes. For instance, Dickinson (1997) has suggested that to promote student autonomy at all levels of education, the learner should be given a more significant role in the construction of the learning agenda, and a greater level of individual responsibility for staying on track with the learning journey that they have helped create. At university, in particular, this is now being reflected in a drive towards knowledge co-construction, in which learners are supported in seeing content through their own personal experiences and asked to be key influencers in how modules are run and assessed (Ahn and Class, 2011). Similarly, schools have shown an increasing willingness to explore the benefits of reciprocal learning, in which knowledge is constructed by accounting for the many different perspectives that individual students bring to the classroom (Cárdenas and Pinzón, 2019). These forms of education focus on the need to work with classroom diversity and therefore increase intrinsic motivation, autonomy and relatedness whilst also increasing levels of personal meaning as students are supported in building connections between their learning and all other aspects of their life.

> **Questions to consider**
>
> Using the key characteristics of SDT, now revisit your own learning experiences at school and/or university. Consider what was done to support your learning and what could have been done to make your learning journey more productive. You are free to interpret the word 'productive' as you wish but make a note of how you are using that term. If you choose to reflect on school and university, then compare your reflections and try to explain how and why they may differ.

The tone of the discussion so far has been on SDT, and the ability to meet the students' basic psychological needs as a predictor of student performance. But through its connections to other psychological states, such as wellbeing, the model's potential to also explain student behaviours at a much more holistic level becomes clear. For instance, SDT assumes that when our psychological needs are not met, then students can act defensively as a coping strategy (Deci and Ryan, 2000). For instance, student behaviour may become more disruptive as they challenge the often-alienating demands being made of them and the authority of teachers to enforce those demands. Such acts are not driven by a need to present intrinsically meaningful or autonomous values and beliefs, but rather to present a counter-narrative to the extrinsic expectations projected towards them. Nor are they specific to the classroom, but to any potentially authoritarian relationship, including their relationship with their parents (Van Petegem, Vansteenkiste and Beyers, 2015). Autonomy has again been found to be of particular significance here; teacher-controlled practices have been found to promote amotivation through need frustration, while autonomy supportive teaching was found to promote need satisfaction and learner engagement (Cheon et al., 2019).

Conclusion

Through the study of motivation and SDT, it should have become clear that all psychological aspects of learning exist in a highly inter-connected space. As such, change in one dimension always creates change in another. Equally, no one learning theory or educational approach creates change in only one area of learner thought or behaviour. As a potential educator, it is therefore your responsibility to fully understand the potential consequences of applying any form of theory or practice. The application of theory always has consequences beyond its primary focus and as such your choice of theory always becomes an act of negotiation between positive and negative consequences. For instance, the use of an extrinsically focused practice may lead to a desired change in student behaviour in the short or long term, but may also potentially carry significant negatives relating to student motivation, performance and wellbeing. As such, to prioritise academic performance alone, which remains the key function of the modern educational process, may be potentially detrimental to the learner as an active and future-orientated whole. In terms of learner motivation, SDT asks you to look at the learner-educational environment as a whole, in order to recognise the potential in what you do, say, create and maintain to meet the psychological needs of learners, specifically autonomy, competence and relatedness.

Recommended reading

Deci, E. L., and Ryan, R. M. (2000) The "What" and "Why" of Goal Pursuits: Human Needs and the Self-Determination of Behaviour. *Psychological Inquiry*, 11(4): pp. 227–268.
This offers an excellent introduction to Self-Determination Theory, as presented by the key theorists of the model. The article both explains the model in full, but also clarifies its place amongst other theories of motivation that can be found in the psychological literature.
Chirkov, V., Ryan, R. M., Kim, Y. and Kaplan, U. (2003) Differentiating Autonomy from Individualism and Independence: A Self-Determination Theory Perspective on Internalization of Cultural Orientations and Well-Being. *Journal of Personality and Social Psychology*, 84(1), pp. 97–110.
This article offers research into the universal value of intrinsic motivation and the ability of SDT to transcend traditional cultural dichotomies of individualism and collectivism.
Milyavskaya, M. and Koestner, R. (2011) Psychological Needs, Motivation, and Well-Being: A Test of Self-Determination Theory Across Multiple Domains. *Personality and Individual Differences*, (50)3, pp. 387–391. https://doi.org/10.1016/j.paid.2010.10.029.
This research piece discusses a study of the relationships between need satisfaction and motivation, and wellbeing. It supports the idea that intrinsic and extrinsic processes promote more holistic consequences than improved performance alone, but highlighting instead their potential to act both positively and negatively at a far more holistic level.
Núñez, J. L., and León, J. (2015) Autonomy Support in the Classroom: A Review from Self-Determination Theory. *European Psychologist*, 20(4), pp. 275–284. https://doi.org/10.1027/1016-9040/a000234
Núñez and León offer an exploration of classroom interventions that seek to support autonomy, and with optimal learner behaviours. Working with real-life practices will help in grounding theory in practice.

References

Ahn, R., and Class, M. (2011) Student-Centered Pedagogy: Co-Construction of Knowledge through Student-Generated Midterm Exams. *International Journal of Teaching and Learning in Higher Education*, 23(2), pp. 269–281.

Burton, K. D., Lydon, J. E., D'Alessandro, D. U., and Koestner, R. (2006) The Differential Effects of Intrinsic and Identified Motivation on Well-Being and Performance: Prospective, Experimental and Implicit Approaches to Self-Determination Theory. *Journal of Personality and Social Psychology*, 91(4), pp. 750–762.

Cárdenas, K. J., and Pinzón, M. M. L. (2019) The Reciprocal Teaching Model in the Development of Writing in Tenth Graders. *Gist Education and Learning Research Journal*, 19, pp. 128–147.

Cheon, S. H., Reeve, J. M., and Yong-Gwan Song, Y.-G. (2016) A Teacher-Focused Intervention to Decrease PE Students' Amotivation by Increasing Need Satisfaction and Decreasing Need Frustration. *Journal of Sport and Exercise Psychology*, 38, pp. 217–235. https://doi.org/10.1123/jsep.2015-0236

Cheon, S. H., Reeve, J., Lee, Y., Ntoumanis, N., Gillet, N., Kim, B. R., and Song, Y.-G. (2019) Expanding Autonomy Psychological Need States from Two (Satisfaction, Frustration) to Three (Dissatisfaction): A Classroom-Based Intervention Study. *Journal of Educational Psychology*, 111(4), pp. 685–702. https://doi.org/10.1037/edu0000306

Deci, E. L., and Ryan, R. M. (1991) A Motivational Approach to Self: Integration in Personality. In R. A. Dienstbier (Ed.) *Nebraska Symposium on Motivation, 1990: Perspectives on motivation*. (pp. 237–288). University of Nebraska Press Lincoln, Nebraska, USA.

Deci, E. L., & Ryan, R. M. (1995) Human Autonomy: The Basis for True Self-Esteem. In M. H. Kernis (Ed.), *Efficacy, Agency, and Self-Esteem* (pp. 31–49). Plenum Press.

Deci, E. L., and Ryan, R. M. (2000) The "What" and "Why" of Goal Pursuits: Human Needs and the Self-determination of Behavior. *Psychological Inquiry*, 11(4), pp. 227–268. https://doi.org/10.1207/S15327965PLI1104_01

Deci, E. L., and Ryan, R. M. (2008) Self-Determination Theory: A Macrotheory of Human Motivation, Development, and Health. *Canadian Psychology*, 49(3), pp. 182–185. https://doi.org/10.1037/a0012801

Dickinson, L. (1995) Autonomy and Motivation: A Literature Review. *System*, 23(2), pp. 65–174.

Jang, H., Reeve, J. M., and Halusic, M. (2016) A New Autonomy-Supportive Way of Teaching That Increases Conceptual Learning: Teaching in Students' Preferred Ways. *Journal of Experimental Education*, 84(4), pp. 686–701. https://doi.org/10.1080/00220973.2015.1083522

Lemos, S. M., and Verissimo, L. (2014) The Relationships between Intrinsic Motivation, Extrinsic Motivation, and Achievement, Along Elementary School. *Procedia – Social and Behavioral Sciences*, 112, pp. 930–938.

Niemiec, C. P., Ryan, R. M., and Deci, E. L. (2009) The Path Taken: Consequences of Attaining Intrinsic and Extrinsic Aspirations in Post-College Life. *Journal of Research in Personality*, 73(3): 291–306. https://doi.org/10.1016/j.jrp.2008.09.001

Nolan, S. B., Horn, I, S., and Ward, C. J. (2015) Situated Motivation. *Educational Psychologist*. 50(3), pp. 234–247. https://doi.org/10.1080/00461520.2015.1075399

Núñez, J. L., and León, J. (2015) Autonomy Support in the Classroom: A Review from Self-Determination Theory. *European Psychologist*, 20(4), pp. 275–284. https://doi.org/10.1027/1016-9040/a000234

Ratelle, C. F., Guay, F., Vallerand, R. J., Senecal, S. L., and Senecal, C. (2007) Autonomous, Controlled, and Amotivated Types of Academic Motivation: A Person-Oriented Analysis. Journal of Educational Psychology, 99(4), pp. 734–746. https://doi.org/10.1037/0022-0663.99.4.734

Ryan, R. M. (1995) Psychological Needs and the Facilitation of Integrative Processes. *Journal of Psychology*, 63(3), pp. 397–427. https://doi.org/j.1467-6494.1995.tb00501.x

Ryan, R. M., Deci, E. L., and Grolnick, W. S. (1995) Autonomy, Relatedness, and the Self: Their Relation to Development and Psychopathology. In D. Cicchetti and D. J. Cohen (Eds) *Developmental Psychopathology: Theory and methods* (Vol. 1, pp. 618–655). New York: Wiley.

Tabernero, C., and Hernandez, B. (2011) Self-Efficacy and Intrinsic Motivation Guiding Environmental Behavior. *Environment and Behavior*, 43(5), pp. 658–675. https://doi.org/10.1177/0013916510379759

Tymms, M., Peters, J., and Scott, I. (2013) Personal Development Planning: Pedagogy and the Politicization of the Personal. *Research in Post-Compulsory Education*, 18(3), pp.257–268. https://doi.org/10.1080/13596748.2013.819264

Tymms, M., and Peters, J. (2020) Losing Oneself: Tutorial Innovations as Potential Drivers of Extrinsic Motivation and Poor Wellbeing in University Students. *Pastoral Care in Education*. 38(1), pp. 42–63. https://doi.org/10.1080/02643944.2020.1713871

Vansteenkiste, M., Lens, W., and Deci, E. L. (2006) Intrinsic Versus Extrinsic Goal Contents in Self-Determination Theory: Another Look at the Quality of Academic Motivation. *Educational Psychologist*, 4(1), pp. 19–31.

Wohlwill, J. F. (1973) The Concept of Experience: S or R? *Human Development*, 16(1), pp. 90–107.

9 Taking a global perspective

The nature and value of comparative and international education (CIE) in UK universities

Leanne Cameron, Rafael Mitchell, Gurpinder Lalli and Brendan Bartram

---

SUMMARY POINTS

- Comparative and international education provides a view into education systems worldwide, but there is ongoing debate in the discipline about what is 'international' and what should be compared.
- The survey from this chapter seeks to better understand what CIE looks like in undergraduate university programmes.
- The survey findings demonstrate that the United Kingdom and Europe in general are the most common geographic areas studied in CIE units, and less emphasis is paid to the ex-Soviet bloc and the Middle East.
- Content analysis showed that CIE units emphasise globalisation, cross-national comparison, and policy transfer but vary greatly in the aspects of education, culture, politics, and social issues that they each cover.

Introduction

From its earliest beginnings where 'travellers' tales' reported on education in far-flung locales, the field of comparative and international education (CIE) has reflected human curiosity in its descriptions of education in societies considered foreign or other. As an academic field, it is relatively young, having emerged in European institutions in the early nineteenth century. The field itself has been positioned to 'improve international understanding and awareness of other cultures and societies' (Crossley and Watson, 2003: 14), often through study of comparative statistics, 'rich' qualitative descriptions, and many other methodological approaches. Even today, the shape of the field itself is in continual flux as research continually expands what is viewed as 'international' and what forms are thus 'compared'.

Within the field, efforts have been made to map the shape of CIE research itself (Davidson et al., 2020; Pizmony-Levy, 2021), but less attention has been paid to the content of CIE university courses. At the end of the twentieth century, Schweisfurth (1999) provided a qualitative exploration of four UK comparative and international education (CIE) university course offerings.

DOI: 10.4324/9781003296935-11

Building on from that work, in September 2020, we issued a call through various professional and social networks, requesting that colleagues share unit handbooks for undergraduate courses which address comparative education, international education and/or globalisation. In response, we received 40 handbooks from 24 universities. We categorised the universities as either 'pre-1992' or 'post-1992'. Post-1992 universities are those polytechnics and other institutions that received university status from the Further and Higher Education Act 1992; they are sometimes called 'new' or 'modern' universities as well. We decided to use this categorisation to systemically explore CIE education and examine if university status impacts what is taught within the discipline. From the total of 24 universities, nine were pre-1992 institutions and 15 were post-1992. A thematic review of the handbooks was supplemented by interviews conducted with seven CIE teachers from four pre-1992 and three post-1992 institutions. As an undergraduate student, why care about the nature of education outside your own context? Especially for more generalist education degrees, preparing students for future careers in UK schools, the study of other educational systems, approaches, and theories may feel like a needless digression. Answers to this question often feature in the coursebook documents that we reviewed, and they are many: to understand the backgrounds of an increasingly multi-national UK school-aged population, to contextualise and question practices that are taken for granted within the UK school system, to expand one's horizons and engage in global citizenship. The field offers an entry point into diverse work environments, informing careers in research, education management, international development, international relations, and beyond.

In relation to our research, some might question the value of auditing what is being taught within CIE units. Surely the study of education in *any* other contexts has some value for future educators. To this proposition, we would point to the social movements of the 2020s, which have kicked off a broad reckoning with what is taught across UK higher education institutions. Undergraduate degrees, by their nature, often provide a broad introduction to an academic field and often present a taken-for-granted 'canon' of coursework seen as foundational for understanding the areas of interest, debate and approaches within that field. As such, and perhaps in contrast with later postgraduate studies, undergraduates may feel less able to question what they are being taught and why. Thus, as this chapter seeks to demonstrate, it is important to understand what is being seen as 'foundational' within the field: as the first step for a future CIE practitioner, professional, or academic, what areas of research, forms of comparison, geographic foci, and theoretical frames are being presented as 'normative' and essential? Who or what is being foregrounded, valued, and lauded, and who or what is being diminished or reduced?

Questions to consider

Have you ever thought about why we focus on some topics in school and ignore others? Who do you think is making those decisions? What kind of values, politics, or reasons are working in the background?

Has your university undergone any curricular investigations or changes as a result of the social movements of the 2020s or postcolonial movements such as Rhodes Must Fall? What impact do you think those changes will have – for you, for students like you, or for students from other backgrounds?

Chapter overview

This brief chapter examines the nature of CIE today through this survey and is, to the best of our knowledge, the first effort to systematically map and analyse what geographic regions, approaches, theories, and concepts are being foregrounded (or, conversely, deemphasised) in modern CIE programming. In the space allotted, we present only a broad sketch on the nature and purposes of CIE programming from the handbook review, with more granular detail to be found in the full report itself, alongside content from the interviews conducted (Mitchell et al., 2021).

Initial findings

The 40 unit handbooks we collected from 24 universities demonstrated a broad range of what may be labelled as CIE. Two decades previously, Schweisfurth (1999: 91) noted that CIE 'as a purely academic course is becoming almost non-existent' but still, 'fragments of the content and methodology of the field continue to permeate other education department programmes at several institutions'. A similar thread is evident in our dataset: the unit handbooks came from varied education-related degrees and ranged from 'general' CIE offerings (e.g. multiple units entitled 'Comparative Education' or 'Globalisation and Education') to course titles that denoted specific emphasis on children, poverty, technology, inequality, special needs, or a particular region of the world. There was also great variety in the documents themselves, ranging from two-page formulaic course overviews to lengthy, detailed module guides with weekly topics, readings, assignments, and questions for discussion.

Unit handbooks were analysed and coded via a content analysis process. First, all documents were also coded for geographic references, with all country references tabulated. Geographic focus varied across units, but there were some clear findings from the data. Ten of the 40, or 25 per cent, did not specifically reference any specific country or region, as with one module which was aimed at 'those students interested in exploring the influence of globalisation on educational provision'. Other units that fell within this categorisation demonstrated the limitations of coding for specific countries: other codes suggested specific geographic focus. Reference to 'OECD', 'World Bank', and 'policy transfer' provide understanding of the probable regions or nations that will be covered or referenced within the class.

For the remaining 75 per cent that did reference countries for study, our review noted a strong emphasis on European nations, appearing in 29 out of 40 unit handbooks, with the UK the most represented country, found in 17 and Germany second, found in eight. Indeed, for the UK in particular, we surmised that the number was likely higher: the UK, like the US, often does not have a country signifier in the title as both nations often function as a 'starting point' for comparison. In 15 handbooks, the UK was contrasted with unnamed 'global' or 'international' contexts 'abroad' or with those spaces where 'global inequalities' operate.

Beyond Europe, Asia and the Pacific, including Australia, was the second most represented region, with a tally of 19, and Africa was third, with 15. The remaining regions were North America (12), Latin America (nine), and the Middle East (none). We noted that country size did not necessarily correlate with coverage: Brazil, for example, only appeared in one reading list, and China, the most populous country and the home of the largest international student population studying in the UK, has just five. The results also demonstrated that little to no attention is paid to ex-Soviet countries in

Eastern Europe and Central Asia, and Russia was referenced by only one coursebook. Again, there were limitations to this approach, as we failed to adequately capture indigenous and boundary-less movements, or those which crossed national borders.

Following geographic mapping, each handbook was assigned between six and 20 keywords based on the content of the document, with the keywords coming from a standardised code set that was developed inductively through the cataloguing process. After the initial assessment, the code set was examined by other team members and similar terms were collapsed; the documents were reviewed twice more as the code set was reduced and revised. A final code set consisted of 86 terms.

For readers unfamiliar with the field of CIE, the content mapping that we present here gives an overview of some of the keywords and themes that have occupied CIE researchers. The first three codes give a clear introduction to topics that matter most within our work: *globalisation* (coded for 28 handbooks), *cross-national comparison* (25), and *policy transfer* (20).

As a code, *globalisation* captured references to trends, including increased contact between nations, shifts in international mobility, the emergence of the global marketplace, etc. It also reflects how higher education – UK universities in particular – have increasingly diverse international student populations and often position themselves as producing 'global citizens' and graduates able to communicate and operate across global contexts. The second code, *cross-national comparison*, is strongly related to approaches used in this field, and reflects the intended learning outcomes of some units, for example: '[students will] be conversant in a range of frameworks and methods that can be used to make comparisons in education'. *Policy transfer*, another term used commonly in the field itself, included references to education policies being intentionally borrowed or imposed. This relates to ideas about education – what pedagogies are 'best', how to prepare teachers, how to use technology, etc. – that may emerge in one country and then implemented in others, for better or worse.

These three codes included general references with more detailed aspects of each (specific policy statements, like the large global propositions such as Sustainable Development Goals (SDGs) and Education for All (EfA), or spaces of specific comparison, like league tables and international large-scale assessments) separately tallied, as seen in Table 9.1.

Grouped into primary themes, the codes provide an overview of the content presented in undergraduate CIE programming in the UK. Handbooks indicate ongoing emphasis on forms and levels of education (e.g. primary school, higher education, Montessori), the characteristics or key aspects of student populations being studied (e.g. SEND, class, rurality), and aspects related to teachers, curriculum, and pedagogy (e.g. language in education, technology, teacher education). Comparative approaches, as tools within the CIE discipline, and theories specific to the field are also foregrounded (e.g. issue-based approaches, capability theory, human capital). Globalisation, including the transfer of global policies and the work of multinational agencies, donors, and banks, along with development (SDGs, inequalities, philanthropy, etc.).

Discussion of findings

When examined together, the geographic and coding data suggest initial findings. Perhaps unsurprisingly, the coding and geographic mapping indicate the ongoing overlaps between CIE and development studies. With a few exceptions, the data demonstrates that lower income countries,

The nature and value of Comparative and International Education   71

Table 9.1 Thematic areas from CIE unit handbooks with five or more references

Key term	Tally	Key term	Tally
Globalisation	28	League tables	7
Cross-national comparison	25	Pedagogy	7
Policy transfer	20	Special educational needs and disability (SEND)	7
Gender	14	UNESCO	7
Inequalities	14	Human rights	6
Sustainable Development Goals (SDGs)	14	Millennium Development Goals (MDGs)	6
Children/youth	12	Neoliberalism	6
Culture	11	Teachers	6
Higher education	11	Alternative education	5
development	10	Capability theory	5
Education for All (EfA)	10	Children's rights	5
Postcolonial/decolonial perspectives	10	Conflict	5
Race	10	International large-scale assessments	5
Inclusion	9	Internationalisation	5
Poverty	9	Primary/secondary education	5
OECD	8	Social change	5
Social justice	8	Sustainable education	5
International non-government organisations (INGOs)/international government organisations (IGOs)	7		

specifically those in Africa, were collocated with social issues such as conflict, poverty, and inequality. In one example from a Year Two post-1992 course, a content description notes that a guest lecturer will discuss their 'research in Tanzania on girls and disability.' Comparison of overall *systems* tended to occur between the UK and high income, European nations, where the national educational approach was examined rather than that nation functioning as a case study for some specific societal ill. Though there were a few examples where Chinese, Japanese, and Cuban models of education were explored at a systems level, high income countries such as those in Scandinavia and Western Europe, were more commonly presented as complete 'systems' for comparison with the UK, as with this content description from a Year Two post-1992 course: 'Comparing schools, teachers and teacher education – culturally situated concepts, France, Denmark, England. Evaluating lessons for France?' However, there were some exceptions to this high income/low-income split, including an entire course focused on education inequalities in higher income countries. Further, the coding did indicate a growing emphasis on postcolonial and decolonial perspectives, which appeared in ten (25 per cent) of the handbooks, which would presumably question why inequalities and such are being relegated to lower income country status.

In sum, this survey indicates myriad directions for more research into current CIE teaching in the UK. For undergraduates, this exploration provides some context in understanding the content of these units and potential assignments; it helps to contextualise what universities might mean when they say that they prepare students to be 'global citizens' or 'internationally-aware'. In deepening our understanding of what content is being foregrounded – and what geographic regions, approaches, theories, and concepts in CIE education, we can have a better understanding of the foundations provided to those entering the field, foundations which establish normative frames that underpin the values, assumptions, and areas of research for the field in the years to come.

> ***Questions to consider***
>
> 1. What are some likely reasons why the UK is emphasised in so many of the units surveyed? Are there issues or problems that might appear with foregrounding the UK?
> 2. Descriptions of CIE have labelled it as everything from multidisciplinary and diverse (Crossley and Watson, 2003) to 'chaotic and disjointed' (Pizmony-Levy, 2021: 447), and, as we have seen in this chapter, there are overlaps with other fields such as development studies. What are the opportunities and the challenges for a disciplinary field that has strong ties with other disciplinary fields?
> 3. If this same research was conducted fifty years ago, it would likely show a very different picture of CIE education. Is it necessary for a field like CIE to grow, evolve, and change its areas of focus? Why or why not?

Recommended Reading

Phillips, D., and Schweisfurth, M. (2014) *Comparative and International Education: An Introduction to Theory, Method, and Practice*. 2nd edn. London: Bloomsbury.

If you are just getting interested in CIE, this book provides an excellent starting point; it even appeared in multiple reading lists from the unit handbooks discussed in our article. The book dives deep into many of the themes introduced here, including forms of educational comparison, globalisation, and the many social, historical, economic, and cultural influences upon education in different systems worldwide.

Pizmony-Levy, O. (2021) Social Network Theory and Analysis in Comparative and International Education: Connecting the Dots for Better Understanding of Education. In T. D. Jules, R. Shields and M. A. M. Thomas (Eds), *The Bloomsbury Handbook of Theory in Comparative and International Education*, pp. 447–458. London: Bloomsbury.

Mentioned in our piece, this book chapter provides a mapping of the many diverse areas of study that fall under the CIE banner. The author uses social network theory to analyse the members and institutions that belong to Special Interest Groups (SIGs) within the North America-based professional group, the Comparative and International Education Society (CIES) to comment on an issue that we briefly touch on: the narrow focus on nation states within the CIE field.

McCowan, T., and Unterhalter, E. (Eds) (2015) *Education and International Development: An Introduction*. London: Bloomsbury.

This edited book provides an accessible overview to the field of education and international development, presenting a number of the key actors, funders, institutions, theories, policies, and practices that underpin education systems and projects primarily in the Global South.

References

Crossley, M., and Watson, K. (2003) *Comparative and International Research in Education: Globalisation, Context and Difference*. London: Routledge.

Davidson, P. M., Dzotsinedze, N., Park, M. F. and Wiseman, A. W. (2020) Themes of Diversity, Comparison, and Contextualisation over Compare's History. *Compare*, **50**(8), pp. 1086–1103. https://doi.org/10.1080/03057925.2020.1831160

Mitchell, R., Lalli, G., Cameron, L., and Bartram, B. (2021) *Teaching Comparative and International Education in the UK: A National Survey of Undergraduate Programmes* (CIRE and Education Observatory Working Paper). Bristol and Wolverhampton: University of Bristol and University of Wolverhampton. https://doi.org/10.5281/zenodo.5148194

Pizmony-Levy, O. (2021) Social Network Theory and Analysis in Comparative and International education: Connecting the Dots for Better Understanding of Education. In T. D. Jules, R. Shields, and M. A. M. Thomas (Eds), *The Bloomsbury Handbook of Theory in Comparative and International Education*, pp. 447–458. London: Bloomsbury.

Schweisfurth, M. (1999) Resilience, Resistance and Responsiveness: Comparative and International Education at United Kingdom Universities. In R. Alexander, P. Broadfoot and D. Phillips (Eds), *Learning from Comparing: New Directions in Comparative Educational Research. Contexts, Classrooms and Outcome*, pp. 89–102. London: Symposium.

10 Being 'international'

The opportunities and challenges of studying education as an international student

Yutong Liu, Rebecca Morris, Tasha Peditto, Lingxi Peng and Ross Purves

---

SUMMARY POINTS

- Although still in a minority, there has been an increase in numbers of international students joining education studies degrees in the UK in recent years.
- International students can elect to study in the UK for various reasons, including perceived prestige and quality of the higher education system, prior familiarity with English language and culture, and links with institutions in their home countries.
- Whilst international students typically enjoy and value the transition to UK study, there can be many personal, linguistic, social, cultural and academic challenges. This group bring distinct perspectives to the study of education which are of great value to home students and staff, but can also find engaging with the complexities of UK education policy and culture difficult at times.
- We offer a range of practical suggestions for how international students can be supported within our subject, and how staff and home students can contribute to a learning environment which benefits and includes everyone.

Introduction

Take a moment to think about your Education Studies classes. Who are your peers? What do you know about their backgrounds or their lives outside of university? Do you know if they are 'home' students or 'international' students? And have you interacted much with students from both of these groups? In this chapter, we consider the experiences and perspectives of international students on Education Studies degrees. We explore the opportunities and challenges that this group of students may face, and reflect upon what this means for aims of equality, diversity and inclusion within higher education. In the spirit of these values, this chapter is aimed at students from all backgrounds – whether home or international. Our chapter, and the contributions and shared experiences from our co-authors, Yutong, Lingxi and Tasha, highlight the wealth of knowledge and insight that international students can contribute to Education Studies courses: as such, we encourage staff and students alike to consider how we can work together to promote a positive, mutually beneficial environment and experience for international students on UK Education Studies courses. Reflecting both the lived experiences of our co-authors and the available literature, some discussion draws particularly on perspectives of international undergraduate education students from

DOI: 10.4324/9781003296935-12

East and South East Asian countries including China, Malaysia, Japan and South Korea. However, we aim to draw out more general considerations as well.

Let's spend a moment reflecting on what we mean by 'international students.' In universities, home or international status is typically used to determine the level of tuition fees students pay for courses. This rather crude distinction essentially places UK-based (home) students into one group and those from all other countries into another group (international). It's also worth pointing out that students from countries within the European Union (EU) and certain other European countries were formerly regarded for official purposes as 'home' students. However, following the UK's exit from the EU this situation has now changed and incoming students from other European countries should check their individual circumstances carefully. Of course, such simplistic groupings are not particularly helpful for those of us interested in students' experiences of education as they ignore the diversity *within* the groups while also reinforcing difference between them. International students, just like those from the UK, are a diverse cohort with varied backgrounds and experiences. For the purposes of this chapter, we want to acknowledge this diversity while also seeking to understand common issues or factors which might influence international students' experiences, and which might be important and relevant for all students and staff working on Education Studies courses.

International students studying education

In recent years, there has been a steady increase in the number of international students joining Education Studies degrees in the UK (Table 10.1). While this group is still in the minority, their share of the total subject cohort grew to nearly 4 per cent in 2020/2021 (HESA, 2022).

We also know that in some universities, proportions of international students are much higher than in others; universities with greater international prestige and/or more pro-active marketing operations have tended to be the ones attracting higher numbers of undergraduate education students (Furlong, 2013). Reduced state funding for HE has produced increased financial incentives to attract international students across the whole UK university sector (Barnett, 2018). The intertwined nature of HE and globalisation is also key here. Universities not only contribute to globalisation, but are also driven by it. These forces have contributed to international student mobilities and increased opportunities for some groups of students to study abroad. (See Marginson (2022) for a helpful, critical discussion of these issues.)

Students' backgrounds and decision to study in the UK

As Seo (2020) notes, some international students, particularly those from East Asian countries, can be attracted to programmes of UK higher education as an investment in graduate career potential:

Table 10.1 Number of UG Education students in the UK

	2018/2019	2019/2020	2020/2021
UK students	69,145	57,855	56,985
International students (including EU)	1,775	1,760	2,225
Total	70,920	59,615	59,210

Source: HESA Student Data, Open Data Tables 22 and 52.

'Educational credentials from globally-renowned universities, as a certificate of accumulating global cultural capital, can determine an individual's access to certain activities' (Seo, 2020: 379). A key attraction of study in the UK is therefore the prestige and social capital associated with educational institutions in this country. Some, but not all, international students will also have a desire to remain in the country for further work or study. Beyond any prestige associated with particular UK universities, however, some international students also draw contrasts between the culture of higher education in the UK and at home. Students from some Eastern Asian countries in particular can perceive that the university education available either at home or in nearby nations is restrictive and lacking in creativity. By contrast, the UK university experience might be regarded as offering greater opportunities for student ideas, reflection and agency, supported by good teaching resources and a strong learning environment. For our co-authors, general attractions of the perceived 'British experience' were further strengthened by a desire for broader-based engagement with education, i.e. going beyond school teaching to embrace economic, political, cultural, historical and social justice perspectives. All the same, international students can experience the same misconceptions about what an education studies degree covers as home students! For instance, it might be interpreted as a preparation for English language teaching.

Yet home students, university staff – and indeed international students themselves – should avoid adopting a 'deficit model' or UK-centric perspective and assuming that the group-based, discursive and collaborative learning approach common within many undergraduate education programmes is superior to educational cultures associated with students' home countries. Whilst our subject can be good at emphasising these forms of learning, not all UK-based degrees might do so to the same extent.

Beyond the style of learning on offer, international students will typically have also considered their choice of host country very carefully, particularly in regard to the necessary language skills. They might have weighed up the various advantages of different English-speaking countries when deciding on the UK. Other European universities might be perceived to have similar benefits to the UK but are less favoured due to the pre-eminence of English language. Perceptions of crime and safety, and their likely reception by the local community are possible further considerations. Moreover, it is worth remembering, of course, that whilst the UK might be perceived by some international students as attractive for its cosmopolitan and global student population, some undergraduate education programmes will be offered at universities located in provincial or even rural areas. This can impact on the cultural diversity in these locations and might, in turn, have a bearing on international students' ease at engaging with the local community. These problems can be exacerbated in smaller institutions and those with a predominantly White British intake (Murphy, 2009).

Whilst international students on undergraduate education programmes might be gaining their first experiences of life and education away from home, this does not necessarily mean they will be newcomers to British (or possibly European) educational cultures. Some will have previously studied at institutions with links to UK universities, and some might have taken advantage of formal institutional links allowing them to transfer to a UK programme partway through. (The latter can cut tuition fees considerably and is thus an attractive option, although joining a programme late from elsewhere in the world can present combined challenges.) As a result of their previous experiences, some international students can arrive in the UK already prepared for aspects of their undergraduate education experience. All three of our student co-authors reflected on prior experiences (such as studying at an international campus of an English university) and skills (such as oral presentations) which prepared them well for their UK-based Education courses.

Other international students might have family or educational ties to other European or English-speaking countries. This again serves as a reminder not to make assumptions about such students' backgrounds. Studying in the UK might present a natural next step. As Hutchinson (2020) argues, some international students consciously develop a cosmopolitan identity based on having successfully navigated a range of prior travel and international study experiences. However, for other international students, these transitions between cultures are much harder to manage. As Seo (2020) notes, it is necessary for them to not only navigate potentially unfamiliar educational cultures and settings, but at the same time reorganise lives and build new social networks. They may also come to re-evaluate aspects of their home culture and education. As a result, it is known that some experience a period of 'transition shock' or 'culture shock' as they manage the various challenges; this has the potential to lead to reduced mental wellbeing. Moreover, some international students feel unable to express how they are feeling to others in their new setting, yet are also unwilling to open up to their families back home for fear of causing them to worry (Hutchinson, 2020).

Questions to consider

Whether you are an international or home student, what were the factors that influenced your decision to study Education at your current institution? Do you recognise similarities with some of the issues and experiences described above?

Advantages and challenges in the Education Studies curriculum

International students can bring distinctive critical perspectives to programmes or modules exploring intercultural or global issues in education. The process of having undergone transitions between education systems themselves positions them well to offer comparative views and to evaluate education systems from objective, detached positions. Indeed, as Wang (2015: 200) notes, in relation to the experience of Chinese international students, 'the interactions of the two cultures of learning accelerate not only the development of the student's intellectual and intercultural maturity but also the formation of an intercultural learning identity'.

On the other hand, international students may not initially be familiar with UK educational policy or practice and its associated vocabulary. Furthermore, securing and completing work placements can be more challenging for international students. They might be less able to draw on existing family/social networks to find relevant placements and less familiar with British workplace culture. By contrast, having navigated paths through the UK education system, home students possess potential advantages when undertaking study or practice in these areas. To draw on ideas from sociologist Pierre Bourdieu (see also Chapter 24 in this book), such partial familiarity might give the impression of a stronger 'feel' for the 'game' of UK education as a whole. Yet, it is important to bear in mind that this system's complexity means that experience with some of its strands does not automatically result in a greater general understanding. Examining issues objectively and within broader contexts is thus just as important for home students as it is for international students; there is probably more common ground between these groups than is often acknowledged. Problems can also occur due to the presence of 'hidden curricula' in the UK context. Specifically, some international students can experience confusion because each member of staff might have slightly different tacit assumptions and expectations (Seo, 2020).

Yet despite potential challenges, our co-authors found that the styles of teaching and learning common on UK undergraduate education programmes – whilst novel to an extent – did not take too much getting used to. Opportunities to reflect on their individual student identities, self-efficacy and metacognition, to explore culture and career planning, and engage in interactive questioning and debate were all highly valued, as were opportunities to undertake personally meaningful research topics.

Feelings of belonging and making social connections

As readers might be aware from their own experiences, travelling to a new country – even just for a holiday – can bring lots of exciting new opportunities to meet people and participate in new social experiences. It can also bring challenges, particularly if you need to communicate in a different language, or if you are less familiar with the social and cultural norms of your host country. To what extent do international students feel integrated and included in the 'social world' of their university? What are the barriers that exist for students to interact socially, both in academic contexts and those beyond the classroom? Many educational studies have revealed that a feeling of belonging and 'fitting in' can be central to fostering academic success and wellbeing. There are many areas to consider in relation to feelings of belonging at university (see e.g. Mackenzie and Morris, 2019; Meehan and Howells, 2019; Mountford-Zimdars et al., 2015). For the purposes of this brief discussion, however, we are going to focus on issues relating to language, labelling and stereotypes which have emerged from the literature and from the co-authors of this chapter.

As we saw in the sections above, an interest in developing and utilising language skills is often a key driver for students wishing to study abroad. While students who arrive from non-Anglophone countries have to produce evidence of English language proficiency (usually via an independent test score such as IELTS or Duolingo English), many still report a range of, often interconnected, challenges. These can include not being easily understood by native speakers (staff and students); not having confidence to practise and 'try out' English usage in real-life academic and social situations; not being able to follow or contribute to conversations; or struggling to translate and use more complex or unfamiliar academic terminology. In a seminar or class situation, this can make it more difficult for those from non-Anglophone backgrounds to contribute to activities such as informal discussions, paired or group work. Magne (2019) and Murphy (2009) point to examples where international, non-Anglophone students are perceived negatively by home students because of their use of English. Magne (2019), for example, found that some BA Education students described a Chinese speaker of English as 'not fluent' or 'wrong' whereas those who had Spanish or French as a first language were judged much more positively for their language and pronunciation.

Questions to consider

What does inclusion 'look like' in your seminar group sessions? How do individuals with different background characteristics contribute to and participate in sessions? How do teaching staff support and facilitate this?

Where international students feel that their English is not as strong as it could be or where they feel less confident to 'have a go' at speaking in English, it is likely to lead to a reluctance to use the language in some academic or social settings. For some students, in some situations, this may result in 'diglossia', where the two different languages are used for different functions i.e. English becomes the language of academic writing and the student's home language is used for social and personal communication (including perhaps conversations with peers in academic contexts). These issues are at least part of the reason why some international students can find themselves gravitating towards working with other international students more than with home peers. Working with those from the same country and with a shared linguistic background might be regarded as providing opportunities for more detailed and clearer discussions, and a less nerve-wracking experience.

One of our co-authors noted that day-to-day English, used in informal communications, both in and out of class, could be difficult because of the use of slang, different cultural norms and references, and the speed of speaking. To avoid the anxiety associated with trying to join in and potentially misunderstanding, she and her peers described working separately in their own group. It was noted that this was not necessarily their preferred way of working but that it provided a more comfortable space for speaking and sharing ideas. Our co-authors, however, are clear that they would have preferred to be more meaningfully included during class and small group discussions, and feel that this would have led to benefits such as supporting their learning and their sense of belonging within the cohort and university.

Often closely linked to the issues of language for international students are concerns around stereotyping and labelling. Gu (2009) and Hutchinson (2020) have both highlighted how East Asian students, particularly those from Chinese backgrounds, are sometimes perceived in UK universities as a homogenous group of learners with similar needs, proficiencies, characteristics and interests. While these may sometimes be framed as positive stereotypes (see e.g. Hutchinson's comments on Chinese students being characterised as 'hard working'), they are stereotypes nonetheless, and thus are unhelpful in terms of the provision of an equitable, fair and supportive learning and social environment for all students. Making assumptions about one's 'hard working' nature with little information other than their cultural background is problematic in itself; however, it also has potentially harmful effects too if, for example, it is coupled with an assumption that because of this hard work they are doing well academically, and thus do not need additional support or guidance with their studies.

How can we work to make things better?

Ideas and suggestions for home students and university staff

As Murphy (2009) notes, individual academic staff and institutions have a role in supporting international students to overcome the issues identified in this chapter. Staff can make significant positive impacts in their teaching, and through roles such as personal tutoring. Moreover, institutional practice and policy can be reviewed to consider how longstanding and potentially tacet conventions and expectations of the UK university experience are perceived by those from elsewhere. Home students have an equally important role to play here. The following recommendations (inspired by contributions from our student authors) are aimed at university staff and home students to support effective inclusion of international students:

- Avoid referring to international students collectively based on this country they are from, e.g. 'the Chinese students'. Labels such as these have the potential to segregate them from home students and imply they might be less familiar with topics under discussion. They may also result in groups of international students working together, emphasising their 'separateness' still further and potentially reinforcing unhelpful stereotypes. Such broad-brushstroke labels are liable to conflict with the individual, nuanced identities of international students.
- During discussion and activities, intentionally mix up students from different countries so that those from outside the UK are encouraged not to revert to their home language. Doing this can further support students' language development skills and can also encourage greater collaboration between different groups of students. Working with students from different countries and backgrounds can be a powerful driver for academic development.
- During class discussions, it is important for staff to balance a desire to support and give attention to international students with the need not to single them out and thus enhance feelings of stress.
- Listen to, and don't interrupt, international students when they are expressing their ideas. Listen *beyond* accents or grammatical errors, and instead engage with the ideas and contributions that international students are making.
- Encourage everyone to start from the premise that we can learn from each other's prior knowledge and experience. Keep an open mind and focus on creating safe, inclusive spaces where everyone has a voice.

In addition, Seo (2020) describes how a peer-assisted learning scheme was beneficial in helping first year international students of BA Education Studies from East Asian backgrounds overcome 'transition shock' and engender a sense of belonging. According to Seo, peer mentors can function not only as role models for international students (since they have gone before them and made a success of this transition), but also as a 'bridge' between international students and staff. The latter is beneficial in helping international students navigate the sometimes 'hidden' assumptions, expectations and implications of small group seminars, individual tutorials and assignment feedback.

Ideas and suggestions for international students

International students can also be pro-active in addressing some of the issues raised in this chapter, and our co-authors have shared the following recommendations.

- It's important to persist in making friends with home students. There is much fun and friendship to be had through sharing language and culture.
- Take the initiative to step out of your comfort zone and introduce yourself properly to the teaching team and other students on your programme. Allow your drive for education to come through in your approach to your studies. Make your passion to learn evident to tutors, who are likely to be very supportive and helpful.
- Be reassured that it's OK to ask staff and students questions about language and context. Similarly, be bold when contributing to class discussions or answering questions. Active engagement in class will result in a better learning experience overall.

- Don't suffer in silence. Be sure to tell someone you trust if you are unhappy about something. One of our co-authors recalls raising concerns about being 'labelled' as part of a group of international students. When she shared this with a trusted staff member, things immediately changed for the better and the staff member also asked other colleagues to be more aware of how they referred to international students.

Conclusion

Education Studies is a subject with diversity and inclusion at its heart. Whether we are thinking about pupils in schools or students at university, those who participate in the education system are entitled to positive, supportive learning environments which promote their achievement and wellbeing. Our co-authors have pointed to a number of great reasons why they would recommend coming to study in the UK. However, our discussions have also shown that for international students, undergraduate study is not always a completely positive experience. It is not just international students who lose out when this happens; home students and university staff are also missing out on a huge wealth of knowledge, insight and enthusiasm if international students are not fully included in their courses, departments and wider institutions.

Higher education in the UK is characterised at present by growing numbers of international students generally, and in Education Studies specifically (HESA, 2022). In light of this, and in line with wider inclusivity movements (e.g. widening participation, decolonisation), universities need to continue working hard to support and enhance the experience for *all* students in their institutions. Ideally, this should be done in collaboration with international students themselves. Their voices and input are needed to bring about and sustain positive change. Education Studies departments and courses are arguably in a strong position to lead on and embrace this work: modelling and embodying the inclusion of international students is likely to have a positive impact for the students, staff and universities involved, as well as for the wider education systems and societies that our students go on to work in.

Despite the challenges that our international student co-authors have shared about their studies, they are keen that we end on a note of optimism. Their hard work and enthusiasm for their studies has led to some ambitious and exciting post-university plans. All will be (or have already) engaged with further, postgraduate study, and are keen to develop their knowledge further so that they can make positive contributions to the field of education and society more broadly. We wish them all the very best with this.

References

Barnett, R. (2018) *The Ecological University: A Feasible Utopia*. Abingdon: Routledge.

Furlong. (2013) *Education - An Anatomy of the Discipline: Rescuing the University Project?* Routledge. https://doi.org/10.4324/9780203078853

Gu, Q. (2009) Maturity and Interculturality: Chinese Students' Experiences in UK Higher Education. *European Journal of Education*, 44(1), pp. 37–52. https://doi.org/10.1111/j.1465-3435.2008.01369.x

HESA (2022) *Where Do He Students Come From?* HE Student Data. Available: https://www.hesa.ac.uk/data-and-analysis/students/where-from (Accessed 23 September 2022).

Hutchinson, V. (2020) *Adults' Perceptions of Their Writing Practices and Development as Writers*. University College London Doctor of Education Thesis.

Mackenzie, H. and Morris, R. (2019) Students' Voiced Experiences of Social Transitions: Facilitating a Sense of Belonging. In P.A. Banerjee, and D. Myhill (Eds) *Transitions from Vocational Qualifications to Higher Education: Examining Inequalities* (pp. 95–110). Bingley, West Yorkshire: Emerald Group Publishing.

Magne, V. (2019) Students' Attitudes Towards Accents of English. *New Vistas*, 5(1), pp. 32–37.
Marginson, S. (2022) Globalisation in Higher Education: The Good, The Bad and The Ugly. In F. Rizvi, B. Lingard, and R. Rinne (Eds) *Reimagining Globalization and Education* (pp. 11–31). Abingdon: Routledge.
Murphy, B. (2009) Great Expectations? Progression and Achievement of Less Traditional Entrants to Higher Education. *Widening Participation and Lifelong Learning*, 11(2), pp. 4–14.
Seo, D. (2020) Helping East Asian International Students Overcome Cultural Differences in Academia: The Importance of Transition Mentoring Programmes as Spaces of Informal Learning. In S. Mawani and A.A. Mukadam (Eds) *Student Empowerment in Higher Education: Reflecting on Teaching Practice and Learner Engagement* (pp. 379–392). Berlin: Logos Verlag.
Wang, L. (2015) *Chinese Students, Learning Cultures and Overseas Study*. New York: Palgrave Macmillan.

11 Learning about research methods

A case study

Louise Gascoine and Laura Mazzoli Smith

SUMMARY POINTS

- A practical exploration of teaching and learning on a research methods module in an education studies undergraduate programme.
- An opportunity for students to reflect on their own research methods journeys, in response to prompts from experiences of both teaching and learning in this case study.
- Meeting the challenge of translating constructivist teaching principles to an approach to research methods that has a strong theoretical underpinning, alongside practice-based relevance and a strong experiential component.

Introduction

This case study is grounded in the practicalities of teaching a research methods module in an undergraduate education studies programme. In this chapter, we will illustrate, with examples from practice, how we have sought to orientate students to research methods through student-centred pedagogy and inquiry. This is an orientation that is grounded in opportunities to explore research methods through constructivist learning where there is a focus on student ownership of their own learning and development. Considering best practice in higher education, McCabe and O'Connor (2014: 355) described 'constructivist, active teaching strategies' as being an effective vehicle for student-centred learning. In our experience, there is often well-intentioned reference to constructivist teaching principles, but translating these into practice-based, experiential learning opportunities is not always straightforward. We would suggest that the complexity of constructivist learning principles is heightened further in the teaching of research methods.

In teaching research methods to education studies students, we have come up against the perception that this is both hard area to engage in and lacks some of the interest of other more topic-led modules. With this in mind, in this chapter we will describe out some of the constructivist activities that we have incorporated into this module, taught and developed over a number of years and in tandem with increased positive student engagement. A focus on the Deweyan orientation of 'closeness to life' as being integral for learning (Cremin, 1959: 163), fits well with our orientation to teaching research methods.

The chapter speaks to our own journeys in teaching research methods, and to our experiences of engaging with students on their research methods journeys in education studies. The metaphor of a

DOI: 10.4324/9781003296935-13

journey reflects the often-winding paths that students weave in research methods learning, as they are encouraged to explore, reflect and be reflexive. It is interesting to draw attention to the use of metaphor at this point, a technique that we value as a means of encouraging student reflection to aid their own meaning-making about research methods. (See Alvesson and Sandberg, 2021 for a detailed exploration of metaphor.) Transformative learning theory gives an account of how disorienting dilemmas can promote learning through reflection on taken-for-granted assumptions (Mezirow, 2018). Considering these assumptions, the journey is a particularly salient metaphor to encourage thinking about:

- Students' own experiential position(s) in relation to the epistemic challenges of understanding educational research methods, and
- The different paths (and iterative process of the journey) where students move from a research idea and question to the summative submission of a research proposal.

Questions to consider

What do I understand about the research I am seeing and reading about?

What are my 'growing edges' (or areas for development) for my understanding of research methods?

What examples of disorienting dilemmas can I draw on to note moments of change or transformation in relation to my understanding? (See the example of *The Spirit Level* below.)

The approach to the design and teaching of the research methods module detailed in this case study, is one that actively encourages engagement in depth with research methods and their underpinnings. Acutely aware of the value of this deep learning (Entwistle and Smith, 2013) for students, we encourage readers to reflect on their own experiences of learning research methods to support and develop their learning in this area.

What follow in this chapter are three examples of aspects of this module designed to foster the above; the example of *The Spirit Level* (Wilkinson and Pickett, 2009) as a seminal case study, the development of a research idea, and thinking inclusively about positionality in relation to research methods.

The spirit level – a seminal case

We use the example of *The Spirit Level* (Wilkinson and Pickett, 2009) to highlight to students the way in which understanding research methods empowers them to engage with, and understand, highly influential research such as this on social inequalities and health. Wilkinson and Pickett's epidemiological study into health and income inequality within societies carries not only an empirical, but also an evaluative, message that has been taken up by political parties of many persuasions. Their argument, which to many is self-evident precisely because of the 'killer graphs' that appear to lead to an incontrovertible conclusion, is that countries with higher levels of income inequality fare worse on a range of health and social outcomes than more equal countries. However, a lengthy critique (Saunders and Evans, 2011) mounts an attack on a series of methodological grounds which necessitates, and thereby fosters, a deep engagement with the material as students are invested in the overall message about equality. The value of this kind of example is that it demonstrates the real-world stakes of understanding research methods, and it is also an influential practical case wherein values and methods intersect. We have found that this particular case can function as a 'disorienting dilemma' for students, in the sense of promoting transformative learning by prompting a reflection on taken-for-granted assumptions. Assumptions that we find they often bring with them at the beginning of their research methods journey.

> **Questions to consider**
>
> Thinking about the example of 'The Spirit Level', what examples of disorienting dilemmas can you draw on to note moments of change or transformation in relation to my understanding?
> What research have you come across that has made you reconsider your own values or views?
> Has there been an occasion when understanding the technicalities of how research has been undertaken has led me to question its quality or value?

Developing a research idea

Opportunity is given, in summative assessment, for students to develop their own research idea which they submit as a research proposal. We provide a structure for students to present their research proposal that is not dissimilar to the kind of information that would be expected by research funders (rationale and aim(s), research question(s), research design and methods, strengths and limitations, and ethical considerations). The research proposal format facilitates this summative assignment as authentic (Villarroel et al., 2018) with the benefits that follow in terms of experiential and constructivist learning.

The importance of situating knowledge, as students develop their own research ideas in a wider, pragmatist orientation to knowledge and truth, is key. A reflexive and iterative process is modelled – we remind students that no two journeys are the same, and that they are a situated part of their planned research as much as any participants might be. Often (and not just at the beginning of developing research ideas) the question 'what is your research question?' is posed, encouraging students to make connections and consider why they make them in a process of relating 'judgements and decisions [that they make] to the question' (Biesta, 2020: 23). Identifying a research question and bringing to light your own understanding about why you pose the question (a question of both positionality and context) are the first part of the journey – the foundations.

If the foundations of research are not clear, then it is likely that what grows from them won't be. This notion of clear foundations speaks also to the importance of defining key terms in writing about research methods and beyond. The example of metacognition (or 'thinking about thinking') (e.g., Flavell, 1979) is a useful way to illustrate this. Desoete (2008: 204) described it as 'How you test is what you get' in relation to assessing metacognitive skills. We draw a parallel here to the research question(s) you ask (including where they come from and your position in relation to them) and how they then influence the research that you do, and the findings that you get.

Drawing on another of Alvesson and Sandberg's (2021: 97) metaphors, this process of students designing their own research idea is something of a 'dance routine', as students are encouraged to move in and out of contact with their ideas, being reflexive (looking inward, considering one's own views, beliefs, and judgements) about their process of arriving at them. Small group seminar sessions are used, and a kind of research proposal 'speed dating' is set up – students each have five minutes to present their idea and pose any questions they have, then peers and tutors give feedback and ask questions. The ensuing discussion is always so fascinating, the back and forth simultaneously challenging and inspiring, and the development in quality and clarity of student thinking clear.

> **Questions to consider**
>
> Set up your own research idea 'speed dating' – take it in turns in a small group to present your research idea. Wait until each researcher has presented before having a discussion and think about these questions:
> Is it clear where the research question comes from?
> Why it is an important question to ask? Who is the research important for and why?
> Where is the researcher in the research?

Thinking inclusively about positionality

The research proposal assignment is preceded by a summative essay, allowing students to first explore at depth, an issue of current importance in educational research. This essay based individual exploration is grounded in learning about broader philosophical and theoretical debates in educational research, fundamental to the development of students' own research ideas later in the module.

We do not avoid challenging debates that are truly inescapable in research methods teaching; we directly explore complex issues including, but not limited to, philosophical and ontological debates and issues around evidence and practice in education. Enabling students to engage with challenging, abstract ontological and epistemological material is brought to life through tangible examples that we use, often directly related to the context we teach in or world around them. We present a schematised overview of research paradigms in multiple visual ways, talking through with students what the adoption of each framework means in practice, but also drawing on American pragmatism and the work of Dewey (Hickman and Alexander, 1998) to demonstrate how multiple positions can be possible to build a better – not necessarily the best or only – version of the world.

> **Questions to consider**
>
> What kinds of knowledge do you have of the room you are in and the things that are in it as you read this chapter?
> How do you know this?
> In what ways might you approach finding out about how you know things?

Thinking inclusively about research design and methods, is something that students have valued for its drive to encourage thinking 'laterally' and being 'dynamic' and 'open to possibilities', as opposed to more fixed views of research methods that students may have encountered before. Veck and Hall (2020) encourage an approach that considers the question of inclusion (who, how and why?) and relationship, by drawing on the work of Martin Buber (1878–1965), particularly '*I and Thou*' (Buber, 2004). Veck and Hall's (2020) challenge to the reader is to consider things like the difference between 'encounter' and 'meeting' in research, as well as research methods and procedures. Students reflexively embraced this way of thinking about research in terms of relationships, their own position and considering what inclusive research means in relation to all aspects of research.

Recommended reading

Schön, D. A. (1992) The theory of inquiry: Dewey's legacy to education. *Curriculum Enquiry*, 22(2), pp. 119–139. https://doi.org/10.1080/03626784.1992.11076093

Donald Schön explores the legacy of Dewey for Education, the metaphor of the 'swamp' in relation to dilemmas in educational research around relevance and rigor is a useful way of thinking about and being reflexive about your own positionality. Schön's conceptualisations of reflection and knowing are a particularly useful way to think about practice based and experiential learning in relation to research methods.

Biesta, G., Filippakou, O., Wainwright, E. and Aldridge, D. (2019) Why educational research should not just solve problems, but should cause them as well. *British Educational Research Journal*, 45(1), pp.1–4. https://doi.org/10.1002/berj.3509

Biesta et al. (2019) explore, in a short editorial piece, some interesting debates around the value of educational research as a vessel to not only solve problems, but also identify and cause problems. In the context of this case study, this speaks to our active encouragement of students to think and be reflexive about what they know, why and what this means in the context of research methods.

Pring, R. (2004) *The philosophy of education*. London: Bloomsbury Publishing.

Pring's *The Philosophy of Education* (2004) is one of the most readable, clear and helpful expositions of philosophical ideas that underpin methodology we have come across. In a short book drawing on real-world examples (including a very memorable idea about social constructionists and aircraft design!), Pring provides an accessible way into the big philosophy of social science ideas that underpin educational research methods.

References

Alvesson, M. and Sandberg, J. (2021) *Re-imagining the research process: Conventional and*

Biesta, G. (2020) *Educational research: An unorthodox introduction*. London: Bloomsbury Publishing.

Buber, M. (2004) *I and thou*. London: Continuum.

Cremin, L. A. (1959) John Dewey and the progressive-education movement, 1915–1952. *The School Review*, 67(2), pp. 160–173. https://doi.org/10.1086/442489

Desoete, A. (2008) Multi-method assessment of metacognitive skills in elementary school children: How you test is what you get. *Metacognition and Learning*, 3(3), pp. 189–206. https://doi.org/10.1007/s11409-008-9026-0

Entwistle, N. J. and Smith, C. (2013) Exploring the nature of academic understanding. *The Psychology of Education Review*, 37(1), pp. 28–36.

Flavell, J. H. (1979) Metacognition and cognitive monitoring: A new area of cognitive — developmental inquiry. *American Psychologist*, 34(10), pp. 906–911. https://doi.org/10.1037/0003-066X.34.10.906

Hickman, L. A. and Alexander, T. M. (Eds.) (1998). *The essential Dewey: Pragmatism, education, democracy* (Vol. 1). Bloomington and Indianapolis: Indiana University Press.

McCabe, A. and O'Connor, U. (2014) Student-centred learning: The role and responsibility of the lecturer. *Teaching in Higher Education*, 19(4), pp. 350–359. https://doi.org/10.1080/13562517.2013.860111

Mezirow, J. (2018) Transformative learning theory. In K. Illeris (Ed.) *Contemporary theories of learning: Learning theorists...in their own words*. (pp. 90–105). Abingdon: Routledge.

Saunders, P. and Evans, N. E. (2011) *Beware false prophets: equality, the good society and the spirit level*. London: Policy Exchange. Available at: https://www.policyexchange.org.uk/wp-content/uploads/2016/09/-beware-false-prophets-jul-10.pdf (Accessed 11 May 2022).

Veck, W. and Hall, M. (2020) Inclusive research in education: Dialogue, relations and methods. *International Journal of Inclusive Education*, 24(10), pp. 1081–1096. https://doi.org/10.1080/13603116.2018.1512659

Villarroel, V., Bloxham, S., Bruna, D., Bruna, C. and Herrera-Seda, C. (2018) Authentic assessment: Creating a blueprint for course design. *Assessment and Evaluation in Higher Education*, 43(5), pp. 840–854. https://doi.org/10.1080/02602938.2017.1412396

Wilkinson, R. and Pickett, K. (2009) *The spirit level: Why equality is better for everyone*. London: Penguin UK.

12 Education for sustainability

Connecting students to outdoor learning via forest school

Dave Cudworth

SUMMARY POINTS

- The promotion of sustainability and the SDGs is an important part of teaching and learning in all educational settings.
- Outdoor Learning supports the development of our health and wellbeing, confidence and motivation to learn, as well as environmental stewardship.
- Forest School is an Outdoor Learning approach that promotes our biophilic connection with the natural world and our relationships with the non-human.

Introduction

As human animals we have been evolutionarily pre-disposed to seek connections with nature and other living things, a concept known as 'biophilia' (Wilson, 1984). Such historic propensity to connect with nature has provided benefits for our psychological health and wellbeing (Chawla, 2015), as well as being responsible for developing our pro-environmental behaviours and ideas of conservation (Zhang et al., 2014).

However, growing concerns of the erosion of our biophilic connection with nature due to the technological advancements of Western Societies (Gullone, 2000) and the creation of artificial environments (Wilson, 1993) correlates to a lack of environmental stewardship, and the need to protect and care for the natural world (Turtle et al., 2015). With humanity facing the multiple crises of climate change and biodiversity, loss of our historical relationship with nature is responsible for harm caused to the natural environment. A new relationship with nature is needed through nature connection, given its strong links with wellbeing and pro-sustainable behaviours. We all need to do our part in thinking about how we can live in a more sustainable way.

Consequently, education has become an increasingly important part of the international sustainability agenda in raising awareness of how we can support action to shape a more sustainable way of life (Rieckmann, 2012). Enshrined in the 2030 Agenda for Sustainable Development or the Sustainable Development Goals (SDGs) (UN, 2015), many universities are well-placed to take a leading role in cementing sustainability as a significant strategic focus (IAU, 2010) by embedding knowledge and understanding of the SDGs as a learning tool. However, with the SDGs often being seen as aspirational and criticised for lacking any credible way of unpacking power relations and wider systemic and structural injustices, it is hard to understand the reality of actions that need to be adopted, particularly at the local level (Sultana, 2018). Furthermore, knowledge

DOI: 10.4324/9781003296935-14

that incorporates action and personal pro-environmental transformation is often quite difficult when teaching takes place indoors (Collado et al., 2020).

However, with global temperatures increasing at worrying rates, and our recent experience of a pandemic, there is a renewed awareness of the need to understand our relationship with non-human animals as well as our individual impact on the wider environment. So, despite the critiques, the SDGs could at least provide a starting point in which to initially begin thinking about our relationship with non-human animals and ideas of sustainability. The purpose of this chapter is to provide details of how one BA Education Studies level five optional module offered at one university supported students' awareness of the natural environment and sustainability by taking learning outside and engaging with the natural world. The emphasis of the module related to this biophilic relationship between our emotional connection and engagement with the natural world outside the 'classroom' and the development of sustainable and pro-environmental behaviours (Braun and Dierkes, 2017).The Outdoor Learning approach used to immerse students in nature was Forest School (FS).

Questions to consider

What is your understanding of the SDGs?
What do you think the relationship is between the SDGs and Outdoor Learning?
In thinking about your own course, how relevant could the SDGs be and how might they be included to enhance or change the experience of students taking the course?

Forest school as a vehicle for outdoor learning

The idea of FS originated in Scandinavia in the 1950s and is culturally rooted in the outdoor ideology of Denmark based on the philosophy of *friluftsliv* (free-air life) (Waller et al., 2017). Since then, it has become an integral part of early years educational practice and remains firmly embedded in their curriculum today (Beery, 2013). A key ethos of FS is to nurture and develop a learner's innate curiosity to explore natural environments and connect with the outdoor which is regarded as 'essential for the health of the individual, society and the planet' (Knight, 2016:1).

The development of FS in the UK can be traced back to 1993 when a group of teachers and early years' practitioners from Bridgewater College, England went over to Denmark to observe FS first-hand. So impressed were they by how children learnt holistically by using the outdoors, on their return they established the first FS in the UK (Knight, 2016). In 2012, the Forest School Association (FSA) was formally launched as the professional association for FS and the governing body for training in the UK with a key philosophy related to connecting children with the natural world (FSA, 2012). As part of its launch, the FSA agreed and formalised six underpinning principles which have continued to guide the practice today (see below).

Since the setting up of the FSA, FS has been gaining in popularity in the UK, although in the main such interest has taken off in early years and primary school settings. However, with an increasing body of evidence highlighting the positive effect of FS in developing learners' confidence and health and wellbeing (Capaldi et al., 2014), their motivation to learn (Skinner and Chi, 2012) as well as environmental stewardship (Turtle et al., 2015), such popularity is spreading across all ages and interest groups, including learners with learning differences, teenagers and adults. This is significant, particularly at a time of a growing appreciation of the damaging effects human behaviour is having on the environment (Wynes and Nicholas, 2017).

The key pedagogic philosophy of FS practice is that the experience offered to learners takes place in a wooded area, is play-based, long term and learner-centred (McCree and Cree, 2017), very much in line with the early pioneers of experiential learning including Froebel, Dewey, Montessori and A. S. Neil (see Cree and McCree, 2012). Learners are free to be spontaneous and choose what they want to do, and practitioners are simply there to facilitate and support activities, make sure learners are safe, and to join in thus breaking down embedded power relations between teachers and learners. It is therefore different from the focus of the neoliberal classroom based on performativity and testing where movement is restricted, and learning is teacher-led (Cudworth and Lumber, 2021). In principle, FS provides learners with a practical real-life learning experience where they are free to explore the outdoor setting and lead their own learning. They gain an understanding of themselves and others including their peers, practitioners and the non-human animals and flora around them, and long-term begin to build a connection with the natural environment (Cudworth, 2020). As learners develop a sense of belonging to the outdoor space, they build an emotional affinity with nature which, in turn, affects their attitudes and behaviours towards the natural environment (Kahn and Kellert, 2002). With increased frequency of visits to these places they develop further a secure attachment to the setting and with others in that setting (Beames and Ross, 2010) fostering caring attitudes towards the natural environment and habitats (Stern et. al., 2008) and a commitment to participate in pro-environmental behaviours (Collado et al., 2013).

The Six Forest School Principles and criteria for good practice (FSA, 2012)

1. **FS is a long-term process of frequent and regular sessions in a woodland or natural environment, rather than a one-off visit. Planning, adaptation, observations and reviewing are integral elements of FS**
   - FS takes place regularly, ideally at least every other week, with the same group of learners, over an extended period of time, if practicable encompassing the seasons.
2. **FS takes place in a woodland or natural wooded environment to support the development of a relationship between the learner and the natural world**
   - Whilst woodland is the ideal environment for FS, many other sites, some with only a few trees, are able to support good FS practice.
   - FS aims to foster a relationship with nature through regular personal experiences in order to develop long-term, environmentally sustainable attitudes and practices in staff, learners and the wider community.
   - FS uses natural resources for inspiration, to enable ideas and to encourage intrinsic motivation.
3. **FS aims to promote the holistic development of all those involved, fostering resilient, confident, independent and creative learners**
   - Where appropriate, the FS leader will aim to link experiences at FS to home, work and /or school education.
   - FS programmes aim to develop, where appropriate, the physical, social, cognitive, linguistic, emotional and spiritual aspects of the learner.

4. **FS offers learners the opportunity to take supported risks appropriate to the environment and to themselves**
   - FS opportunities are designed to build on an individual's innate motivation, positive attitudes and/or interests.
   - Any FS experience follows a Risk–Benefit process managed jointly by the practitioner and learner that is tailored to the developmental stage of the learner.
5. **FS is run by qualified FS practitioners who continuously maintain and develop their professional practice**
   - School practitioners, who are required to hold a minimum of an accredited Level 3 FS qualification.
   - The FS leader is a reflective practitioner and sees themselves, therefore, as a learner too.
6. **FS uses a range of learner-centred processes to create a community for development and learning**
   - A learner-centred pedagogical approach is employed by FS that is responsive to the needs and interests of learners.
   - Play and choice are an integral part of the FS learning process, and play is recognised as vital to learning and development at FS.
   - Reflective practice is a feature of each session to ensure learners and practitioners can understand their achievements, develop emotional intelligence and plan for the future.

Question to consider

Thinking about the FS approach to learning and the six principles above, do you think that key elements of its practice, purpose and principles can be adopted and embedded in wider areas of mainstream teaching and learning and if so, what would this look like in practice?

The module

Due to an increased awareness and growing interest in FS and on qualifying as a FS Leader in 2018, I became increasingly interested in providing our Education Studies students with a practical insight into FS practice. I was keen to offer them a real-life, experientially informed learning opportunity that embodied a more horizontal approach to learning particularly in relation to staff and student relationships. It was important to provide a more hands-on approach to learning in order to enable students to immerse themselves in the natural environment and see more clearly the links between educational theory and its relationship with outdoor learning practice. Hence my decision to create a module that focused on FS as a vehicle for Outdoor Learning.

The module consisted of 12 × two-hour workshops. Two thirds of the workshops took place on campus, with some classroom input, and outdoor activities around the campus and a local park, with the other third being totally practical. These latter practical sessions took place off campus within an open natural space. Practical sessions involved a variety of activities including observational nature walks and mindfulness, den-building, playing games, lighting fires, cooking, creating art using natural materials, using tools and making artefacts.

Furthermore, as part of the module each student also undertook a FS placement at a local primary school where they gained further experience of FS in practice in a school setting. The school had a designated FS Leader (a qualified teacher who has also taught at the school for 25 years) and an FS area and offers a block of four to five afternoon sessions for each class from Years 3–6, on a specific afternoon per week over the year. Students chose a block that complemented their timetable, and were able to commence the placement before, during or after the module took place. This provided the students with a work-based learning opportunity where they also gained experience working with children in the outdoors, and again it provided them with an opportunity to relate theory to practice. Many of the students that elected to take the module, went on to complete their third-year dissertation on FS, and would often return to the school to collect data and carry out further placements as participant observers.

For the assessment, students produced an FS teaching pack for a six-week learning programme. This included a planning sheet detailing a six-week programme (six two-hour sessions), complete with learning and development objectives, resources, a risk assessment and teacher notes. The teaching pack made links with some aspects of education policy and guidance (for example, DCSF, 2007; DfES, 2006; Ofsted, 2008) as well as key theories and literature that discussed the benefits of outdoor learning and FS in particular. (See reference list and further reading below.)

With FS being a communal experience and learner-led, such involvement in the module provided students with the tools in which to become more confident and effective communicators as well as developed their understanding of others. Further, by engaging with the natural environment they also developed an affinity with the natural world which can often promote a sense of wider connectedness with the environment and an understanding of its relationship with environmental sustainability and the SDGs.

It soon became increasingly clear that, in undertaking the practical activities in particular, students got a lot of enjoyment from the module and were able to develop their mental health, whilst at the same time gaining an understanding of the SDGs and a respect for the natural world and others.

Reflective practice

Reflective practice is a key element of all learning and something that is embedded in FS practice (see principle six above). Consequently, at the end of each practical session off campus students were asked to share their informal reflections about the session. They were under no pressure to share these reflections if they did not want to. However, many students did share their reflections as they developed their confidence and ability to share their thoughts in other seminars and tutorials across their degree. These reflections were later captured more formally in a feedback questionnaire at the end of the module. Some examples of this feedback are offered here.

What, if anything, do you think you will take away from the module?

> *I have found that my personal connection to nature keeps me happy and that it is essential to open up FS to all children. As it allows for the children to gain skills and incorporate them into learning.*
> *That learning is in many forms, not just the traditional academic learning in a classroom.*

Has the module benefitted you in any way? If so, in what ways?

I think it has made me want to get out more and just appreciate nature and what it has to offer. There is so much you can do outdoors, and I don't think we take advantage of it.

The reason for doing this degree was the FS module. I no longer want to spend my time working inside, I want to be outside, enjoying the environment and contributing towards maintaining and improving our environment.

Would you say that the module has increased your understanding of the SDGs? If so, in what ways?

Yes, I understand the indirect effect of our behaviour with nature in going towards many SDGs. I didn't know the meaning of this term and now I am more aware of how we can be more sustainable

> **Questions to consider**
>
> Considering these reflections, what would you suggest were the key learning objectives achieved by these students?

Conclusion

Fundamentally, the environmental problems facing us all in part relate to our (dis)connection from/to the natural world. It is the responsibility of all governments to play their part in supporting and helping us to live more sustainably. Education is an important vehicle in which to encourage and support this thinking as well as embedding action. Universities are well-placed to align their curricula and policies with the principles of sustainable development and equally play their part. One way of achieving this is to take learning outside as much as possible and immerse students in the natural environment. To give the new generation a sustainable future, I argue that we urgently need to recognise how outdoor learning can support the understanding of our biophilic relationship with nature and the non-human others that we share this planet with. It's time for all of us to get outside and develop a renewed affinity with the natural world and promote pro-environmental behaviours and sustainability.

Recommended reading

Cree, J., and Robb, M. (2021) *The Essential Guide to Forest School and Nature Pedagogy*. Abingdon: Routledge.
This book provides a complete guide to Forest School and Nature Pedagogy. By drawing on real-life examples and session plans it brings together systems, approaches, viewpoints, and the principles that underlie teaching in nature.

Sackville-Ford, M. and Davenport, H. (2017) *Critical Issues in Forest Schools*. London: Sage.
This book takes a critical look at the challenges, barriers and tensions surrounding the implementation of Forest School practice in schools and beyond.

Waite, S. (Ed.) (2017) *Children Learning Outside the Classroom: From Birth to Eleven* (2nd Ed). London: SAGE.
This is a popular textbook complete with a companion website available at https://study.sage.pub.com/waiteze. It brings together a wealth of methods, perspectives and different approaches to support students and professionals understand the importance of taking children outside of the classroom with lots of ideas and activities for teachers and practitioners to embed in their curriculums.

References

Beery, T. H. (2013) Nordic in nature: Frilufsliv and environmental connectedness. *Environmental Education Research*, **19**(1), pp. 94–117. https://doi.org/10.1080/13504622.2012.688799

Braun, T. and Dierkes, P. (2017) Connecting students to nature: Ow intensity of nature experience and student age influence the success of outdoor education programs. *Environmental Education Research*, **23**, pp. 937–949. https://doi.org/10.1080/13504622.2016.1214866

Capaldi, C.A., Dopko, R.L. and Zelenski, J.M. (2014) The relationship between nature connectedness and happiness: A meta-analysis. *Frontiers in Psychology*, Article 976, pp. 1–15. https://doi.org/10.3389/fpsyg.2014.00976

Chawla, L. (2015) Benefits of nature contact for children. *Journal of Planning Literature*, **30**(4) pp. 433–452. https://doi.org/10.1177/0885412215595441

Collado, S., Staats, H. and Corraliza, J.A. (2013) Experiencing nature in children's summer camps: Affective, cognitive and behavioural consequences. *Journal of Environmental Psychology*, **33**, pp. 37–44.

Collado, S., Rosa, C. D. and Corraliza, A. Jose (2020) The effect of nature-based environmental education program on children's environmental attitudes and behaviors: A randomized experiment with primary schools. *Sustainability*, **12**, pp. 1–12. https://doi.org/10.3390/su12176817

Cree, J. and McCree, M. (2012) A brief history of the roots of Forest School in the UK. *Horizons*, **60**, pp. 32–34.

Cudworth, D. (2020) Promoting an emotional connection to nature via Forest School: Disrupting the spaces of neo-liberal performativity. *International Journal of Sociology and Social Policy (Special Edition: Towards a Critically Posthumanist Sociology)*, **41**(3/4), pp. 506–521. https://doi.org/10.1108/IJSSP-09-2019-0188

Cudworth, D. and Lumber, R. (2021) The importance of forest school and the pathways to nature connection. *Journal of Outdoor and Environmental Education*, **24**, pp. 71–85. https://doi.org/10.1542/peds.2017-1498

DCSF (2007) *Effective Practice: Outdoor Learning*, Nottingham, Department for Children, Schools and Families. Available at www.urbanforestschool.co.uk/PDF/3_3b_ep.pdf (Accessed 12 November 2021).

DfES (2006) *Learning Outside the Classroom Manifesto*. Nottingham: DfES. Available at: https://www.lotc.org.uk/wp-content/uploads/2011/03/G1.-LOtC-Manifesto.pdf (Accessed 14 March 2021).

FSA (2012) *What Is Forest School*. Available at: https://forestschoolassociation.org/what-is-forest-school/ (Accessed 12 November 2021).

Gullone, E. (2000) The Biophilia hypothesis life in the 21st century: Increasing mental health or increasing pathology? *Journal of Happiness Studies*, **1**, pp. 293–321. https://link.springer.com/article/10.1023/A:1010043827986

IAU (International Association of Universities) (2010) *Sustainable Development*. Available at: http://www.iau-aiu.net/sd/index.html (Accessed 16 March 2021).

Kahn, P.H. and Kellert, S.R. eds. (2002) *Children and Nature: Psychological, Sociocultural, and Evolutionary Investigations*. Cambridge, MA: The MIT Press.

Knight, S. (2016) *Forest School in Practice for All Ages*. London: Sage.

McCree, M. and Cree, J. (2017) Forest School. In S. Waite (Ed.), *Children Learning Outside the Classroom: From Birth to Eleven* (2nd Ed), (pp. 222–232) London: Sage.

Ofsted (2008) *Learning Outside the Classroom: How far should you go?* Available at: https://www.lotc.org.uk/wp-content/uploads/2010/12/Ofsted-Report-Oct-2008.pdf (Accessed 14 March 2021).

Rieckmann, M. (2012) Future-orientated higher education: Which key competencies should be fostered through university teaching and Learning? *Futures*, **44**, pp.127–135. https://doi.org/10.1016/j.futures.2011.09.005

Skinner, E. A. and Chi, U. (2012) Intrinsic motivation and engagement as "active ingredients" in garden based education: Examining models and measures derived from self-determination theory. *Journal of Environmental Education*, **43**(1), pp. 16–36. https://doi.org/10.1080/00958964.2011.596856

Sultana, F. (2018) An(Other) geographical critique of development and SDGs. *Dialogues in Human Geography*, **8**(2), pp. 186–190. https://doi.org/10.1177/2043820618780788

Turtle, C. Convery, I. and Convery, K. (2015) Forest Schools and environmental attitudes: A case study of children aged 8-11 years. *Cogent Education*, **2**(1) pp.1–14. https://doi.org/10.1080/2331186X.2015.1100103

United Nations (UN) (2015) *The 2030 Agenda for Sustainable Development*. Available at: https://sustainabledevelopment.un.org/post2015/transformingourworld (Accessed 4 March 2021).

Waller, T., Arlemalm-Hagser, E., Sandseter, E. B. H., Lee-Hammond, L., Lekies, K. S. and Wyver, S. (Eds) (2017) *The Sage Handbook of Outdoor and Learning*. Sage: London.

Wilson, E. O. (1984) *Biophilia*. Cambridge, MA: Harvard University Press.

Wilson, E. O. (1993) Biophilia and the conservation ethic. In S. R. Kellert and E. O. Wilson (Eds), *The Biophilia Hypothesis* (pp. 31–41). Washington DC: Island Press.

Wynes, S. and Nicholas, K. A. (2017) The climate mitigation gap: Education and government recommendations miss the most effective individual actions. *Environmental Research Letters*, **12**, p. 074024. Available at: https://iopscience.iop.org/article/10.1088/1748-9326/aa7541 (Accessed 28 September 2022).

Zhang, W, Goodale, E. and Chen, J. (2014) How contact with nature affects children's biophilia, biophobia and conservation attitude in China. *Biological Conservation*, **177**, pp. 109–116. Available at: https://doi.org/10.1016/j.biocon.2014.06.011 (Accessed 28 September 2022).

13 The role and value of arts-based learning for education studies

Cheryl Cane

SUMMARY POINTS

- Arts-based learning is a complex concept and needs defining for particular contexts.
- Arts-based learning can promote learning experiences that are inspired by artistic processes: open-ended with moments of surprise, taking time for perception and imagination, demonstrating coherence between form and content, showing awareness of feelings and senses.
- There are limitations and challenges inherent in arts-based learning activities and they require careful planning, organisation and practice.

Introduction

Perhaps one of the most interesting starting points in a discussion about arts-based learning is a discussion about definitions. This chapter highlights a number of ways that arts-based learning has been described, or implied, in relevant literature. It does not claim to be inclusive of all theoretical perspectives, but it does outline the difficulty that emerges in theorising about a concept that presents itself in multiple ways for different contexts. The chapter highlights two arguments that are pertinent to the discussion: engaging in arts practices in education (for example taking part in dance, drama, music, visual arts and so on) does not necessarily mean that arts-based learning is being employed, and second that the presence of arts-based learning does not require the use of a recognisable art form, product or professional artist. To understand these ideas in more detail it is important to consider what can be meant by arts-based learning and to recognise that there are 'many different art worlds to consider' (Cannatella, 2020: 39).

Art worlds and the difficulties of terminology use

One of the complications with exploring the use of the arts in education is that the different art worlds have their own 'specific qualities and artistic conceptual interests' (Cannatella, 2020: 41). A mapping of twenty years of arts-based methods in higher education by Chemi and Du (2018) notes that conceptual choices can link to different scholarly traditions such as 'arts education, arts in education… arts-based interventions' (Chemi and Du, 2018: 1–2). There are also the specific arts subject disciplines and training programmes for dance, drama, music and so on (Meltzer and Schwencke, 2020). The choice to discuss arts-based *methods* for Chemi and Du is a deliberate choice to embrace the wide range of intentions and practices with, or without, the presence of professional artists and with, or without, a focus on specific arts products within the field of arts in education.

The arts within education has a long history of debate around its various functions, revealing tensions such as the claim that using the arts *for* education can be potentially detrimental to the arts in a number of ways. First, if the use of the arts is claimed to boost achievement in other subjects, then any incidences where achievement measures are not positively evidenced can lead to the arts being dismissed (Eisner, 1998). Furthermore, to use the arts in service to other subjects can promote a hierarchy that places the arts in a subsidiary role and presents the arts as a 'kind of add-on' (Chemi, 2014: 371). Lajevic has warned of the dangers of devaluation where the arts are 'readily used for decorative purposes and treated without integrity' (2013: 42). A further argument to this, prevalent in the field, is that if all educators can claim arts processes as their own, then this can also undermine the place and purpose of professional artists within education.

These tensions remain relevant to any discussion involving the arts and education but do not need to be a barrier to identifying the particular use of arts-based learning as a pedagogic choice. Furthermore, the use of arts-based learning as AN educational process, does not attempt to replicate or replace the professional training of specific arts subjects. Taking part will not lead to the birth of a professional musician, dancer, photographer and so on, although professional training for arts professions can incorporate aspects of arts-based learning within their pedagogic choices. In addition, arts-based learning does not attempt to replace the inclusion of specific arts subjects, or the services of professional artists, within a curriculum design. The parameters are clear: arts-based learning is the use of arts-based processes and concepts to characterise the learning atmosphere in a particular educational context. It relates to learning methods that are 'founded on experiential, experimental and exploratory learning processes' (Meltzer and Schwencke, 2020:8). Arts-based learning then has a unique place in education, at all levels, and can sit alongside arts subjects and professional arts training under an umbrella term of arts-based methods (Chemi and Du, 2018). What is particular is the focus on utilising arts-based processes *for* learning within the context of any topic or subject. The characteristics of the learning environment are that it is infused with the qualities of arts-making with teachers and students working through artistic processes and becoming *artists* (Eisner, 2009) within their educational work. It is a learning process that uses artistry and artfulness at its core.

Eisner and arts' *lessons* for education

Elliot Eisner was a leading scholar of arts education and not only advocated for the importance of the arts in any curriculum setting, but introduced a series of improvements that he felt the field of education could learn from the arts. Eisner identified that educational improvement had relied significantly upon 'scientific methods' (2009: 6) and he encouraged those involved with educational improvement (practitioners, policy makers, leaders) to utilise 'methods that are deeply rooted in the arts' (2009: 6). Eisner's arguments called for releasing education from the confines of a hyper-rationalised approach based on measurement rather than meaning (Eisner, 2009). He urged all educators to embrace the working approaches of artists and for education to redress the balance of scientific ideals with an awareness of what an artistic approach could add to the learning environment. His later work extended into wider arts-based conceptualisations that defined arts-based

Table 13.1 Eisner's key lessons for educational improvement

Eisner's lessons that those involved with educational improvement can learn from the arts:

- Form and content cannot be separated – Eisner argued that form and content are inherently connected, and one cannot be altered without altering the other.
- Everything interacts – there is no form without content and all activity is relative to the activity around it.
- Nuances matter – individual interpretations are important, and teaching (and by relation learning) is an art.
- 'Surprise is not to be seen as an intruder in the process of inquiry but as a part of the rewards one reaps when working artistically' (2009:8) Surprise can, and should, be welcomed in the learning process.
- Perception requires a slowing down – Eisner (influenced by John Dewey) encouraged a movement away from 'recognition' in learning to 'perception' and that can only be achieved by taking time to experience moments rather than rushing to end points.
- The limits of language are not the limits of cognition – that we can understand more than we can describe and 'we know more than we can tell' (2009: 8).
- Somatic experience is a powerful indicator – bodies and senses can be powerful allies in the learning process – individuals can sense and feel directions, reactions, outcomes even when they might not be able to capture the feeling in words.
- Open-ended tasks permit the exercise of imagination.

Source: Adapted from Eisner (2009).

educational research (Barone et al., 2011), carrying implications not just for the learner as artist but also the educational researcher as artist. Eisner's lessons for education can be a useful way to characterise the presence of an arts-based learning approach within any learning activity or environment as Table 13.1 helps to illustrate.

> **Questions to consider**
>
> What are the implications of Eisner's lessons for educational experiences in general?
> Think about a recent educational activity that you have been involved in as a learner or teacher. Can you recognise any of Eisner's arts processes in the activity? If you were to re-work a particular activity to embrace some of Eisner's points, how might the activity become (for example) more open-ended with opportunities for surprise within the learning experience?

Learning journeys as artistic processes: Characteristics of an arts-based learning approach

Arts-based learning is characterised specifically as an educational experience built on the use of artistic processes within the learning design. Practitioners and researchers of arts-based learning approaches have recognised potential benefits to learners within a range of settings but there is no set terminology used by all. The examples that follow may not even use the specific term 'arts-based learning', but it is possible to recognise them as this due to the methods and learning processes being artistic. As outlined earlier, there can be fluidity and overlap between terms such as arts-integration or arts-in-education. The examples selected here demonstrate alignment with the explanation of learning as explorative, creative, and innovative. Interestingly, the very same terms arts-integration, arts-in-education can also be used to discuss activity that would not meet the criteria to be designated as arts-based learning. Students watching a performance from a visiting theatre or dance company might well be experiencing highly valuable educational arts activities but are not necessarily examples of arts-based learning by the definition employed here.

In a three-year study of activity termed as 'arts integration' in Canadian schools, Smithrim and Upitis (2005) found that there were increased benefits for students in the arts-based schools than in the control schools. Students' engagement with learning and their wellbeing were both evaluated as greater in the schools that had employed arts-based approaches across the curriculum. Interestingly, a similar positive evaluation followed with teacher engagement and teacher wellbeing within the arts-based schools. Another large study in Danish schools examined the characteristics of teacher-thinking and artist-thinking in order to promote a way of working that could embrace both through the 'artful teacher' (Chemi, 2014: 380). The study found that artful teaching transported learners away from 'a linear movement to a longer, more challenging and obscure journey' (Chemi, 2014: 380) where teachers needed to be confident to take artistic detours. The learning resulting from these detours was found to be 'embodied, easier, more fun, more personal, and more motivating' (Chemi, 2014: 380).

For students of education, arts-based learning can create a valuable way to explore their own subject and experiences through a variety of lenses and, for undergraduate and postgraduate initial teacher education students, it can offer opportunities to approach the task of learning design in innovative and interdisciplinary ways. Furthermore, arts-based seminars can support trainee teachers in examining their teacher-identities, enabling them to 'examine their frames of reference and eventually transform them' (Bhukhawala et al., 2017: 624). Just as Chemi (2014) outlined in the requirements for the artful teacher, this way of working also persuades students to become artful students. An arts-based learning classroom or studio contains artful learners – teachers and students alike working through artistic processes together.

Challenges and limitations of an arts-based learning approach

Whilst this chapter promotes arts-based learning as a valuable approach in education at all levels, and particularly for students in higher education, it is important to point out some significant limitations and challenges for educators desiring to use such an approach. The theoretical base for underpinning curriculum design is not clearly delineated, as mentioned previously. Another challenge can be that the necessary approaches required to create an arts-based experience demand qualities in the learning atmosphere that might not be familiar, comfortable, or easily achieved for educators or participants. These artistic atmospheres, embodied by qualities of ensemble and togetherness, need to be carefully negotiated, and managed, by all group members. There is also the difficulty of assessment that has not been the direct focus of this chapter but does need acknowledging and will be further discussed below.

Introducing arts-based learning to an undergraduate education course

A starting point for any arts-based learning practitioner is to collect, understand and action working definitions whilst being transparent about their origins and influences. This process can also allow for conversation and reflection throughout the learning experience, and it offers opportunity for regular re-thinking and reframing of the working definitions being used by the group. In short, it is important that participants understand the theoretical background to how they are working but are also empowered to question, challenge and even help to re-frame when they bring themselves and their own experiences to the process, in the company of other learners.

My own experience of introducing an arts-based learning module to an undergraduate education course began with a process of framing the conceptual background for the module. Generic university module approval paperwork can often create a particular frame that can seem at odds with an arts-based learning approach. Any statement of open-endedness, surprise, the importance of senses and feelings within the educational process (Eisner, 2009) can seem incompatible with fixed statements of module learning objectives or outcomes and can create a tension between policy and practice. That said, the value of an arts-based learning module, or even a session within a learning programme, is in that very opportunity to offer variety and difference within the curriculum diet and such differences will require different policy frameworks.

The module was designed as a ten-week block of weekly workshops to take place during the second or third year of an undergraduate education course and involving further activity and individual exploration between workshops. The module was also set up to be selected as an optional module for students from other degree programmes, allowing opportunities for interdisciplinary learning relationships with students across various university departments.

The main activity of the workshops involved being introduced to various learning dilemmas, or explorations, through arts-based approaches. This progressed towards the creation of student designed arts-based learning experiences for all to present towards the end of the course. Workshops can vary each year offering the opportunity to pick up on issues of local, national, or international importance. The arts-based learning processes remain consistent features ensuring that there is opportunity to reflect on the learning process through activities that are collaborative, open-ended, with no clear pre-set outcomes and where the destination reveals itself during the journey. Arts-based learning students might find themselves immersed in a group role play scenario, they might explore a piece of literature through drama education techniques. They might be learning about the importance of the protection of bees in the story of human existence but beginning as a bee-waggle dance and progressing into a climate change challenge. They might examine complicated issues of inclusion, ethics, equity and decolonisation but through a fictionalised world where they are invited to problem-solve as active community members faced with a human-rights issue. Arts-based learning allows itself to adopt some rehearsal or creation practices from the worlds of specified arts subjects (Cannatella, 2020), but it is not confined to working with methods from one or more arts subject. Arts-based learning also borrows from non-arts subjects and can create experiences that do not resemble any recognised art form at all. What remains consistent is that every session allows opportunity to explore a topic or a subject through an artistic process with designated linked knowledge but open-ended outcomes.

Undergraduate students' own arts-based learning designs that have developed during the module have been impressively diverse. One student coming from a Philosophy course (additional module), with a future place to study for a Maths PGCE, decided to explore how the use of role play could enhance the teaching and learning of statistics. For him, the arts-based learning module helped him to connect his understanding of statistics to his aspiration to link Maths to real people and real stories in teaching and learning situations. In his plan, learners met and explored people's stories and situations as an essential part of understanding the statistics that represented them. Another education student decided to examine how poetry might materialise from rhythm, games and music explorations resulting in students, who had actively avoided poetry since leaving secondary education, becoming engaged poets innovating form. Other examples have included arts-based contexts for second language learning, scientific concept exploration through movement and role, history experienced through the sounds and music of time-periods.

Assessing and grading the arts-based learning module

Assessment for the module remains an interesting tension. The arts-based learning programme is clear from the outset that, throughout the module, students must experience the content in a Dewey-inspired way: they need to engage with the experience of the learning, to see the light, the shade, walk through the shadows (Dewey, 2005). Students are not learning *about* arts-based learning but rather learning *through*, with the intention being to nurture confidence in themselves as practitioners in future educational settings. The assessment of the module includes an opportunity to define and frame their own understanding of arts-based learning using a range of academic readings either from the course recommendations or from their own research. This is followed by an opportunity to plan and deliver an arts-based learning experience for others (either within the module group or within a local setting such as a business or a school). However, it is worth noting that there remains an interesting feature in the assessment of students on the module because their final grading is based on the writing they complete *about* their arts-based learning practice rather than assessing the practice itself. This opportunity to capture and reflect on the creativity, insights, challenges and perspectives after the event in writing can be incredibly important, but the question remains whether the arts-based learning itself can be assessed. This is an area for further development and research.

Conclusion

Arts-based learning can be seen as a distinct area of education studies and can offer students (at all levels of learning) the opportunity to experience learning through artistic processes embracing actions that are open ended, nuanced, surprising and where the methods employed (form) are coherent with the topic studied (content) (Eisner, 2009). Arts-based learning can be viewed separately to the arts subjects of dance, drama, music and so on, respecting their individual places within any curriculum design. In addition, arts-based learning can be found under practice that is titled as arts integration, arts-based methods, arts in education but the term particularly highlights education practice and learning processes modelled on the artistic. As an interdisciplinary tool arts-based learning is available to all. It is an approach that can be utilised by any subject and all practitioners. Of course, arts-based learning is not alone in offering alternative educational experiences but what is unique about it is the reliance on arts processes as inherent to the design and experience of learning. Embracing arts-based learning for all, is an important feature within the palette of pedagogic approaches available to all educators and students, and particularly within the study of education.

Recommended reading

Barton, G. and Baguley, M. (Eds) (2017) *The Palgrave Handbook of Global Arts Education*. London: Palgrave Macmillan. https://0-doi-org.pugwash.lib.warwick.ac.uk/10.1057/978-1-137-55585-4

This handbook provides an insight into how the arts can play a vital role in learning and teaching contexts around the globe. It brings together academic contributions from leading voices in arts education representing many different perspectives.

Du, X. and Chemi, T. (Eds) (2018) *Arts-Based Methods in Education Around the World*. Gistrup: River Publishers. https://ebookcentral.proquest.com/lib/warw/detail.action?docID=5306342

This collection of academic papers explores links between the arts, humanities and business in higher education with a particular focus on arts methods and processes. It is a helpful starting place for students and scholars interested in mapping and exploring the range of perspectives that make up this growing but fragmented field.

References

Barone, T., Eisner, E.W. and Barone, T. Jr. (2011) *Arts Based Research*. London: Sage Publications. https://ebookcentral.proquest.com/lib/warw/detail.action?docID=996367

Bhukhawala, F., Dean, K. and Troyer, M. (2017) Beyond the student teaching seminar: Examining transformative learning through arts-based approaches. *Teachers and Teaching*, 23(5), pp. 611–630. https://doi.org/10.1080/13540602.2016.1219712

Cannatella, H. (2020) Knowledge and learning in arts education: Neglecting theory and practice. *Journal of Aesthetic Education*, 54(2), pp. 39–55. https://go.exlibris.link/JTcxXKsZ

Chemi, T. (2014) The artful teacher: A conceptual model for arts integration in schools. *Studies in Art Education: A Journal of Issues and Research*, 56(1), pp. 370–383. https://go.exlibris.link/Cyr1WSqX

Chemi, T. and Du, X. (2018) Tracing arts-based methods in higher education. In T. Chemi and X. Du (Eds) *Arts Based Methods and Organizational Learning: Higher Education Around the World* (pp. 1–18). Switzerland: Springer Nature.

Dewey, J. (2005) *Art as Experience*. London: Perigree Books.

Dewey, J. (1963) *Experience and Education*. New York: Macmillan.

Eisner, E.W. (2009) What education can learn from the arts. *Arts Education*, 62(2), pp. 6–9.

Lajevic, L. (2013) The lost and found space of the arts in education. *International Journal of Education through Art*, 9(1), pp. 41–54.

Meltzer, C. and Schwencke, E. (2020) Arts-based learning in vocational education: Using arts-based approaches to enrich vocational pedagogy and didactics and to enhance professional competence and identity. *Journal of Adult and Continuing Education*, 26(1), pp. 6–24. https://doi.org/10.1177/1477971419846640

Smithrim, K. and Upitis, R. (2005) Learning through the arts: Lessons of engagement. *Canadian Journal of Education*, 28(1/2), pp. 109–127. https://doi.org/10.2307/1602156

Section 3
Challenge and change in education studies

Mark Pulsford

The seven chapters in this section are focused on education studies' relationship with power, privilege and social inequality. The chapters reveal that this relationship has two dimensions. First, the importance in education studies of recognising injustice, pushing for education systems that are more equitable and examining education's fundamental role in shaping national and global citizenship. Second, how the experience of taking an education studies' degree can be transformative because it promotes students' reflexivity about their identities, social positioning and agency to create change. Education studies' role in advancing students' personal and professional understanding is therefore inherently linked with concerns for social justice, social inclusion, and individual and social transformation. As you read the chapters in this section, you are encouraged to think critically and constructively about your engagement with these wider issues, as well as how you can positively influence your own education studies course on these matters.

The first two chapters in this section offer theoretically informed perspectives on education's role in society, examining democracy and social justice respectively. Chapter 14 by Ted Fleming draws on influential philosophers Habermas and Dewey to argue that a decline in public, democratic dialogue in contemporary society means that the role of education is ever more important because it can promote open, free and inclusive discussion of key issues. This can – and indeed should explicitly aim to – develop citizens who are fully engaged with social, political and environmental issues, in the hope of generating more democratic, more just and more caring societies. Education studies is therefore important because it can advocate for models of education that promotes this, and its graduates can act to challenge narrow and more individualised visions of schooling and educational success. Jenny Hatley's Chapter 15 follows this with the idea that education studies programmes would benefit from integrating a theory of social justice throughout their curricula. Using Fraser's theory of Democratic Justice, Hatley develops an argument that it is important to move beyond a surface-level conception of justice as 'fairness' and that instead the focus on *recognition, redistribution* and *representation* offers a framework to structure a deep analysis of education systems and experiences.

Hatley also uses Fraser's notion of *participatory parity* to raise awareness of how some groups are denied equitable means to be involved in and contribute to educational ideas, which connects to Fleming's discussion of the declining public sphere and points us toward the other chapters in this section. In different ways, the next five chapters amplify the voices of students in education studies and draw on their perspectives to chart emerging priorities in the area. In Chapter 16, Jawiria Naseem and Zhu Hua report on a project involving BA Education students to decolonise undergraduate education curricula. The chapter gives a detailed background to decolonising the

DOI: 10.4324/9781003296935-16

curriculum, and goes on to consider what this means in practice on an education studies degree. In asking critical questions such as *who owns knowledge* and *whose knowledge counts*, the chapter makes key points about belonging and social inequality, and the imperative for educators to reflect on their own role in silencing certain voices, histories and worldviews. This challenge is carried into Chapter 17 by Heather Knight and Emma Jones, who turn our attention to anti-racist pedagogy. Using personal reflections about teaching (from Knight) and learning (from Jones, a former education studies student), the chapter explores how racism education is typically approached. It argues that learners and teachers need to embrace fear, shame and uncomfortable emotions in learning about Whiteness, power and privilege. Both chapters are calls for education studies' students and tutors to forego some of the comfort that we all look for and accept the challenge of difficult learning in order to break down barriers to justice and equity.

The call to become reflective practitioners and raise our self-awareness is emphasised in Talitha Bird and Rajvir Gill's Chapter 18. They write about student–staff interactions as a way of challenging entrenched ideologies of gender and race, encouraging students to think about which staff members they ask for help and who they go to for advice, for example. Addressing concerns of identity, positionality and intersectionality, the chapter invites students to recognise the social dimensions that shape their own and their lecturers' identities, and to find ways to collectively challenge the stereotypical roles we are often assumed to fulfil. The idea of stereotypical social roles comes through in the chapter I was an author on, too. Chapter 19 draws on the experiences of five men who have studied education at undergraduate level, where themes of privilege and marginalisation are highlighted. As an underrepresented yet 'in-demand' group in education, the men describe a mixed picture that reflects wider assumptions about men's social role and perceptions of 'typical' masculine pursuits and priorities. The chapter considers what the education studies community might do to minimise traditional and essentialist notions of gender that are restrictive to both men and women. The last in this section, Chapter 20 connects many of the themes and issues that have been discussed here. This innovative chapter is co-written by education studies lecturers and students and offers an open, honest account of a collaborative project to develop a Special Educational Needs and Disability module. It guides us through a process of knowledge co-construction and demonstrates that authentic and meaningful change can be achieved through prioritising the perspectives and needs of marginalised groups, by dissembling the hierarchical barriers between staff and students, and nurturing safer spaces for exploring our identities, values and collective interests in education studies.

14 Education and democracy

The public sphere reclaimed for educational study

Ted Fleming

SUMMARY POINTS

This chapter explores

- The democratic notion of the 'public sphere' – spaces where public opinion can be formed which influences Government policy – and why this is curtailed because of the influence of the media, the economy and other powerful forces in society;
- How the study of education helps to understand these issues and in particular focus on the relationship between education – with its ideal of open and free processes of discussion – and democracy;
- The value of taking an education studies degree programme as a way of engaging in increasingly complex debates about the role of education and its relationship to democracy;
- How education can pave the way for more democratic ways of living together that are more just, more caring and more supportive of difference and equality.

Introduction

Governments are interested in education not just because it involves bringing children through a process of growth and development. They are also concerned that the education system delivers students who can contribute the necessary knowledge and skills to the economy. Yet governments must also have an interest in producing mature, insightful and active members of a society because democracies need each generation to participate in social debates and decision making. Democratic governments and the education system share these projects, yet there are often conflicting positions taken about how these aims might be achieved. For these reasons, the role and purpose of education itself has been controversial for hundreds of years and is still unresolved. Education studies as a discipline engages in the contemporary version of this conflict. Topics that are new and about the future, such as climate change, are therefore of concern for education studies, because how these topics are understood (how they are learned about and discussed) shapes the action that the public will take.

This chapter explores the nature of the conversations that are needed and the spaces – the 'public sphere' – in which they take place to support each person to become a more engaged citizen and better educated in democratic ways of living. We rely on famous German critical theorist Jürgen Habermas to understand the public sphere as an essential part of democracy. This is our way of arguing that education provides the path towards engaged citizens and more democratic ways of living together that are more just, more caring and more supportive of difference and equality.

> **Question to consider**
>
> Take a moment to consider your initial thoughts about the relationship between education and democracy. What is the relationship between education and the 'public sphere' of free, open conversation and debate?

The public sphere

Jürgen Habermas (1989) describes the 'public sphere' as an area 'of our social life in which something approaching public opinion can be formed,' and to which 'access is guaranteed to all citizens' in an 'unrestricted fashion' (1974: 49). More recently Axel Honneth (2014: 254), another member of the Frankfurt School for Social Research, defines the public sphere as 'a social space in which citizens form generally acceptable beliefs through deliberative discussion, beliefs that form the principles to be obeyed by the legislature in accordance with the rule of law'.

In the past, coffee houses in England and *Tischgesellschaften* [table societies] in Germany were the spaces in which status was disregarded and issues of common interest were discussed in inclusive debates – inclusive, at least in theory. In this public sphere of free and open conversations, opposing views could be expressed leading to consensus as to what actions ought to be taken up by the legislature and be made into laws. For Habermas (1989: 52), the public sphere is a 'society engaged in critical public debate'.

In what might be seen as idealistic situations, free conversations of citizens take place under no duress or intimidation and the expressed views, interests and needs get taken up by governments. In a public sphere, citizens form 'a public' and public opinion is thereby constituted; it is through this process that citizens regulate or moderate the considerable power of the state. Governments that pay attention to the public sphere increase their legitimacy as they engage citizens in areas of interest to the public and implement policies that address the emerging needs, i.e., in public health, public education and public ownership. Today, it is mostly through opinion polls that governments keep in contact with the opinions and needs of society.

The ideal public sphere makes political freedom real and 'the rights to vote, to assemble and to form associations' are one concrete expression of this freedom (Honneth, 2014: 259). The public sphere enables people to recognise the equal importance of each citizen. Such freedom to engage acknowledges the mutual right to be recognised as entitled to 'equal participation in the nation state' (Habermas, 1974: 49). However, this raises an important difficulty with the public sphere concept because it is an aspiration; it involves an *ideal view* of democracy. In the real world, not everybody experiences equality. Gender, class, race, sexual orientation, ability and education attainment continue to divide. Negt and Kluge (1993) are two important social theorists with an active interest in education who sharply critique Habermas because he neglects the differences between the ideal version of the public sphere and how it is experienced in the real world that is quite divided and stratified.

Women were always excluded from the public sphere and as a result the public sphere itself is a contradiction. Nancy Fraser eloquently critiques women's exclusion and confinement to the private sphere of the family. Other groups are also excluded and this, she states, has led to the formation of 'subaltern' or 'counter publics' (Fraser, 1992: 116, 123). These are parallel discursive spaces providing oppositional interpretations of women's needs, interests and identities. Movements for climate change, disability rights and LGBTQ+ recognition also started in this way.

If one is denied access to public spaces these exclusions function, according to Honneth (1995), as *misrecognitions*. His recognition theory holds that these exclusions undermine individual self-worth and social inclusion. One's identity is undermined by exclusions and misrecognitions in the public sphere (Fleming, 2022). As such, this is an example of how political or social activities can negatively impact on individual identity. Conversely, policies that seek to secure new inclusions in the public sphere (such as LGBTQ+ rights) increase social solidarity and enhance individual identity.

Questions to Consider

Reflect on how much you feel part of the 'public sphere' – the free, open conversations about social issues that inform Government policy: to what extent is this related to your social positioning?

Also think about and discuss how connected you and your peers feel to the processes of Government policy and law making.

The demise of the public sphere today – counter publics

The same forces or impulses that brought about the public sphere also contribute to its decline. For instance, discussions about how to support business and trading were often the subject of such conversations in the public sphere, but the self-interest of the participants became an obstacle to addressing the common good. Today, one of the most pressing problems in society concerns how governments and the political system seem to be much more responsive to the needs and demands of powerful groups that are willing to exercise their power in overt and covert ways. There is a sense that the power of citizens is more fleeting compared to the power exercised by the wealthy in society, and Habermas has used the word 'colonized' to describe the ways these forces have invaded the public sphere.

The rather idealised version of the public sphere (including its obvious exclusions) leads critics to explore the role of television and other media as a possible public sphere that claims to act in the public interest. Although newspapers and public service broadcasting (such as the BBC in the UK) might be seen as good examples of public spheres, media are often involved in reducing public discussions through controlling debates, and they are often closely allied with political interests and the interests of their owners. Moreover, the amalgam of information, entertainment and education provided by television is presented to viewers as a totally pre-packaged system. This leads to what Hansen, in her introduction to Negt and Kluge (1993: xxiv), calls the 'industrialization of consciousness'; the collective view is often packaged ready for the media consumer, rather than presented in ways to prompt meaningful debate and active citizenship. Referring to media and television organisations, Negt and Kluge state that 'the real interests and needs which people would be prepared to fight for in a serious way play no role' (1993: 101).

We might consider that social media represents a valid contemporary public sphere. However, these platforms tend to reduce their public sphere potential to a user-friendly on-line experience of interpersonal communication. Yes, they are easily accessed. They are influential. They can mobilise young people and highlight sensational aspects of important subjects. However, media advertising and private ownership have curtailed debate in the traditional sense of a public sphere. This tends to eliminate the social, economic or discursive political dimensions, meaning that they rarely function to translate critical public debate into proposed actions for Governments; they do not act as a mediating space between Government and the governed. Splichal (2022: 211) calls this the 'banalization of the public sphere' where debate and disagreement become routinised yet are disconnected from the potential to influence wider policy change. Therefore, there is a challenge to the development of contemporary public spaces in which the real needs of citizens can be articulated. We suggest that these concerns are central to the purpose of education today and vital for students of education to consider: with a diminished public sphere, what role must education have in society?

Question to consider
Based on the critical reflection presented here, in what ways could you apply this kind of criticism to your own favourite social media platform, e.g., Instagram, TikTok?

The public sphere and education

A significant debate took place one hundred years ago between Walter Lippmann (1922), a well-known American journalist, and John Dewey (1922), America's most famous philosopher of education. The debate question was: can an ordinary citizen have sufficient knowledge to take part effectively in complex debates in the public sphere? Lacking specialised knowledge and distracted by busy lives citizens are, according to Lippmann, 'outsiders in all but a few aspects of life' (1922: 251). Today, when we consider the knowledge required to understand global migrations, climate change or food security, for example, we too can wonder whether it is possible to know enough to meaningfully discuss vital issues.

In addition, the knowledge we accept as genuine may depend on the perspective we hold and habits of thinking we have acquired. Our ways of understanding are not neutral and emerge from our individual life history and culture. They are hard to change. Our modern understanding of resistance to antibiotics, for example, is based on an understanding of evolution by natural selection. So too is the idea of a mutating (Covid) virus. Yet, some may not accept evolution as scientific fact and this impacts on public opinion. Similarly, when the credibility of experts, public figures and government is subject to much suspicion, this affects our confidence in the information we are being given.

Lippmann (1922) was calling attention to the limited knowledge of individual citizens. Yet John Dewey (1922) was not convinced that locating the problem in the individual was correct. He proposed that groups of citizens in collaborative discussions could overcome these limitations and that the individual is 'moved and regulated by his [sic] associations with others...' (Dewey, 1922: 188). This sounds like the beginning of a good argument for educating citizens who would harness the 'cumulative and transmitted intellectual wealth of the community' (Dewey, 1922: 218). The key for Dewey is the development of communities that are well organised and in a position to tap into collective strengths. We suspect this is what he meant by asserting: 'the outstanding problem of the public is discovery and identification of itself' (1922: 185).

Dewey was also aware of problems posed by 'prejudice, bias, misrepresentation and propaganda' (1927: 212), and held the view that a democratic society has the responsibility to improve the 'methods and conditions of debate, discussion and persuasion' (1927: 208) through education. Hence the development of the public sphere, where inclusive discussion and debate forms consensus and can generate positive change, begins to look important and indeed essential for our society. This is consistent with Dewey's belief that education has a mandate to assist every citizen reach their 'full stature' (Dewey, 1922: 286) – in today's language, their full potential.

Dewey certainly sees education as part of the solution. Though many aspects of reality have changed in the hundred years since Dewey/Lippmann, this may be a good moment to re-examine these ideas. We can accept, with Dewey, that citizens play an important role in making public decisions, even if accessing the required knowledge is a challenge. We might also accept that the focus is less on individual knowledge and expertise. We also recall that Dewey thought that knowledge cannot exist without community; we know things better when we combine our enquiries. He also asserted that 'a democracy is more than a form of government; it is primarily a mode of associated living, of conjoint communicated experience' (Dewey, 1966: 91).

This gives education and democracy a shared purpose. To engage in discussions and debates between those who have expert knowledge and those seeking to acquire it is one way forward. More listening is required between politicians and experts and citizens. Education might accept responsibility to train citizens so that all sectors of society would be able to join in a public sphere informed by critical and well-informed conversation and a rich imaginative pursuit of knowledge:

> Democracy demands a more thoroughgoing education than the education of officials, administrators, and directors of industry. Because this fundamental general education is at once so necessary and so difficult to achieve, the enterprise of democracy is so challenging. To sidetrack it to the task of enlightenment of administrators and executives is to miss something of its range and its challenge.
>
> (Dewey, 1922: 288)

Educators, even a hundred years ago, were engaged in these debates and there are many who in more recent times illuminate this agenda. Jack Mezirow (2000) and Paulo Freire (1972) are two prominent figures, and this final section draws on their thinking.

Classrooms in universities and schools can be seen as democratic public spheres where teachers and students pursue issues for the common good (Hooley, 2008). Yet there are problems with the education system, not least of which is that it has been colonised by the functional imperatives of the (neoliberal) economy; the drive to deliver workers to the marketplace with skills to serve the economy. However, the purpose of education should at least be a contested topic, and so the question might be how to balance and rectify the conflicting approaches offered by the different views of education: whether educational systems and the experiences offered should be driven by pre-set knowledge (disciplines); or by the needs of society for worker skills; or by the need for critically engaged citizens through the development of a model of education that is more critical, more aware of and more interested in solutions to social issues. We call the latter a *critical pedagogy*.

In a more critical model of education, studying education means to discuss social issues and engage in conversations in a public sphere, generating issues, ideas and concerns. This involves questioning assumptions and pre-existing knowledge and creating moments of democratic debate. The theory of *transformative learning* describes the learning required to engage critically in examining assumptions that underlie our ways of interpreting the world around us. According to Mezirow (2000: 22), transformative learning is:

> …the process of becoming critically aware of how and why the structure of our psychocultural assumptions has come to constrain the way in which we perceive our world, of reconstituting that structure in a way that allows us to be more inclusive and discriminating in our integrating of experience and to act on these new understandings…

Conclusion

Education is an important issue in individual lives and in society. It is important to study education because it develops our understandings of this. Education is about the future and about how society will develop. Education studies is vital because its students will play a role in establishing cultures of public discussion through their ability and confidence to challenge taken for granted ideas and models of education that may diminish people. Students of education right now must be interested in debating controversies and should engage in these debates during their time at university. This involves developing meaningful, critical discussions about change and inclusion and democratic processes as these are fundamental to what it means to be 'a student of education'. Even if as individuals we inherit great opportunities in life, our thinking is influenced by our gender, by race, wealth and social class. For many, education has become the opportunity to rise, to transcend, to overcome prescribed possibilities. Education studies involve the exciting prospect that society will become, through becoming better educated, a more just and caring place in which to live.

How can this be done? We suggest by creating the kinds of public spheres in classrooms that encourage debate, argumentation, reasoned discussions, evidence-based making of cases and respect for each participant. This includes a public debate about teaching, learning, life and the role of education in a society of citizens, in a democracy. It means making classrooms a public sphere, a democracy, a discursive space.

Questions to consider

In your opinion, what should each of us know in order to be a more informed and engaged citizen? How might one acquire this knowledge?

What might you do to participate in the public sphere? Why is this important for students of education to do?

Recommended reading

The Public Sphere Project
This project promotes more effective and equitable public spheres around the world. Their website supports researchers and activists and provides a broad framework for a variety of interrelated activities and goals. See https://publicsphereproject.org/about

This project believes a thriving public sphere is necessary to support people's ability to manage public affairs fairly and effectively. New digital technologies are a major source of opportunities and challenges for those interested in the public sphere.

Ueno, M. (2016) *Democratic Education and the Public Sphere: Towards John Dewey's Theory of Aesthetic Experience*. Abingdon: Routledge.

This book is a collection of chapters that takes the discussion a step further.

YouTube: Habermas – The Structural Transformation of the Public Sphere

The public sphere as described by Habermas is updated to take into account recent issues https://www.youtube.com/watch?v=R1K46oK3xTU

YouTube – Jürgen Habermas Interview

An interview with Habermas saying what interests him most: the need to develop democracy especially following the Nazi experience; the importance of developing our ability to be more reasonable in our everyday conversations, interactions and discussions. https://www.youtube.com/watch?v=jBl6ALNh18Q

References

Dewey, J. (1922) Public Opinion - Review. *The New Republic*, **30**, pp. 286–288.

Dewey, J. (1927) *The Public and its Problems*. New York: Holt.

Dewey, J. (1966) *Democracy and Education*. New York: The Free Press.

Fleming, T. (2022) Critical Theory and Transformative Learning: Making Connections with Habermas, Honneth and Negt. In A. Nicolaides, S. Eschenbacher, P. Buergelt, Y. Gilpin-Jackson, M. Welch, and M. Misawa (Eds) *The Palgrave Handbook of Learning for Transformation*. London: Palgrave. https://doi.org/10.1007/978-3-030-84694-7_2

Fraser, N. (1992) Rethinking the Public Sphere: A Contribution to the Critique of Actually Existing Democracy. In C. J. Calhoun, (Ed) *Habermas and the Public Sphere* (pp. 109–142). Cambridge, MA: MIT Press.

Freire, P. (1972) *Pedagogy of the Oppressed*. London: Penguin.

Habermas, J. (1974) The Public Sphere: An Encyclopedia Article (1964). *New German Critique*, **3**, pp. 49–55. Available at: http://www.jstor.org/stable/487737 (Accessed 20 April 2022).

Habermas, J. (1989) *The Structural Transformation of the Public Sphere: An Inquiry into a Category of Bourgeois Society*. Cambridge, MA: MIT.

Honneth, A. (1995) *The Struggle for Recognition: The Moral Grammar of Social Conflicts*. Cambridge: Polity.

Honneth, A. (2014) *Freedom's Right*. Cambridge: Polity.

Hooley, N. (2008) Teacher Education as Democratic Public Sphere. *Australian Educational Researcher*, **35**(3), pp. 37–51. Available at: https://doi.org/10.1007/BF03246288. (Accessed 20 April 2022).

Lippmann, W. (1922) *Public Opinion*. New York: Transaction Publishers.

Mezirow, J. (2000) Learning to Think like an Adult. In J. Mezirow and Associates, (Eds) *Learning as Transformation: Critical Perspectives on a Theory in Progress* (pp. 3–33). San Francisco: Jossey-Bass.

Negt, O. and Kluge, A. (1993) *Public Sphere and Experience: Toward an Analysis of the Bourgeois and Proletarian Public Sphere*. Minneapolis, MN: University of Minnesota Press.

Splichal, S. (2022) The Public Sphere in the Twilight Zone of Publicness. *European Journal of Communication*, **37**(2), pp. 198–215. Available at: https://doi.org/10.1177/02673231211061490 (Accessed 20 April 2022).

15 The role of social justice theory in education studies

Jenny Hatley

SUMMARY POINTS
- Education is often touted as having the potential to equalise society through social mobility. However, society is far from equal and social differences are reflected in educational outcomes and experiences.
- Education cannot be considered in isolation but must be viewed in light of its relationship with multiple social, political and economic factors which lay bare the need for social justice.
- The role of social justice, while superficially present in education studies programmes, can be strengthened using a theory of social justice.
- Nancy Fraser's theory of democratic justice, with its focus on recognition, redistribution and representation, is ideally placed to provide a conceptual framework for understanding social justice in education in all its interconnected facets.
- This can equip students on education studies programmes with the tools to understand the mechanisms behind injustice, to pose concrete solutions and make connections that lead to a deeper and more nuanced understanding.

Introduction

One of the biggest claims made of education is its potential to enhance social mobility. As stated by Ravitch (2010 cited in Smith, 2018), schools are still the main way a democracy enables citizens to attain social mobility. Education is, supposedly, the great equaliser. However, the global pandemic highlighted in a very public way that pupils' home circumstances can make all the difference. Closing schools and putting education online has shown the intersections between education and society in a stark light. Learners in homes with multiple digital devices, a decent internet connection, private and quiet spaces to learn and carers with the ability, desire and means to provide support generally fared better than those without. Research has shown that after the first lockdown in 2020 'the relative learning loss for disadvantaged pupils was equivalent to undoing between a third and two-thirds of the progress made in the last decade in closing the disadvantage gap in primary schools' (DfE, 2021: 9). Clearly, to tackle disadvantage, education must be examined in light of the multiple social, political and economic factors that influence educational outcomes. After all, as Smith (2018: 207) notes, 'the *most* important factors in determining future life chances lie firmly outside the school gates'. Without a comprehensive understanding of the mechanisms behind these inequalities and the ability to pose concrete solutions, there is a danger that sticking-plaster

DOI: 10.4324/9781003296935-18

solutions continue to be posed for complex issues. A theory of social justice can provide the conceptual framework for this understanding, enabling you as students to more fully appreciate the systemic nature of justice on multiple scales and equip you to truly understand and navigate the systems you will work within as future educators.

This chapter begins with an examination of the place of social justice within education studies programmes and suggests that a more thorough approach is needed if education is to be a vehicle for social justice. It then explores the purpose and role of theory and suggests Fraser's theory of democratic justice as one approach that can support students to gain an understanding of justice beyond simply what is 'fair'. This is then applied to a scenario of those with protected characteristics, which illustrates how theory can be applied within education studies programmes. Finally, the chapter considers how Fraser's theory can enhance students' interconnected thinking and how an understanding of theory, and the key questions it enables us to ask, can form a strong framework of justice within which to examine education and one's own place as a socially just educator.

Education studies and social justice

Education studies programmes were created in response to a need to expand the study of education outside of teacher training (Bartlett and Burton, 2020). The subject takes a broad view of education and provides opportunities for students to examine its sociological, historical, philosophical and psychological aspects. Indeed, these four areas are considered the foundations of education alongside more recent additions of political, economic, technological and international perspectives. The power of education studies programmes lies in the way that they open our minds to different ways of thinking. This contrasts with teacher training which arguably trains students to reproduce the status quo in the classroom, stripped of the time to really debate and take a critical view of current practice.

Indeed, Yogev and Michaeli (2011, cited in Tezgiden Cakcak, 2016: 131) summarise the 'problem of teacher education' generally as follows:

> Contemporary teacher training demarcates itself within the boundaries of inculcating disciplinary knowledge, developing didactic skills, and nurturing self-awareness. Graduates of traditional teacher training ... perceive themselves mainly as knowledge brokers and do not think about or question the basic concepts of the system in which they work, the curriculum they teach, or the teaching methods they apply.

One of the freedoms of education studies programmes is the space to question how things are and how things should be, and in order to do that a critical approach needs to be developed. The QAA Benchmark Standards (QAA, 2019) define education studies programmes and they mention criticality nine times, including critical *engagement, capabilities, analysis, reflection, debate and understanding*. Hence it is clear that critical skills play a central role in the subject, and it is this questioning, debate and new thinking that enables problems to be explored and a different future for education to be imagined. By comparison, social justice is explicitly mentioned only twice (QAA, 2019: 9) but it is implicit in several other statements. For example, that education studies programmes will cover: 'the role of education in human rights and ecological issues' (p. 4); debates about values and social engagement as they relate to communities and societies (p. 4); and that students are to accommodate new ideas related to social inclusion (p. 7).

> **Questions to consider**
>
> In the benchmark statements, why do you think that 'critical' is so prevalent yet 'social justice' is not? Do you think that social justice should be made more explicit and what might the advantages or disadvantages of this be?

There are different ways of looking at social justice. Political parties all make claims to social justice, but each with very different means to achieve it and these are hotly contested. (For a good discussion of this, see Smith 2018, Chapter 1.) Political claims to social justice appear to rest on ideals seen by each proponent as common sense, rather than an in-depth examination of what may work that is grounded in theory. Theory helps us to understand the mechanisms behind what is happening. It enables us to gain a deeper understanding and as Costley states, 'theories make us think!' (Costley, 2006: 5). Without theory, there is a risk that we build interventions based on untested assumptions, our own life experiences, intuitions ('folk intuitions') and gut feelings (Muthukrishna and Henrich, 2019), whereas theory can tune our intuition so that we can spot when something feels off (Costley, 2006).

Theory also provides principles for specific predictions. Without these, disparate notions of social justice may be drawn upon to justify a chosen course of action, yet injustice remains because those notions are weak or 'surface level' and may in some cases reinforce the social inequality they are trying to redress. When things are disconnected from theory or based on 'folk intuitions' (Muthukrishna and Henrich, 2019), moves towards social justice for all will be hampered. Our efforts may be well intentioned, but they will be inherently limited. Nevertheless, theory is not a panacea. No theory is perfect and none can account for every influencing factor; but theory can provide the best framework for analysis, prediction and the planning of actions which are based on thorough reasoning and tested thinking which is more likely to have a greater chance of success.

> **Questions to consider**
>
> Do you think theory can provide concrete benefits as described above or do you think that theory is abstract and does not link to everyday experiences? How far do you think teaching and learning often relies on untested assumptions or 'folk intuitions'?

As shown through the benchmark statements, some notion of social justice should already be present in education studies programmes. However, how this is discussed can sometimes rely on an arguably surface level approach rather than a structured theory which can provide a framework for the deeper critical questioning needed for the achievement of social justice. Often, social justice is introduced to students in terms of justice as harmony, justice as equity and justice as equality (Ruitenberg and Vokey, 2010, cited in Smith, 2018: 15). This is helpful for an introduction to ideas around social justice during the first year of an undergraduate programme and it is often repeated across modules for emphasis, but this is often not developed to any greater depth through the second and third years and this represents a missed opportunity to achieve that deeper understanding.

The theory presented here, Fraser's theory of Democratic Justice (Fraser, 2010), provides a framework for looking at social justice within the current political era of globalisation. It examines systems and processes that influence people's participation in social life but which people may be powerless to affect. There are other theories of social justice that also offer valuable insights to education. For example, Sen's Capability Approach focuses more on an individual and their ability to do or be things they value (their 'capabilities') so that they live a life they find meaningful (Vaughn and Walker, 2012). Both theories have much to offer a study of education, but Fraser's focus is arguably more objective, enabling a systemic examination of justice on many different scales and for all groups within society. Fraser's theory enables examination of justice across many topics and areas of study which may or may not be things an individual values personally, but nonetheless remain important to someone's role as a future educator.

Fraser's theory of democratic justice

For Fraser, social justice is defined as 'participatory parity' (Fraser, 2010: 16). Participatory parity means that everyone is able to participate equally as peers in social life. For there to be justice, there must be participatory parity and for this to occur, Fraser's three 'fundamental dimensions of justice' must be satisfied (Fraser, 2010: 16):

- The dimension of **redistribution** (and the associated injustice of **maldistribution**) typically relates to economic structures, and states that resources and opportunities must be equally distributed to all. Keddie (2012, cited in Vincent 2020: 43) notes some of the consequences of maldistribution stating that 'Principles of distributive justice recognise the links between poverty, poor schooling performance, early school leaving and future economic deprivation and social discontent/dysfunction.' Lynch and Lodge (2002) also state that distribution of resources and opportunities based on other social differentiations, including gender, are comparable to differentiations of social class in depth and scale.
- The dimension of **recognition** (and associated injustice of **misrecognition**) states that everyone must be given equal status and respect in society, otherwise cultural domination by more powerful groups may occur.
- The dimension of **representation** (and the associated injustice of **misrepresentation**) states that everyone must have their voices heard equally in decision-making. Lynch and Lodge (2002) describe it well: 'Having political equality is about ensuring that one's definition of the situation is not disregarded, that one's voice is equal to that of others, that one is given the space and capacity to act autonomously' (Lynch and Lodge, 2002: 6).

All three dimensions relate to structures and practices within institutions (including schools) and within societies, from the local to the global, that may prevent people from participating equally as peers in social life (Fraser, 2010). Fraser's theory has something to say to the issues experienced in education and schooling today because not everyone participates equally as peers and because through asking questions about recognition, redistribution and representation it draws attention to the cultural, economic and political aspects of social life – foundational aspects on which the study of education rests.

Fraser's theory has been used to examine education in various ways, all of which apply to topics within education studies programmes. Participatory parity has been applied to the structures of institutions such as schools (Lynch and Lodge, 2002; Keddie, 2012), national policy affecting Scottish young people (Mackie and Tett, 2013), rural science education (Eppley, 2017), educational access of mobile children in India (Dyer, 2010) and Lifelong Learning in light of Sustainable Development Goal 4 within UNESCO (Vargas, 2017). Whether it is the treatment of those with SEND, the difference in resources between schools in urban, rural and coastal areas, the needs of child carers or those of minority communities, Fraser's theory takes us beyond our own ideologies and deeper into the systemic causes of, and mechanisms behind, such barriers. It arguably avoids 'folk intuitions' and can contribute to concrete predictions about successful action.

Applying Fraser's theory to education studies programmes

Common to education studies programmes is an exploration of the schooling experiences of minority groups, including those with protected characteristics, and Fraser's theory can be applied to this. For example, as students, you may explore scenarios of pupils with protected characteristics in school, perhaps pupils who either identify as LGBTQ+ themselves and/or come from same-sex families. Their position in school may be demonstrated through a lack of visibility in textbooks and curricula resources, or visibility may be present but in a way that reinforces negative stereotypes or heteronormativity. Posters placed in school may display a purely heteronormative family ideal, for example. If this is combined with teacher-talk and materials, such as reading books, which repeat this ideal and do not recognise diversity, then learners from same-sex families do not see themselves represented. They are not afforded equal status and they suffer the injustice of **misrecognition**. Further, they may be denied, either explicitly or implicitly, the opportunity to discuss their families and see them celebrated in the classroom. They receive the message, spoken or unspoken, that they do not hold the same cultural power as other groups. It would take a very courageous child to speak about their family and risk the rejection of dismissal in an environment which implicitly tells them their families are not as valuable. In turn, this weaker cultural status and powerlessness to change it may contribute to 'marginalisation and subordination' (Phillips 1999 in Lynch and Lodge 2002: 195), representing **maldistribution**.

In being unable to challenge this directly or simply to talk about their own family, they suffer **misrepresentation** – their definition of the situation is disregarded, and their voice is not equal to those of others (Lynch and Lodge, 2002). These pupils are not able to participate equally in discussions about families which is a common topic certainly in primary classrooms, and hence they are denied **participatory parity**. In this scenario, we see all three of Fraser's dimensions of justice but at its heart is the injustice of misrecognition, which has been generative of the injustices of maldistribution and misrepresentation.

On your degree programme, you may also study educational policy and legislation. You may look at the Equalities Act 2010 and note that it is illegal to discriminate on the basis of sexual orientation. You may examine some school policies and note that there is no mention of LGBTQ+ pupils or diverse families in curriculum policies. Lynch and Lodge (2002) examined school policy and found that where groups were invisible in the discourse of policy, staff did not have the vocabulary with which to discuss an issue with pupils which led to **misrecognition** and prejudicial attitudes in schools. Using Fraser's theory as a lens to form questions, you can begin to interrogate policy from the perspective of social justice. Drawing on your previous exploration of pupil's experiences in school, you can now include policy as well and develop a deeper understanding of whether the educational environment is just or unjust, not only at a personal level but at a systems level too, since policy so strongly influences behaviour at multiple levels within an organisation.

When you go on to consider issues of race, gender and disability in education, you can use the theory to explore intersectionality. For example, what is the experience of **participatory parity** for people who are LGBTQ+ and have a disability? What are some of the additional nuances within this experience and how might action to achieve participatory parity change in light of multiple injustice? Beyond simply knowing that the experience may be 'unfair', you are empowered – through the use of theory – to ask specific questions and consider specific actions that might need redress. Might action on policy help? Might action on classroom resources help? Might it help to set up fora where those experiencing the injustice can be heard? Could it be all these things and more? What might the knock-on effects of these actions be for other groups and how might we evaluate the justice of that?

Questions to consider

Consider your education studies programme overall. Where are opportunities given to discuss social justice? In what way is social justice described?

Choose an example where protected characteristics have been discussed on your course, and apply Fraser's three dimensions of justice: can you see how Fraser's theory can bring a greater depth to your understanding?

Conclusion

Social justice theory equips us to analyse situations, make connections and ask critical questions. Using it, you are empowered to understand the mechanisms behind issues of injustice and consider concrete actions. Having this understanding alongside other key threads of your education studies programme, including personal reflection on your values as future educators and what you may choose for your careers, you have the tools available to recognise your own place within social justice and to plan actions to make education in the coming years more just.

Recommended reading

Vincent, C. (2020) *Nancy Fraser, Social Justice and Education*. Abingdon: Routledge.
This edited volume explores some of the philosophical aspects of Fraser's theory and deals with some of its main critiques. This will aid understanding of her theory in a more nuanced way, beyond what has been possible in this chapter.

Lynch, K. and Lodge, A. (2002) *Equality and Power in Schools: Redistribution, Recognition and Representation*. Abingdon: Routledge.
This applies Fraser's theory to the Irish school system and provides a comprehensive account of the many different aspects of education present in schools, both in terms of systems and different group identities.

Smith, E. (2018) *Key Issues in Education and Social Justice* (2nd Edition). London: Sage.
This latest edition explores social justice more broadly including some intersections between education and society. It provides a helpful introduction to the topic for those new to the area whilst also serving as a concise reminder of the main debates.

References

Bartlett, S. and Burton, D. (2020) *Introduction to Education Studies (Education Studies: Key Issues)*. London: Sage.

Costley, K. (2006) Why do we have theories? *ERIC*, online submission, Available at: https://eric.ed.gov/?q=why+use+theory&ft=on&ff1=souOnline+Submission&id=ED491769 (Accessed 5 July 2022) ERIC Number: ED491769.

DfE (2021) *Understanding Progress in the 2020/21 Academic Year - Complete Findings from the Autumn Term.* Available at: https://www.gov.uk/government/publications/pupils-progress-in-the-2020-to-2022-academic-years (Accessed 20 April 2022).

Dyer, C. (2010) Education and social (in)justice for mobile groups: Re-framing rights and educational inclusion for Indian pastoralist children. *Journal Educational Review,* **62**(301), p. 313. https://doi.org/10.1080/00131911.2010.503601

Eppley, K. (2017) Rural science education as social justice. *Cultural Studies of Science Education,* **12**(1), pp. 45–52. https://doi.org/10.1007/s11422-016-9751-7

Fraser, N. (2010) *Scales of Justice-Reimagining Political Space in a Globalizing World.* New York: Columbia University Press.

Keddie, A. (2012) Schooling and social justice through the lenses of Nancy Fraser. *Critical Studies in Education,* **53**(3), pp. 263–279. https://doi.org/10.1080/17508487.2012.709185

Lynch, K. and Lodge, A. (2002) *Equality and Power in Schools: Redistribution, Recognition and Representation.* London: RoutledgeFalmer.

Mackie, A. and Tett, L. (2013) 'Participatory parity', young people and policy in Scotland. *Journal of Education Policy,* **28**(3), pp. 386–403. https://doi.org/10.1080/02680939.2012.761729

Muthukrishna, M. and Henrich, J. (2019) A problem in theory. *Nature Human Behaviour,* **3**(3), pp. 221–229. https://doi.org/10.1038/s41562-018-0522-1

QAA (2019) *Subject Benchmark Statements: Education Studies.* Gloucester: QAA. Available at: https://www.qaa.ac.uk/docs/qaa/subject-benchmark-statements/subject-benchmark-statement-education-studies.pdf?sfvrsn=3ae2cb81_5 (Accessed: 31 January 2022).

Smith, E (2018) *Key Issues in Education and Social Justice* (2nd Edition). London: Sage.

Tezgiden Cakcak, Y. (2016) A critical review of teacher education models. *International Journal of Educational Policies,* **10**(2), pp. 121–140.

Vargas, C (2017) *Lifelong Learning from a Social Justice Perspective.* Education Research and Foresight - Working Papers. Paris: UNESCO.

Vaughn, R. and Walker, M. (2012) Capabilities, values and education policy. *Journal of Human Development and Capabilities,* **13**(3), pp. 495–512. https://doi.org/10.1080/19452829.2012.679648

Vincent, C. (2020) *Nancy Fraser, Social Justice and Education.* Abingdon: Routledge.

16 Inclusive curriculum matters

Co-creating a decolonised education curriculum through student voices

Jawiria Naseem and Zhu Hua

SUMMARY POINTS
- There is no single definition of 'Decolonisation'.
- Decolonisation is a process and therefore should be viewed as on-going discussions and reflections about curriculum and pedagogy.
- Decolonising education programmes at undergraduate level is central to addressing issues of belonging and social inequalities.
- Student and staff partnerships are inherent to successful decolonial activities.
- A change in belief systems is necessary before a change in knowledge system.

Introduction

Ever since the 2015 Rhodes Must Fall campaign in Cape Town, South Africa, where students called for the removal of British Imperialist Cecil Rhodes's statue, decolonisation of the curricula has become a prominent concern internationally in higher education (HE) (Nyamnjoh, 2016). Today, decolonising the curriculum has become a pedagogical matter in HE, especially in predominantly White universities located in the Global North, that is to say, in countries entrenched with colonial histories (Bhambra et al., 2018). Within the UK, for instance, there have been several student-led campaigns that demand a review of their university curriculum and the importance of seeing themselves reflected in all aspects of their learning (e.g., UCL students' campaign on 'Why is My Curriculum White?' in 2014) which echo similar efforts from within the sector (e.g., Universities UK's '#ClosingtheGap' report in 2019). Despite the pressing demand from students, increasing coverage in the media and news and growing commitment among HE staff, there is very little knowledge about how to translate the commitment to decolonisation into practice and how to reframe knowledge and pedagogies for an inclusive and diverse curriculum (cf. Keele University, Kingston University). This lack of progress makes it difficult to implement decolonising initiatives, share good practice or even create an environment welcoming to the idea of decolonisation. In this chapter, we discuss our and our students' collaborative efforts to engage in decolonial work in the School of Education at the University of Birmingham and reflect on the challenges, the successes, and the ways forward.

Conceptual framing: What does decolonisation of the curriculum entail?

'Decolonisation' can mean different things to different people in different contexts. The Cambridge dictionary, for instance, refers to 'decolonisation' as 'the political independence received by European colonies (i.e., a country or area controlled politically by a more powerful country) in Africa and Asia after World War II' (Cambridge Advanced Learner's Dictionary and Thesaurus, 2020). From a 'decolonial' lens, this very definition requires questioning as the wording (i.e., 'independence *received*') undermines the reality experienced by millions of people, their liberation struggles against oppression, and the fights they *won* against Eurocentric domination. In other words, independence was never 'handed-over' but was fought for over several centuries. As such the term 'decolonisation', although contested, calls for a different 'way of thinking about the world which takes colonialism, empire and racism as its empirical and discursive objects of study' (Bhambra et al., 2018: 2).

Why universities should engage in decolonial work has received much attention in recent years (for detailed discussions, see Arday and Mirza (2018), Mamdani (2019) and Morreira and colleagues (2020)). To foreground our collaborative strategy of implementing decolonisation, we will briefly discuss the key thinking that informs our work below.

A decolonisation of the university curriculum means critically engaging with the questions of *who* owns knowledge, *whose* knowledge counts, *how* to improve the system and the structure to eradicate institutional racism, and *how* to develop a meaningful partnership with students, in particular marginalised groups in educational matters (Zhu et al., forthcoming). '*Whose* knowledge counts' is a question that also considers *what* or *whose* knowledge is 'left out' and subsequently asks what impact this has on those who own this 'disregarded' knowledge or associate with it (Jansen, 2019). University curriculum is criticised for maintaining white power and privilege by over-representing knowledge produced by White male scholars, thus excluding scholars who find themselves at the intersection of minority statuses such as minority ethnic and/or female scholars (Arday, 2019). This unbalance in knowledge production or, in other words, refusal to recognise the multiplicity of knowledge systems beyond White male and Eurocentric writers and theorists, sustains unequal power relations in the production and dissemination of knowledge.

Decolonising knowledge in HE thus entails revisiting existing curriculum, not through a process of replacement (e.g., White with Black), but a process by which knowledge is decentred and presented without the white western prism. Diversity and pluralism of knowledge seek to destabilise these unequal power relations in knowledge production, 'allowing new forms of knowledge which represent marginalised groups – women, working classes, ethnic minorities, lesbian, gay, bisexual, and transgender (LGBT) to propagate' (Begum and Saini, 2019: 3). Revisiting a narrow and restrictive curriculum, therefore, has significant implications for you as learners in HE. It offers opportunities for all students to be exposed to, and be able to critically engage with, all forms of knowledge.

> **Questions to consider**
>
> What does 'decolonisation' mean to you?
> What does decolonising the curriculum mean for education studies?

Why co-create a curriculum through students' voices?

Educational curricula are dis-empowering and alienating students who already feel a sense of non-belonging in HE, mirroring societal racism (Joseph-Salisbury, 2019). Minority ethnic students, especially, need to see themselves in their learning by a validation of their experiences in a decolonised space, which no longer ignores the contributions of marginalised thinkers. This is particularly important since knowledge production is embedded in each and everyone's identities and histories and thus a white curriculum reinforces a sense of isolation and dis-engagement among minority ethnic students which subsequently contributes to these students' low attainment as compared to their White peers (Arday *et al.*, 2020). A decolonised curriculum thus addresses the intellectual, emotional and psychological needs of students growing up in a diverse and global environment by accessing alternative ways to view and interpret the world. Such a curriculum, therefore, benefits all students (and not just those who are known to be marginalised) as it is an 'opportunity to *experience*, not just learn *about*, how the centralisation of [minority] worldviews/ways of being and knowing influence common understandings about dominant cultural locations' (Phillips *et al.*, 2005: 7).

It is precisely due to these implications for students that, we believe, decolonial activities in HE cannot be successful without a partnership between you, as learners, and us, as teachers. How can power relations be altered or rebalanced if those ascribed the inferior position are not heard and not given an equal status? Positioning the voices of students at the heart of our project was a prominent feature; it enabled us to understand how our students could see themselves reflected in their curriculum and how we could support the endeavour of decolonising education studies in our institution.

Questions to consider

Is your voice being heard on your education programme?
    Does your programme offer opportunities for student and staff collaboration?
    How essential do you think such a partnership is in facilitating your learning?

Decolonising education studies: Taking a module-level approach

Despite the small yet steady increase in the minority ethnic students' enrolment between 2014 and 2020, as of 2020, the undergraduate cohort in education studies remained overwhelmingly white (82.98 per cent) and had a lower population of minority ethnic students (17.02 per cent) than the overall undergraduate population (26.18 per cent). Some minority ethnic groups are more affected than others; for instance, Black students made up 8 per cent of all undergraduate students in 2020, but only 5 per cent of the education cohort (HESA, 2019/2020). These disparities mirror those experienced by minority ethnic academics who, in 2020, constituted only 9.7 per cent of all academics in education studies (Advance HE, 2020). These representational inequalities have significant impact on the aspiration and success of minority ethnic students, contributing to feelings of non-belonging and the widening of their attainment gap (UUK and NUS, 2019).

In September 2020, together with two other colleagues, we initiated a project embedding decolonial work into pedagogical practices with the aim of addressing the above issues in the delivery

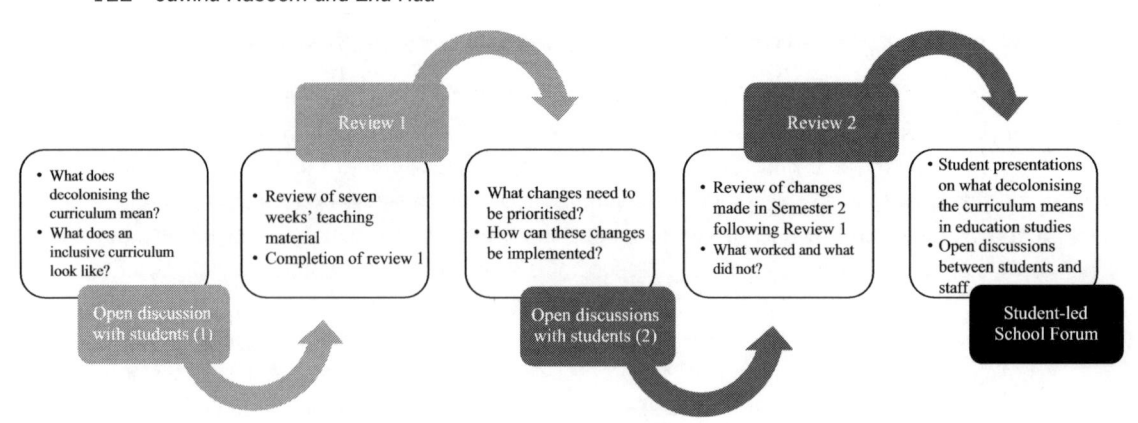

Figure 16.1 A detailed overview of the student–staff collaborative stages

and design of our School's education studies degrees at undergraduate and postgraduate levels. The project was envisaged as a process of rethinking and reframing current knowledge and pedagogies through critically engaging students, both White and minority ethnic. We invited undergraduate students in education studies and postgraduate students in the field of disability, inclusion and special needs in education to take part in the project. Here, we discuss work conducted with our undergraduate students.

The undergraduate students were tasked with conducting a review of a Year 1 compulsory module called *Contemporary Issues in Education* which ran in Semesters 1 and 2 during the academic year 2020/2021. As its title suggests, the module is concerned with contemporary educational matters in the UK and beyond. This module draws on sociological, psychological and historical perspectives in examining educational matters and is taken across the three undergraduate programmes we offer. In total, 15 students in Years 1–3 volunteered. Students formed a mixed group including international students, White British students and British minority ethnic students. All participants were female.

We adopted a module-level approach to decolonising our pedagogy and practice by actively involving students as project partners. This module level approach aimed to assess the entire module's curriculum by asking three core questions:

1. Are students able to see themselves reflected in the module? (representation)
2. How accessible is the module? (accessibility)
3. Does the module equip students to work in a global and diverse world? (employability)

> **Questions to consider**
>
> To what extent do modules on your degree programme address our three core questions? Can you identify ways that these questions could be effectively addressed?

As a first step, students were invited to take part in a workshop (on-line, due to the Covid pandemic) exploring the meaning and importance of adopting a decolonial pedagogy and curriculum in order to create a more inclusive learning environment. Following these conversations, the 15 students reviewed the module content and seven weeks' teaching materials. They were encouraged to question all aspects of the module, from learning outcomes to the assessment strategy, available on the module's online platform against each of the above three core questions.

Following the first review, we collated the students' response into two documents; the first showcased all aspects that students highlighted as being in line with the above aims, while the second suggested changes to be made to the module to move towards these aims. Students discussed these documents with us in a follow up workshop and focused on the second one (with the suggested changes). This was important since aspects viewed by some students as inclusive were challenged by others. For instance, some students considered that having the option to select a question from a list for their assignment was an inclusive strategy as it gave students opportunity to draw on their particular interests and strengths. However, some students saw this very list of question as restrictive since they felt that the questions did not necessarily allow students to reflect on topics beyond the UK/the West. The aim of the discussion was therefore to provide a platform for students to voice their views in a collaborative way. As a group, we then asked ourselves two questions: *What changes need to be prioritised?* and *How can these changes be implemented?*

We agreed on three changes in relation to the assessment, reading list and essential reading tasks. The students agreed on the following:

1. **Assessment**: to provide opportunities to answer essay questions by focusing on a country of their choice, thus enabling discussions of contemporary issues in education beyond the UK
2. **Reading list**: to include readings in a way that acknowledges contributions of authors from the Global South
3. **Essential reading**: to provide a list of guiding questions to support students for whom English is not a first language, to access the content and focus on key issues raised

We implemented these changes in two steps: some changes were made during Semester 1 while others were implemented in Semester 2. Thus, unlike other opportunities for students to voice their views (such as end of module feedback), students were able to *experience* the suggested changes (rather than changes being experienced by the following cohort). These changes were then assessed again in a second review of the module during Semester 2. The project culminated with a student-led Department-wide forum (open to both staff and students) which offered students an opportunity to discuss their views on decolonising matters and share their experience as partners in the project.

Successes and challenges: How to navigate between multiplicity of views and beliefs

Without doubt our co-participatory, collaborative and conversation approach brought together academics and students for group as well as personal transformations. Reflecting about students' experiences, we witnessed transformation both at a personal and research level, with students motivated by addressing inclusivity and social inequalities. For instance, one of the students joined the university's Reverse Mentoring Scheme to promote a more inclusive, diverse and equal study environment by working closely with a senior university level colleague. One international student is now aiming to pursue doctoral studies to address inequalities experienced by minority ethnic groups in their own country.

For us, on a personal level, we also found ourselves at the intersections of new spaces allowing reflections of our own positions as minority ethnic female academics. I (Jawiria) believe that my intercultural experience growing up as a Muslim Pakistani woman remain subsumed under my lived experiences in the Netherlands, France and the UK. Putting my module bare in front of the students, a module I have been leading for three years, allowed me to engage in a self-reflective exercise by drawing on students' voices. This allowed me to question my own assumptions and made me more sensitive towards questions of ownership and belonging among students and how these are ongoing processes that require continuous exploration of my pedagogy and practice as an educator.

As a transnational scholar with training in China and the UK and a scholar in multilingual and intercultural communication, I (Zhu Hua) have become acutely aware of the dominance of the Eurocentric norms and English in academia over the years. The co-creation project provided a concrete opportunity to appreciate both conceptual complexity and practical challenges of decolonising the curriculum. For me, the success of the project lies in breaking-down the dichotomy of teachers vs. learners and the reversal of the hierarchy. The challenge, however, remains as to how to bring together multiple perspectives and experience of multilingual and multicultural students and staff. Yet, this challenge can be addressed by decentring Eurocentric knowledge in the curriculum through a focus on accessibility, representativeness and employability (Meda, 2020).

Through these activities, our students were also claiming a practical right to lead in these decolonial efforts. For instance, the first change (in relation to the assessment) offered students the opportunity to voice their views on educational matters from their own perspective and also educate us along the way. Indeed, changes to the assessment provided a platform for students to direct their research towards countries of their own interest or countries with which they shared a personal history, *and* guide teachers towards often unknown literature, expanding our knowledge as well. This mutual learning process is precisely rooted in what Guzmán Valenzuela (2021) called a relational strategy. Guzmán Valenzuela (2021) argues that a relational strategy can be a successful approach for decolonising efforts as it is concerned with the development of 'relationships among all involved – recognising that everyone is different – and based especially on values of care, respect, and solidarity' (p. 14). We decided to move together as a learning community towards a decolonised education curriculum by drawing on the voices of our students; no one claimed ownership of any form of knowledge or superiority in what knowledge can or cannot be brought into discussions of educational issues. Collaboratively, we opened doors to knowledge that has been silenced and remained narrowed for a long time.

> **Questions to consider**
>
> What knowledge has been 'silenced and remain narrowed' on your education studies degree programme?
> What do you think are the main challenges to decolonising the curriculum on your degree programme?

Yet, we also found ourselves in an unexpected situation as we thought through the proposed changes. *How can we reconcile pre-existing knowledge, reconcile White and minority ethnic students as well as the multiplicity of views among minority ethnic students?* This question was particularly sensitive as it related to the relationships between our diverse group of UK and international students and how learning could be sustainable for all. In addressing these issues, several factors were considered: how to provide a comfortable and safe space for all to share their views; how to validate all views while also decentring Western knowledge; and how to provide 'opportunities to interpret unfamiliar forms of knowledge and ways of producing knowledge' to all, especially for White students (Phillips et al., 2005: 7). It is through a focus on graduate qualities such as 'critical thinking, problem-solving, interdisciplinarity, reflection, and ethics' that we addressed these issues as these qualities are conducive to the development of intercultural competence (Harvey and Russell-Mundine, 2018: 793).

Considering 'the education triad' of academics, students and the curriculum highlights that we cannot focus on decolonising matters in isolation (Vandeyar, 2020: 783). Thus, partnership with and between staff is a key component for success, yet lack of commitment from academics is the Achilles' heel – to use Vandeyar's (2020) expression – of any decolonising agenda. This is particularly salient in a subject like education which is, in theory, conducive to questioning and challenging social justice issues. But how do you change belief systems when these are, unlike knowledge, most resistant to change (Schraw and Olafson, 2002)? We do not necessarily have a one-size-fits-all answer to this question, but we do believe that by sharing experiences – of having difficult conversations – we can produce a shift in personal belief systems and therefore overcome resistance and gain support.

Concluding remarks: Where do we go next?

By cultivating an environment which would expand existing curriculum, by way of embracing intellectual contributions of all authors – White and minority ethnic alike – the project aimed to create an academic space in which all students would feel that they belong to, and identify with; a space where stereotypes, prejudice and patronising views are broken down to encourage intellectual stimulation for all. This commitment to capture the richness of knowledge from both the global North and South helped everyone question what is taught and how it is taught, opening the possibility to question and challenge any knowledge.

Nevertheless, our module-level approach is only a small step forward, not a leap into the reforming of colonised spaces. As Phillips and his colleagues (2005) argued, the real success of decolonised efforts is 'dependent more upon the broader university landscape than the content and teaching approaches within the confines of a single subject' (p6). A whole-university level approach can significantly address prominent issues such as degree classification awarding gaps between students as has been demonstrated at other UK universities (see. for example, Mcduff et al. (2018) for the successful work conducted by Kingston University in closing the attainment, where its proportion of minority ethnic students obtaining first and upper-second class degrees increased from 45 per cent in 2012 to 70 per cent in 2017).

It is thus vital for the teaching and learning spaces, as well as the curriculum, to be revisited with a decolonial lens. It is often assumed that staff and students on education studies programmes are predisposed and committed to ideas of inclusivity, diversity and social justice. However, such assumptions can create barriers for self-reflection and recognition that silenced voices, histories and knowledges are being excluded. The goal of decolonising the curriculum, therefore, as Harvey and Russell-Mundine (2018) state, should not only involve the development of students but also 'staff (academic and professional) as well as broader institutional culture change' (p. 790).

Recommended reading

Bhambra, G.K., Gebrial, D. and Nişancıoğlu, K. (2018) *Decolonising the university*. London: Pluto Press. http://library.oapen.org/handle/20.500.12657/25936

This edited volume offers a broad discussion of calls to decolonise the university drawing on student and staff's experiences and suggestions for concrete practices situated in specific theoretical questions of what decolonisation in higher education in the Global North means.

Schucan Bird, K. and Pitman, L. (2020) How diverse is your reading list? Exploring issues of representation and decolonisation in the UK. *Higher Education*, 79, pp. 903–920. https://doi.org/10.1007/s10734-019-00446-9

This article discusses the role of reading lists in decolonising UK universities by reviewing two modules at a renowned HE institution. It argues for a diversification of reading lists in higher education and highlights challenges that can be encountered in this decolonial work.

Motala, S., Sayed, Y. and de Kock, T. (2021) Epistemic decolonisation in reconstituting higher education pedagogy in South Africa: The student perspective. *Teaching in Higher Education*, 7(8), pp. 1002–1018. https://doi.org/10.1080/13562517.2021.1947225

The article focuses on students' perspectives in discussions of decolonised curriculum in the context of South Africa, where the Rhodes Must Fall movement started. In particular, the paper examines students' relationships with staff, the use of language and their experiences at two HE institutions.

Shaik, A. and Kahn, P. (2021) Understanding the challenges entailed in decolonising a Higher Education institution: An organisational case study of a research-intensive South African university. *Teaching in Higher Education*, 7(8), pp. 969–985. https://doi.org/10.1080/13562517.2021.1928064

This article examines challenges that universities experience in implementing a coherent and collective strategy to decolonisation. It presents examples from a university in South Africa drawing on conceptual discussions of cultural identity.

References

Advance HE (2020) Equality in higher education: Statistical report 2020. Available at: https://www.advance-he.ac.uk/knowledge-hub/equality-higher-education-statistical-report-2020 (Accessed 2 January 2022).

Arday, J. (2019) Dismantling power and privilege through reflexivity: Negotiating normative Whiteness, the Eurocentric curriculum and racial micro-aggressions within the Academy. *Whiteness and Education*, 3(2), pp. 141–161. https://doi.org/10.1080/23793406.2019.1574211

Arday, J., Zoe Belluigi, D. and Thomas, D. (2020) Attempting to break the chain: Reimaging inclusive pedagogy and decolonising the curriculum within the academy. *Educational Philosophy and Theory*, 53(3), pp. 298–313. https://doi.org/10.1080/00131857.2020.1773257

Arday, J. and Mirza, H.S. (2018) *Dismantling race in higher education: Racism, whiteness and decolonising the academy*. Cham: Springer. https://doi.org/10.1007/978-3-319-60261-5

Begum, N. and Saini, R. (2019) Decolonising the curriculum. *Political Studies Review*, 17(2), pp. 196–201. https://doi.org/10.1177/1478929918808459

Bhambra, G.K., Gebrial, D. and Nişancıoğlu, K. (2018) *Decolonising the university*. London: Pluto Press. http://library.oapen.org/handle/20.500.12657/25936

Cambridge Advanced Learner's Dictionary and Thesaurus (2020) 'Decolonization', Available at: https://dictionary.cambridge.org/dictionary/english/decolonization (Accessed 4 January 2022).

Guzmán Valenzuela, C. (2021) Disrupting curricula and pedagogies in Latin American universities: Six criteria for decolonising the university. *Teaching in Higher Education*, 7(8), pp. 1019–1037. https://doi.org/10.1080/13562517.2021.1935846

Harvey, A. and Russell-Mundine, G. (2018) Decolonising the curriculum: Using graduate qualities to embed Indigenous knowledges at the academic cultural interface. *Teaching in Higher Education*, 24(6), pp. 789–808. https://doi.org/10.1080/13562517.2018.1508131

HESA (2019) Table 24 – UK domiciled undergraduate students of known ethnicity by subject area and ethnicity 2014/15 to 2018/19. Available at: https://www.hesa.ac.uk/data-and-analysis/students/table-24 (Accessed 4 January 2022).

HESA (2020) Table 53 – UK domiciled undergraduate students of known ethnicity by CAH level 1 subject and ethnicity 2019/20. Available at: https://www.hesa.ac.uk/data-and-analysis/students/table-53 (Accessed 4 January 2022).

Jansen, J. (2019) *Decolonisation in universities: The politics of knowledge*. Johannesburg: Wits University Press. https://doi.org/10.18772/22019083351

Joseph-Salisbury, R. (2019) Institutionalised whiteness, racial microaggressions and black bodies out of place in Higher Education. *Whiteness and Education*, 4(1), pp. 1–17. https://doi.org/10.1080/23793406.2019.1620629

Mamdani, M. (2019) Decolonising universities. In Jansen, J. (Ed.) *Decolonisation in universities: The politics of knowledge*. Johannesburg: Wits University Press. https://doi.org/10.18772/22019083351

Mcduff, N., Tatam, J., Beacock, O. and Ross, F. (2018) Closing the attainment gap for students from black and minority ethnic backgrounds through institutional change. *Widening Participation and Lifelong Learning*, 20(-1), pp. 79–101. https://doi.org/10.5456/WPLL.20.1.79

Meda, L. (2020) Decolonising the curriculum: Students' perspectives. *Africa Education Review*, 17(2), pp. 88–103. https://doi.org/10.1080/18146627.2018.1519372

Morreira, S., Luckett, K., Kumalo, S.H. and Ramgotra, M. (2020) Confronting the complexities of decolonising curricula and pedagogy in higher education. *Third World Thematics: A TWQ Journal*, 5(1–2), pp. 1–18. https://doi.org/10.1080/23802014.2020.1798278

Nyamnjoh, F.B (2016) *# RhodesMustFall: Nibbling at resilient colonialism in South Africa*. Langaa RPCIG. Available at: muse.jhu.edu/book/67106. (Accessed 4 January 2022).

Phillips, J., Whatman, S., Hart, V. and Winslett, G. (2005) *Decolonising university curricula – reforming the colonised spaces within which we operate*. In Proceedings The Indigenous Knowledges Conference – Reconciling Academic Priorities with Indigenous Realities, Victoria University, Wellington, New Zealand. Available at: https://www.researchgate.net/publication/27468178_Decolonising_University_Curricula_-_reforming_the_colonised_spaces_within_which_we_operate (Accessed 4 January 2022).

Schraw, G. and Olafson, L. (2002) Teachers' epistemological worldviews and educational practices. *Issues in Education*, 8(2), pp. 99–148. https://doi.org/10.1891/194589503787383109

UUK and NUS (2019) *Black, Asian and minority Ethnic student attainment at UK universities: #Closing the gap*. Available at: https://www.universitiesuk.ac.uk/policy-and-analysis/reports/Documents/2019/bame-student-attainment-uk-universities-closing-the-gap.pdf. (Accessed 4 January 2022)

Vandeyar, S. (2020) Why decolonising the South African university curriculum will fail. *Teaching in Higher Education*, 25(7), pp. 783–796. https://doi.org/10.1080/13562517.2019.1592149

Zhu, H., Kiwan, D. and Youdell, D. (Forthcoming). *Decolonising schools*. Chartered College of Teaching.

17 Speaking through silence

Embracing fear and shame in anti-racist education

Heather Knight and Emma Jones

> **SUMMARY POINTS**
> - In educational settings where most staff and students are White, both students and educators need opportunities to explore feelings of fear and resistance that can arise when learning about racism.
> - Critical pedagogy offers a way forward for engaging in dialogue about racism that goes beyond surface learning and instead explores issues that learners find troubling.
> - Shotwell's theory of 'negative affect' provides a framework for exploring uncomfortable feelings that can become transformative learning moments.

Introduction

Discussing issues of race and racism in educational contexts is often experienced as uncomfortable or disturbing. Fear of looking racist (Leonardo, 2009) or 'getting it wrong' can lead to silences and avoidance of the subject matter. The issue is exacerbated in predominantly White areas, where a common belief exists that anti-racist education is unnecessary (Gaine, 2005; Asare, 2009). However, in a globalised world, as communities are becoming more diverse, students growing up in predominantly White and rural areas are likely to find themselves living and working in increasingly diverse contexts. Yet students and educators who have had little access to experiences of racial diversity may find they have limited understanding of the existence of racism, its impact, and the implications of racial and cultural difference (Asare, 2009). Lack of contact with people of colour, the absence of an anti-racist curriculum and fear of engaging with discussions about race and racism can lead to avoidance, resistance and disengagement from learning and implementing changes (Knight, 2018). Even those who would like to move forward as part of the solution may feel uncertain about what to do (Gaine, 2005). Consequently, when education does not address issues of race and racism and focusses primarily on the needs of the dominant ethnic group, children of colour can be left unsupported in their educational settings and restricted by educators who are unable to meet their needs (Maylor, 2014).

In this chapter, an education studies lecturer and a former education studies undergraduate student (now a further education lecturer) critically reflect on learning moments during anti-racism lectures with a mainly White cohort. These lecturers take a critical pedagogy approach (Freire, 1970), recognising the importance of providing opportunities for dialogue. We argue that this is especially important when learning about racism, because if people do not express their ideas, they cannot change them. We embrace Shotwell's (2011) notion of 'negative affect', which proposes paying attention to uncomfortable emotions such as fear and shame and utilising these as pivotal moments for change. This chapter forms part of a continued effort to explore ways forward for developing anti-racist practice on education studies courses.

> **Questions to consider**
>
> Consider your own feelings when having conversations about ethnicity and racism. What type of emotions do you feel? Do you find it easy or uncomfortable to engage in these conversations? Why do you think this is?
>
> When growing up, what assumptions did people around you have about ethnicity and racism? How were conversations about these topics approached in your schools? What does this tell you about attitudes towards ethnicity and racism in these contexts?

Racism in mainly white communities: Challenging the 'No problem here' myth

The context for this chapter is an education studies course located in a city with a predominantly White population in a rural area of Southwest England. Whilst slowly emerging as a more multicultural city (Burnett, 2011), at the time of writing the education studies course still attracts mainly White students. Many of these students state that they have grown up in White areas with little, if any, experiences of racial diversity in their lives and school education. Minimal contact with people of colour often leads White people to adopt the false assertion about racism that that there is 'no problem here' (Gaine, 1995) and thus no need to learn about racism. Gaine (1995) highlighted that 'no problem here' is a misconception. He explored attitudes amongst White children living in predominantly White areas and found much negativity towards ethnic minority groups and embedded beliefs about people with brown skin being allegedly dangerous and undesirable.

The existence of racism in predominantly White areas is well documented (Gaine, 2005; Burnett, 2011; Myers and Bhopal, 2017). Yet, Myers and Bhopal (2017: 126) found that in schools there is 'an entrenched discourse of White culture unhappy to acknowledge that racism flourishes in such spaces'; when racial hostility is reported, it is often dismissed due to beliefs that such reports are a threat to the image of the school. Not dealing with racism and presenting an image that seeks to obscure it can be seen as a form of structural racism that puts White people first and disadvantages people of colour (Delgado and Stefancic, 2012). However, whilst some acts of racism are deliberate, structural racism may not always be done deliberately with the intention of harm. Indeed, Taylor (2009) argues that the predominantly White teaching population contribute to the racial achievement gap through their practice while being unable to recognise what they are doing. This suggests that even well-meaning people can unwittingly contribute to racial harms, despite good intentions.

We argue that in areas where there is little opportunity to have assumptions changed due to a lack of experiences of racial diversity, learning about racism becomes *more* necessary, not less. However, teaching about racism can be problematic when educators too have had limited opportunities to mix with and learn from diverse communities. Recent figures showed that only 53 per cent of newly qualified teachers felt that teacher education prepared them well to teach pupils from all ethnic backgrounds (Ginnis *et al.*, 2018). Lander (2015) argues that teachers are ill prepared and unsure about how to tackle racism; they receive very little training on race and there is limited space for critical reflection around racism in initial teacher education (ITE). Davies (2021) highlights restrictions that can inhibit such work in ITE, including time constraints, lack of confidence amongst White teacher educators, and superficial student satisfaction measures that can lead to the avoidance of topics such as racism which may be perceived as uncomfortable or challenging. Yet, we argue that engaging in dialogue about race is a necessary part of the learning process for both students and educators. Education studies degrees can provide opportunities to engage in challenging conversations and deeper learning about racism in ways that may prove more difficult in ITE, highlighting how important such degree programmes should be because they grow future educators who can help develop anti-racist practice in schools and education settings.

Education studies practice: Dialogue and emotionally critical reflection

The teaching on education studies programmes is often informed by critical pedagogy. Critical pedagogy is a transformation-based education approach that seeks to raise awareness of oppressive and discriminatory systems and enable people to take action to transform lives. Paulo Freire (1970), one of the key thinkers on critical pedagogy, proposes that education either *domesticates* or *liberates*. Domestication education replicates the status quo with all its inequalities, while liberation education seeks to transform it. Freire (1970: 53-55) likens traditional education to 'banking', whereby teachers 'deposit' information into students' heads. Freire argues that this dehumanises students because they remain passive in this process and do not develop critical consciousness.

Banking education can include students not receiving an anti-racist education and instead being told how they must – or must not – speak about race and ethnicity. Knight (2018: 250) found that in schools, when students mention aspects of ethnicity, they are often shut down and told, 'you can't say that'. When ideas about racism and ethnicity are not explored and instead are prescribed and enforced in punitive ways, students may learn what teachers expect of them without gaining deeper understanding of why prejudiced beliefs are untrue and harmful (Richardson and Miles, 2008). Richardson and Miles (2008) argue instead for an approach that includes transforming the underlying cultural discourses that allow derogatory ideas to fester. We argue that this approach necessitates a pedagogical shift from teaching methods that require students to 'bank' information about race, and instead facilitate discussions that encourage the examination of one's beliefs and assumptions. Freire's (1970: 60) theory of 'liberation education' provides a useful framework. This involves learners engaging in critical dialogue to explore issues in ways that relate to their own lives, including fears and doubts. Freire argues that not addressing fears and doubts leads to blocks and silences.

Silences can also arise when teachers do not feel confident to facilitate dialogue about racism. In such incidences, conversations and questions can be shut down, resulting in students not being given a chance to discuss issues that they find difficult or confusing nor engage in conversations that could develop their thinking (Knight, 2018). Leonardo (2009) proposes that White people's feelings of fear and individual guilt block the ability to engage in critical dialogue about race. Therefore, the emotional aspects of difficult dialogue also need to be addressed. Hence, we combine critical pedagogy with 'negative affect'. Shotwell (2011: 74) describes 'negative affect' as a collection of negative emotions, such as 'guilt, sadness, panic, shame, embarrassment', which arise following certain behaviours towards and conversations about race. She argues for 'leaning in' to the sharp points of discomfort rather than 'cushioning ourselves from it' (p. 80). She maintains that if we do not meet and work with negative affect, we lose a potentially useful tool. With this in mind, in what follows we offer insights into pivotal moments in our own teaching and learning journeys.

Heather's story

I am a White working class lecturer. I teach about racism on an education studies course. Each year, the majority of students state that their school education contained almost no content about Black roles models, such as scientists, mathematicians, authors, and other historical figures. Some White students express that due to the absence of diversity education when growing up, they do not feel confident to work in racially diverse settings, let alone tackle racist incidents. Some students have revealed that they fear going into diverse school contexts, feel nervous about working with children from diverse religious and cultural backgrounds, and are unsure how to overcome these feelings. When introducing the topic of racism, I have found it beneficial to begin by exploring how conversations about race make students feel, which can lead to revelations about discomfort and fear of 'getting it wrong'. It has proved useful to introduce Shotwell's (2011) theory of negative affect, highlighting her assertion that recognising and engaging with discomfort can be an important part of the learning process, which alerts us that there is something that needs to be examined and changed.

Emma's story

Waiting for the racism lecture to begin, a familiar feeling occurred: one of complacency and resignation. As a mature student from a rural, predominantly White area, I anticipated this lecture to follow certain expectations; I would be taught that discrimination or treating individuals differently simply because of their ethnicity or race is unacceptable, followed by an introduction to culturally, ethnically and racially diverse groups, identifying how each group lives and how, essentially, 'they' are no different to 'the rest of us' and should be included in education and offered the same opportunities. It did not occur to me that those thoughts were harmful and were a product of previous inadequate racism education.

My feelings about what I was about to experience were compounded when my lecturer entered the room. A White, seemingly middle-class female lecturer made me feel comfortable and unthreatened; here was a person I could relate to, one who was not going to make me feel challenged. However, within the first few minutes of the lesson, I realised I was about to experience something very different. There was no gentle lecture, no learning about Diwali or Rosa Parks, no mention of the importance of equality and the laws created to protect against racism, but an instant encouragement to open a dialogue identifying what racism is and what it means, introducing concepts of Whiteness, power and privilege.

Questions to consider

Think about lectures and seminars on race and racism that you have attended. What approach did those sessions take? Did they provide you with an opportunity to explore current behaviour, including your own? How did you feel before, during and after those lectures or seminars?

Heather's story

Understanding Whiteness, power and privilege has been a core part of my own learning journey. My story arises from wanting to make a difference to the pervasive structures of racism, which I came to recognise through being a mother to dual heritage children. I found myself frustrated by the repeated denial from people around me that racism existed. Trying to make sense of racist pain in a culture of denial fuelled my desire to develop my own understanding. However, I initially positioned myself as a 'good' White anti-racist, not recognising how Whiteness gave me privileges, shaped my worldview, and led to racialised blind spots. Farr (2014) argues that many well-intentioned White people are fine with talking about race as long as this does not go deep enough to challenge their own identity and privilege. This can lead to positioning others as the problem and not recognising our own role in preserving White advantage. Applebaum (2005: 278) argues that it is not enough to consider oneself a 'good moral anti-racist citizen' because it is often those very people who are 'contributing to the perpetuation of systemic injustice'; belief in one's own moral position can act as a barrier to seeing White privilege. Thus, even White people who are seeking to be part of the solution need to be self-vigilant to their own assumptions. A dialogical approach that allows us to critically reflect on our own stories can be a way forward. This inevitably means embracing discomfort (Shotwell, 2011) in our own reflections and in classroom discussions.

Emma's story

The uncomfortable silence that initially occurred in that lecture was patiently allowed by the lecturer. The dialogue tentatively began without using certain terms to avoid offending or inadvertently outing oneself as racist. With encouragement and guidance, the conversation became more involved, exploring those words, phrases and ideas that may otherwise have been shut down, and facilitated by drawing on Freire's and Shotwell's pedagogical methods. Without the use of critical pedagogy and instead a reliance on 'banking' knowledge, my experience of learning about racial studies would have continued to reinforce the existing ideas I held. By moving away from considering the learner as someone who receives information, to seeing a learner as a person of discovery, transformational learning can occur. The discomfort I experienced led to reflection: "why did I feel uncomfortable? What can I learn from this discomfort?" Shotwell posits that the avoidance of negative affect is often prompted by an 'implicit idea that the purpose of life is to be endlessly comfortable and at ease' (2011:80). Yet learning about controversial topics can be anything but comfortable when seeking to dig deeper and go beyond surface learning.

The knowledge I now had regarding the benefit of discomfort and negative emotion led to personal transformation following a critical moment that occurred while on a teaching placement with mature students who were discussing the headline news. The article identified Shamima Begum as the 'ISIS bride' who wished to return to the UK, and the story centred around the acts she had allegedly committed (Busby and Dodd, 2019). The students were expressing opinions that suggested intolerance or suspicion directed towards the Muslim community and I realised, to my shame, that my instant, initial response was similar. Shotwell (2011) states that it is not easy to admit feeling a sense of shame: it gives us an unpleasant, uneasy feeling of discomfort that is difficult to verbalise. Because my mind kept returning to this incident, I raised it with my lecturers, exploring why my initial reaction occurred. Had I embodied racial and Islamophobic intolerance without even realising it? It was not easy to admit to such thoughts but by doing so I could begin to understand why they occurred and what could be done to provoke change. If I had buried those feelings and shied away from the revelations they prompted, I would not have recognised the pervasive nature of institutional or structural racism and how my actions may be contributing to racism, despite my belief in the opposite (Jones, 2020). This recognition was beneficial – it raised my awareness that my thoughts and actions are influenced by societal structures that favour White people, and that I have an obligation to contribute to dismantling them. Identifying systemic privilege holds the dominant culture accountable.

Heather's story
Change does not come easily. First comes recognition of the ways that our own ethnic identities shape how we see the world. As Rollock (2013: 500) argues, 'White researchers… are not neutral enquirers in conversations about race. They sit within and are part of a wider system of race inequity characterised by performances of privilege, power and entitlement'. During my time as a PhD student, I was asked to consider ways that my Whiteness shaped my understanding. I remember feeling troubled and thinking…surely, I am not the one affected by racist assumptions…am I? The idea that our thoughts might be racialised can lead to fear that we might be perceived as bad people (Shotwell, 2011). Indeed, I felt that my identity as a 'good' White person was being challenged, which led to the 'negative affect' of guilt, shame, and frustration at being questioned. I was committed to researching, raising awareness of, and challenging racism, so why did I feel resistance to this question? Leonardo (2009:264) argues that White guilt can become a paralysing sentiment: 'White guilt blocks critical reflection because Whites end up feeling individually blameworthy for racism'. Leonardo posits that when this happens people become overly concerned with whether or not they 'look racist' rather than exploring the structural aspects of racism. This can lead to defensiveness and resistance to learning.

To move beyond this, Shotwell (2011) argues that we can reposition negative affect as a disruptive moment that opens up a gap to try something new. I argue, therefore, that reflective-shame can offer the gift of opportunity for change by providing insights. I realised that questions about how Whiteness shaped my understanding were not accusations, but came from a place of care and a desire for equality; a wish for researchers and educators to better understand how White privilege operates and therefore seek to 'undo' it. Garner (2007: 6) offers insight by arguing that the purpose of using Whiteness as a conceptual tool is to '…insert a conceptual crowbar between Whiteness as "looking White" and Whiteness as the performance of culture and the enactment of power'. This can lead us to be more mindful of power and privilege so that we might take action to change this.

This experience drew my attention to the pitfall of positioning oneself as a 'good' White person who is 'not racist'. White people may believe they are not racist if they do not engage in deliberate acts of racial hostility, yet may not recognise ways that our own behaviours contribute to the structural advantages of a world that prioritises Whiteness. Indeed, the very act of positioning oneself as a 'good' non-racist White person can be seen as an act of White privilege because it impedes the understanding that we all exist within a society structured by race, and this will inevitably have impacted on how we experience the world and act within it (Rollock, 2013). By engaging in critical reflection around our own assumptions and behaviours, we can seek to recognise and undo harmful enactments of privilege. Such recognition can prompt us to act differently now and in the future. Although this realisation will likely be experienced with discomfort, in order to develop anti-racist practice we must engage anyway.

> **Questions to consider**
>
> Consider what emotions you have experienced when talking or learning about race and racism. Have you experienced shame or fear? If so, what impact did this have on your thinking and learning? How might you utilise these emotions to develop insights about racism, power and privilege?

Emma's story

My previous experience of 'anti-racism education' relied on incorporating lessons about diversity and ethnic groups at various times of the school year, such as Ramadan or Chinese New Year. This tokenistic method of diversifying curriculum arguably accentuates rather than eliminates the position of 'Others', reverting to Freire's 'banking' pedagogy by depositing information about others in what I would now argue to be a superficial approach, albeit one that appears to promote inclusion. However, simply establishing racial or culturally specific celebration into mainstream White culture can lead to the 'colour-blindness' that many White people rely on as an acceptable way to 'prove' their non-racist behaviour, with its intention to eliminate deliberate, direct discrimination. However, this approach does little to address subconscious or indirect discrimination that often forms the basis of structural racism. Using critical pedagogy, Freire (1970) specifies that students should be encouraged to develop a critical consciousness within their educational and living situations, which begins with looking at oneself and inevitably leads to an awareness of personal responsibility for social justice - making equality a personal problem, as well as a social one.

Conclusion

In this chapter, we offered insight into our own intertwining stories and uncomfortable learning moments in pursuit of an effective anti-racist education. We have found that Freire's critical pedagogy provides a useful framework for teaching and learning about racism in classrooms with predominantly White students. This moves away from prescribing a 'correct' way to think and behave, avoids simplistic notions of blame and assumptions about whether or not students are 'getting it right', to utilising critical reflection to find ways forward. Shotwell's (2011) framework encourages transformative learning by leaning in to discomfort rather than pulling away, challenging existing schema and accommodating the development of new ones by a process of exploration and acquisition of new knowledge. This process inevitably involves messy conversations and difficult dialogue as educators and students grapple with trying to understand Whiteness, power and privilege and seek ways to dismantle this. We argue that within an education studies classroom environment, it is essential that these conversations begin with establishing an expectation of discomfort and the volatility of this process. Deficient racism education in previous settings may mean that White learners default to the defensive position of verbalising only what they believe is 'safe' and 'correct', and it will take the educator's understanding of critical pedagogy to facilitate meaningful discovery.

Recommended reading

Freire, P. (1970) *Pedagogy of the Oppressed*. London: Penguin Books.
This seminal text explores the relationship between oppression and education arguing for a pedagogy that liberates communities through dialogue and critical reflection.
Maylor, U. (2014) *Teacher Training and the Education of Black Children: Bringing Color into Difference*. Abingdon: Routledge.
This book challenges dominant educational discourses about Black children's education and achievement and creates new understanding for initial teacher education about 'race' and 'difference'.
Shotwell, A. (2011) *Knowing Otherwise: Race, Gender and Implicit Understanding*. Pennsylvania: The Pennsylvania State University Press.
This book explores the role of embodied knowing, such as emotions that can shape people's understanding of racism and gender discrimination. It explores ways that educators can work with 'negative affect' to transform understanding.

References

Applebaum, B. (2005) In the name of morality: Moral responsibility, whiteness and social justice education. *Journal of Moral Education*, 34(3), pp. 277–290.
Asare, Y. (2009) Them and Us': Race equality interventions in predominantly white schools. *The Runnymede Trust*. Online: http://www.runnymedetrust.org/companies/130/182/Them-and-Us.html (Accessed: 24 July 2017).
Burnett, J. (2011) *The New Geographies of Racism*. London: Institute of Race Relations.
Busby, M. and Dodd, V. (2019) London schoolgirl who fled to join Isis wants to return to UK. *The Guardian*. 14 February. Available at: https://www.theguardian.com/world/2019/feb/14/london-schoolgirl-who-fled-tojoin-isis-wants-to-return-to-uk (Accessed: 01 May 2019).
Davies, J. (2021) Opening the "Can of Worms": Preparing teachers to address issues relating to "Race". Frontiers in Education. Vol 5. Online: https://www.frontiersin.org/article/10.3389/feduc.2020.489407 (Accessed: 4 May 2022).
Delgado, R. S., & Stefancic, J. J. (2012) *Critical Race Theory: An Introduction*. 2nd Edition. New York: NYU Press
Farr, A. (2014) Racialised consciousness and learned ignorance: Trying to help white people understand. In G. Yancy and M. Del Guadalupe Davidson, (Eds) *Exploring Race in Predominantly White Classrooms* (pp. 102–109). Abingdon: Routledge.
Freire, P. (1970) *Pedagogy of the Oppressed*. London: Penguin Books.
Gaine, C. (1995) *Still No Problem Here*. Stoke on Trent: Trentham Books.
Gaine C. (2005) *We're all White Thanks: The Persisting Myth about All White schools*. Stoke on Trent: Trentham Books.
Garner, S. (2007) *Whiteness: An Introduction*. Abingdon: Routledge.
Ginnis, S., Pestell, G., Mason, E. and Knibbs, S. (2018) Newly qualified teachers annual survey 2017: Research report September 2018. Department for Education. Available from: https://assets.publishing.service.gov.uk/government/uploads/system/uploads/attachment_data/file/738037/NQT_2017_survey.pdf (Accessed: 5 March 2021)
Jones, E. (2020) Work-based learning and an investigation into racial hostility, an autoethnographic study. *The Plymouth Institute of Education Online Journal*, 1(1). http://hdl.handle.net/10026.1/16085
Knight, H. (2018) 'The Impact of Arts Education Programmes on Anti-Racist School Practice in the South West of England'. PhD Thesis. Plymouth University.
Lander, V. (2015) 'Racism, It's Part of My Everyday Life': Black and minority ethnic pupils' experiences in a predominantly White school. In C. Alexander, D. Weekes-Bernard, and J. Arday, (Eds) *The Runnymede School Report: Race, Education and Inequality in Contemporary Britain*. London: Runnymede Trust.

Leonardo, Z (2009) The colour of supremacy: Beyond the discourse of "White privilege". In E. Taylor, D. Gillborn and G. Ladson-Billings, (Eds) *Foundations of Critical Race Theory in Education* (pp. 261–276). Abingdon: Routledge.

Maylor, U. (2014) *Teacher Training and the Education of Black Children: Bringing Color into Difference.* Abingdon: Routledge.

Myers, M. and Bhopal, K. (2017) Racism and bullying in rural primary schools: Protecting white identities post-Macpherson. *British Journal of Sociology of Education*, 38(2), pp. 125–143.

Richardson, R. and Miles, B. (2008) *Racist incidents and bullying in schools: How to prevent them and respond when they happen.* Stoke on Trent: Trentham Books.

Rollock, N. (2013) A political investment: Revisiting race and racism in the research process, *Discourse: Studies in the Cultural Politics of Education*, 34(4), pp. 492–509.

Shotwell, A. (2011) *Knowing Otherwise: Race, Gender and Implicit Understanding.* Pennsylvania: The Pennsylvania State University Press.

Taylor, E. (2009) The foundations of critical race theory in education: An introduction. In E. Taylor, D. Gillborn and G. Ladson-Billings, (Eds) *Foundations of Critical Race Theory in Education* (pp. 1—13). Abingdon: Routledge.

18 Understanding identity and positionality through student–staff interactions on an education studies undergraduate programme

Talitha Bird and Rajvir Gill

SUMMARY POINTS

- It is important for students to understand their positionality and how their experiences and views shape their perspectives and their interactions with others.
- Students should also consider how their lecturers and tutors are positioned in relation to identities such as gender, ethnicity, disability.
- In the process of becoming critically reflective learners, students should consider how their interactions with staff reflect, maintain, or challenge existing social inequalities that are often discussed in the education studies classroom.

Education is about more than simply telling future generations about ideas and facts; it is about challenging future generations to innovate and transform the world we live in, including everyone not just those in power. We cannot expect our students to revolutionize the world unless we as educators give them a voice and the knowledge to do so

(Liegeot, 2020: 11)

Introduction

When they begin their undergraduate programmes, students bring various identities and social positions with them, and students on education studies courses are no different. These identities and social positions are likely to shape students' experiences of academic life, with one notable aspect being their interactions with tutors and lecturers. Whilst the majority of undergraduate students studying education are female and White with no known disability, there has been a steady growth in the number of students from ethnic minority groups and those with a disability (HESA, 2020/2021). HESA (2021) report a similar growth in the diversity of academic staff on these programmes since 2016/17, meaning that groups who have historically been marginalised in educational spaces are better represented. However, while there have been some increases in diversity this seems to be course specific rather than sector wide, as the dominant profile of 'an academic' in the United Kingdom is male, White and heterosexual, with almost half of all professors aged over 56 (HESA, 2022). In this context, it is important to raise the question about student–staff interactions: to what extent do these entrench societal expectations around particular identities, and how can we positively challenge that?

DOI: 10.4324/9781003296935-21

This chapter will highlight the importance of understanding positionality so as to critically reflect on identity. We will focus on aspects of gender, race and ethnicity. It is crucial to establish that lessons about social inequality are not only relevant to the university classroom and are not only about 'other people'; when we teach and learn about ethnicity and schooling, for example, those same issues resonate in students' and staff experiences of university, too. For that reason, identifying and reflecting on everyday interactions between students and staff will support students in developing awareness and understanding of both those issues and their own positionality. We suggest that conversations during formal taught sessions, tutorials or informal discussion can be used as a way to understand how students and staff can bring about change now and in their future working environments.

> **Questions to consider**
>
> If you had a problem with your university work, which members of staff would you contact about it? Why do you think that is the case? Think about their identities and social attributes in relation to your own. Reflect on the assumptions that are made about who is available to help.

Identity, positionality and intersectionality

It is important to define identity, positionality and intersectionality before exploring any potential impact on students and staff in education studies.

Our identities are who we are, often understood in relation to the socially constructed ideas of: ethnicity, gender, class, disability, sexuality and culture, and it is our blend of identities which contribute to our positioning. Acevedo *et al.* (2015: 32) suggest that 'when we think about our "position" in the world, and more specifically about our position in society, we reflect on the different roles that occupy us in our lives'. The roles we play as members of a family, as employees, as teachers, as students, as friends, and in informal and formal social situations may differ. Therefore, we can think of our identities and positions as being fluid. According to Liegeot (2020: 4) 'positionality is the idea that identity can change over time based on historical and social changes happening around the person'; it develops through our lived experiences and are shaped by the social constructs we encounter. Therefore, if we draw on the definitions above, we can suggest that our interactions become a crucial element in shaping our positions and our identities.

In order to fully understand the interactions and experiences which position students and their tutors, we also need to acknowledge the intersecting identities of all these stakeholders. The term 'intersectionality', coined by Crenshaw (1991), acknowledges the multidimensional identities created through experiences of gender, race, class and disability, and how they intersect to 'produce complex relations of power and (dis) advantage' (Nichols and Stahl, 2019: 1). Crenshaw (1989: 149) provides us with this analogy:

> discrimination, like traffic through an intersection, may flow in one direction, and it may flow in another. If an accident happens in an intersection, it can be caused by cars traveling from any number of directions and, sometimes, from all of them.

This suggests that discrimination is not linear, and it can affect individuals in a variety of ways.

Showunmi (2020: 50) summarises intersectionality as an examination of 'how formal and informal systems of power are deployed, maintained and reinforced in social structures, policies and practices through notions of race, class and gender'. For example, in Showunmi's study of White and ethnic minority women in HE leadership, she concludes that intersectionality is key as White women reported difficulties which attributed to their gender and social class, whereas ethnic minority women discussed gender and racial barriers. However, Kapilashrami (2021) suggests that we should extend this definition of intersectionality to also include one's language proficiency, level of deprivation, socio-political and cultural lives. Therefore, when discussing positionality, intersectionality provides a critical lens in which all identifiers can be equally considered.

Positionality is a concept that is entangled with pedagogy and education at all levels. When Liegeot (2020) writes about her positionality as a teacher and as a student, she emphasises the importance of understanding positionality in order to acknowledge the various viewpoints and opinions which will guide and shape her practice and behaviours in the classroom. This takes on more significance when we consider Goffman's (1990) suggestion that we are all careful to construct roles and identities through our everyday interactions to elicit a specific response from others. Educational issues always intersect with societal norms and pressures, according to Brown and Stern (2018: 174), and therefore discussions on education will always intersect with 'culturally assigned attributes' (Acevedo *et al.* 2015: 33), or identities, such as: gender; race; sexuality; age; ethnicity; class; religious practice, and political affinity. Therefore, drawing on our previous discussion, we can suggest that the interactions students have with their tutors and support staff will be *tied with*, and shaped by, pre-existing identities and positionality.

To learn about equality, and to take this forward into professional practice, it is crucial that students and tutors do not view the issues as mere 'topics' to be covered or as experiences disconnected from the 'real world'. Instead, students and tutors need to develop the skills and awareness to critically position themselves within these discussions. With various multifaceted identities, students develop particular positions throughout their educational experiences and use them to guide their understanding in the classroom. Just like the teachers mentioned by Liegeot (2020), students also come into the classroom settings with their own viewpoints and opinions which could alter the positionality and experiences of the staff they interact with (Hearn, 2015). Therefore, because our cultural attributes/identities and our positionality will be drawn upon in our interactions and communications, they are powerful instruments in addressing equality and social justice. For this reason, it is important that we acknowledge and utilise these identities, not try to minimise them or ignore their significance.

Understanding positionality and intersectional dimensions in education are important for the move into professional practice, but they are just as important to be aware of during undergraduate study. Students not only need to become aware of their own positionality, but also of how their staff are positioned. Given that education studies programmes have a pre-dominance of female academics and students, it is important to consider how the multi-layered identities of academic staff lead to particular positionings which do not necessarily benefit them.

Gender

Shared identities can be inspirational and powerful motivators. However, sharing an identity does not always mean that prejudice and discrimination are avoided. For example, in 1964 Jessie Bernard wrote about 'academic momism' as a way to describe the perception of female staff as more nurturing, and six decades later research still suggests that female members of staff are more often called on to perform the 'emotional labour' of supporting students (Berry and Cassidy, 2013). As a form of work that is rarely acknowledged in institutional workload calculations, we feel that students should be aware of these issues so that shared identities might also mean shared understanding.

Within the higher education [HE] sector, female academics continue to be underrepresented in senior academic and leadership roles, they are more likely than men to work part-time and on fixed-term contracts, and there is a gender pay gap (Advance HE, 2021a). Furthermore, a systematic review from Westoby et al. (2021) on the barriers for female academics in HE found that women were more likely to be assigned lower-status work roles, and are more likely to take on additional teaching, pastoral and administrative work. These findings reflect an earlier study by Ashencaen Crabtree and Sheli (2019: 1) who also found 'essential and essentialized roles, where "mothering" duties and "housekeeping" academic roles are allocated primarily to women academics'. We can suggest that these experiences of everyday sexism will inevitably impact on positive levels of physiological well-being.

Students on education studies courses may well be 'learning' that these pastoral and support roles are indeed female, or feminised, through their daily interactions with their academic team. These interactions then reinforce gender difference by assuming it is female academics who are best placed to inhabit these roles. As potential educators of the future, it is essential that students recognise the connection between these gendered identity constructions and the roles that women are assumed to be most effective at fulfilling within educational settings. Becoming aware of this can lead to challenging the status quo. What we mean by this is that it is not always female members of staff who are best placed to provide pastoral support and, equally, that male members of staff are not always the most knowledgeable about a subject or hold the authority to make decisions.

Race and ethnicity

Building on the discussion around intersectionality, identities and gender, ethnicity remains another key strand to understanding positionality of women of colour in HE. Whilst the number of ethnic minority staff has increased over the years in HE, academics of colour still remain underrepresented in senior positions and permanent contracts (Advance HE, 2021b). Moreover, staff bodies are not representative of student characteristics; students from ethnic minority backgrounds are less likely than White students to see themselves represented in their university teaching staff. Universities UK and the National Union of Students (2019: 17) identified this as an issue because ethnic minority staff are more likely to 'become overburdened with the responsibility of acting as role models and mentors' for students from similar backgrounds. This can lead to additional work for women of colour.

This means that it is important to consider intersectionality. It has become an essential component of education studies curricula and students are expected to consider the multi-layered identities of different groups. This should also include the staff who are teaching them. Sian (2019: 79) writing about the teaching experiences of women of colour refers to this as 'double exclusion' where women of colour experience structural racism and patriarchal gender bias that 'makes them more exposed and vulnerable to hostility from students'. Sian (2019) highlights a number of issues that women of colour face from their students, such as challenges to their knowledge and regular interruptions during teaching sessions. These experiences are not restricted to student interactions but are often present within HE institutions more widely (Arday and Mirza, 2018).

Some staff experience their identities as 'out of place' in university settings because of entrenched racist and sexist assumptions about intelligence and social roles. These deeply engrained social biases can seep through into the ways that students interact with staff and the differential expectations they have of lecturers. For example, Adam et al. (2022: 788) in a large study investigating student evaluations of teaching found gendered differences in student's expectations of staff behaviour and teaching practice. They concluded that gendered expectations about staff particularly disadvantaged women staff who were 'actively punished' for failing to confirm to their gender roles. This is important because these expectations and assumptions affect how staff do their job; it impacts on their positioning and experiences within the institution, in the same way that we acknowledge how staff assumptions affect students' experiences.

Therefore, it is essential that students on education studies courses not only understand their positionality within HE settings, but that they are also aware of the impact they have on the experiences of staff and how this affects their own identity positions. Students can do this by challenging their own perceptions and acknowledging the identities of individuals/staff they seek support from beyond the classroom setting. This will require students to make a conscious effort in recognising their assumptions about staff, and actively working to break those down by confronting the ways the staff roles and responsibilities fall along gendered and racialised lines.

Conclusion

This is ultimately a call for equity in education. Importantly, this is not something we can pick and choose our way through; deciding which aspect of equality best fits our own social positions and avoiding others. Equality education must encompass all aspects of inequality, regardless of whether they reflect our own histories and experiences. As educators and as students, we will encounter others whose positions and identities are diverse and different to our own, and therefore we must acknowledge the power of our communications in either challenging or maintaining inequality and social injustice. If the inequalities discussed throughout this chapter are not made visible and challenged in students' university experience and early career steps, then it could be suggested that these inequalities will be perpetuated and become self-fulfilling once students move into roles working with, supporting, and leading others. Bringing to the surface how issues of identity and positionality shape student–staff interactions can generate change now and for the future.

Although this chapter has focused on gender and ethnicity, we also need to be aware that our positionality is affected by a host of other identities that can be equally important, such as disability, accent, appearance and sexuality. In the process of 'becoming' critically reflective learners, students can be encouraged to consider how their interactions with staff reflect, maintain, or challenge the educational inequalities that are often discussed in seminars and lectures.

Our experience tells us that students strongly oppose discrimination and prejudice, and seek out ways to change education for the better. Yet, inequality in education can be reinforced through the everyday interactions that students are part of during their HE experience. Through identifying these moments, students and staff are able to build a community of not only reflective learners but also critical educators who can challenge social inequalities through their everyday interactions.

> **Questions to consider**
>
> Keep a reflective journal during your time as an undergraduate student to record your thoughts on the questions and prompts below. Do your views change during your time as a student?
>
> What are your initial thoughts about your lecturers and tutors? Think about identity and social attributes
>
> How have you arrived at these conclusions? What are they based on?
>
> Do you change your 'position' when communicating with your lecturers and tutors? Why do you think this is?
>
> If you have an academic problem, who do you communicate with about it most often? What are their identities and social attributes?
>
> If you have a pastoral problem, who do you communicate with about it most often? What are their identities and social attributes?

Recommended reading

Berry, K. and Cassidy, S. (2013) Emotional labour in university lecturers: Considerations for higher education institutions. *Journal of Curriculum and Teaching*, 2 (2), pp. 22–36. https://doi.org/10.5430/jct.v2n2p22

This article defines what emotional labour is, suggests the effects it has on individuals, and why it prevails in education and specifically HE, through comparisons of emotional labour levels across different occupations.

Liegeot, J. (2020) *My positionality as a teacher: My testimony as educator with a global perspective*. Available from:https://www.unilim.fr/trahs/2978 (Accessed 17 May 2022)

This article provides a teacher's testimony in examining their positionality in education and how this has shaped their views and teaching practice in the classroom.

Tsaousi, C. (2020) That's funny…you don't look like a lecturer! dress and professional identity of female academics. *Studies in Higher Education*, 45 (9), pp. 1809–1820. https://doi.org/10.1080/03075079.2019.1637839

This paper focuses on female academics in the UK and the construction of their professional identities in reference to dress, body and academic identity. It focuses on the challenges of being a female academic in HE and navigating the workplace.Bozalek, V., Braidotti, R., Shefer, T. and Zembylas, M. (Eds) (2018/2020) *Socially just pedagogies: Posthumanist, feminist and materialist perspectives in higher education*. London: Bloomsbury Publishing.

Specifically focus on the work in Part Two (Ethics and Response-ability in Pedagogical Practice). These bring a keener focus on the importance of identifying and understanding interactions, or 'intra-actions' as the authors suggest.

References

Acevedo, S., Aho, M., Cela, E., Chao J-C., Garcia-Gonzales, I., MacLeod, A., Moutray, C. and Olague, C. (2015) Positionality as knowledge: From pedagogy to praxis. *Integral Review*, 11 (1), pp. 28–46.

Adams, S., Bekker, S., Fan, Y., Gordon, T., Shepherd, L.J., Slavich, E. and Waters, D. (2022) Gender bias in student evaluations of teaching: 'Punish[ing] those who fail to do their gender right'. *Higher Education*, 83, pp. 787–807. https://doi.org/10.1007/s10734-021-00704-9

Advance HE (2021a) *Gender equality in higher education*. York: Advance HE.

Advance HE (2021b) *Equality in higher education: Statistical report 2021*. Available at: https://www.advance-he.ac.uk/news-and-views/equality-higher-education-statistical-reports-2021 (Accessed 14 May 2022).

Arday, J. and Mirza, H.S. (2018) *Dismantling race in higher education: Racism, whiteness and decolonising the academy*. Cham: Palgrave MacMillan.

Ashencaen Crabtree, S. and Sheil, C. (2019) "Playing Mother": Channelled careers and construction of gender in academia. *Sage Open*, pp. 1–14. https://doi.org/10.1177/2158244019876285

Bernard, J. (1964) *Academic women*. University Park, PA: Penn State University Press.

Berry, K. and Cassidy, S. (2013) Emotional labour in university lecturers: Considerations for higher education institutions. *Journal of Curriculum and Teaching*, 2 (2), pp. 22–36. http://dx.doi.org/10.5430/jct.v2n2p22

Brown, A. and Stern, M. (2018) Teachers' work as women's work: Reflections on gender, activism, and solidarity in new teacher movements. *Feminist Formations*, 30 (3), pp. 172–197. https://doi.org/10.1353/ff.2018.0046

Crenshaw, K. (1989) Demarginalizing the intersection of race and sex: A black feminist critique of antidiscrimination doctrine, feminist theory, and antiracist politics. *University of Chicago Legal Forum*, 1 (8), pp. 139–167.

Crenshaw, K.W. (1991) Mapping the margins: Intersectionality, identity politics and violence against women of color. *Stanford Law Review*, 43 (6), pp. 1241–1299. https://doi.org/10.2307/1229039

Goffman, E. (1990) *The presentation of self in everyday life*. Harmondsworth: Penguin.

Hearn, M.C. (2015) Positionality, intersectionality, and power: Socially locating the higher education teacher in multicultural education. *Multicultural Education Review*, 4 (2), pp. 38–59. https://doi.org/10.1080/2005615X.2011.11102893

HESA (2020/2021) *What do HE students study? Personal characteristics*. Available at: https://www.hesa.ac.uk/data-and-analysis/students/what-study/characteristics (Accessed 17 May 2022).

HESA (2021) *What areas do they work in?* Available at: https://www.hesa.ac.uk/data-and-analysis/staff/areas (Accessed 17 May 2022).

HESA (2022) *Higher education staff statistics: UK, 2020/2021*. Available at: https://www.hesa.ac.uk/news/01-02-2022/sb261-higher-education-staff-statistics (Accessed 17 May 2022).

Kapilashrami, A. (2021) *Embracing intersectionality to interrogate and action equality, diversity and inclusion in teaching and learning*. Available at: https://www.advance-he.ac.uk/news-and-views/embracing-intersectionality-interrogate-and-action-equality-diversity-and-inclusion (Accessed 14 April 2022).

Liegeot, J. (2020) *My positionality as a teacher: My testimony as educator with a global perspective*. Available from: https://www.unilim.fr/trahs/2978 (Accessed 17 May 2022).

Nichols, S. and Stahl, G. (2019) Intersectionality in higher education research: A systematic literature review. *Higher Education Research and Development*, 38 (3), pp. 1–14. https://doi.org/10.1080/07294360.2019.1638348

Showunmi, V. (2020) The importance of intersectionality in higher education and educational leadership research. *Journal of Higher Education Policy and Leadership Studies*, 1 (1), pp. 46–63. http://dx.doi.org/10.29252/johepal.1.1.46

Sian, K. (2019) *Navigating institutional racism in British universities*. Cham: Palgrave Macmillan.

Universities UK and NUS (2019) *Black, Asian and Minority Ethnic student attainment at UK universities: #closingthegap*. Available at: https://www.universitiesuk.ac.uk/sites/default/files/field/downloads/2021-07/bame-student-attainment.pdf (Accessed 14 May 2022).

Westoby, C., Dyson, J., Cowdell, F. and Beuescher, T. (2021) What are the barriers and facilitators to success for female academics in UK HEIs? A narrative review. *Gender and Education*, 33 (1), pp. 1–24. https://doi.org/10.1080/09540253.2021.1884198

19 Men and masculinities on undergraduate education studies degrees

Mark Pulsford, Ryan Cazley, Abdullah Daya, Rowan Godfrey, Shenghao Lyu and Taiwo Okutubo

SUMMARY POINTS
- Men make up just 15 per cent of students on undergraduate education degree courses.
- When men choose to take education studies, it can prompt surprise and even incredulity from friends and family because of gendered assumptions about 'appropriate' study and career routes.
- On their education studies courses, though, men can experience a privileged position because of being seen as rare and in-demand in the field of education.
- However, they may also experience isolation and some marginalisation as education studies classrooms may not feel like spaces where men belong.
- Education studies' communities can take steps to break down essentialist and binary notions of gender that are restrictive to all students.

Introduction

Around one in seven students on undergraduate education degree courses in the UK are listed as male (HESA, 2021). This figure – about 15 per cent – is perhaps expected given the wider underrepresentation of men in careers working with children and young people or involving care and community work. Although there is a wealth of research on the career choices and experiences of men in such fields (especially teaching) little is known about men on undergraduate education degree courses, and we suggest that this is a missing element in the understanding of men's trajectory into a field that has been numerically dominated by women. Understanding more from men studying in this area can help both students and staff on education studies courses gauge the influence of gender on our everyday, typical study experiences. Addressing this can also help male students feel better prepared to pursue a career in education or related fields where they are likely to encounter many of the same issues; it also has the potential to support more men to choose these degree programmes in future if such issues are acknowledged and foregrounded.

The chapter is based on five of the authors' recent experiences studying for an undergraduate degree in education studies. Through those varied accounts, we discuss the conflicts that emerge due to dominant ideas of masculinity as we grapple with the obstacles presented by – yet also the privileges accrued from – gender stereotypes in education (Warin, Ljunggren and Andrä, 2020). Discussion of the themes that emerge from our written accounts follows a background section where some context is given to the issues that men on women-majority degree courses can often

DOI: 10.4324/9781003296935-22

face. The concluding section then considers the significance of the issues raised and, in light of that, identifies steps that your education studies community can take.

> **Questions to consider**
>
> To what extent do you notice gender as part of your student/learner identity? Is this prominent in your experience or does it not feel relevant? Why do you think that is the case?
> Reflect on how ideas of gender roles may have influenced your choice of degree subject, study experiences and career aspirations. Why do you think this is important to be aware of?

Background: University degree choice and men studying in women-majority subject areas

From very early in our lives, through our families and during our school experiences, we get a sense of what paths are appropriate for us to follow – and these are often highly gendered (Davies et al., 2013). Girls are often encouraged to value the capacity to care, nurture and support others, meaning they're more likely to feel that a career drawing on these attributes would suit them, whilst boys are often socialised to reject these facets of themselves and hence make different study and career choices. Here, we are thinking about the power of socially constructed ideas of gender that often fall into binary categories (traits, expressions or interests that are erroneously seen as *either* male or female) which become layered on top of biological attributes of sex. In this way, we can see how social characteristics such as gender influence our motivations to go to university and the subjects we choose to take. For example, Chevalier's research (2002) found that men are more likely to say they chose their degree subject because of anticipated future income, whereas women are more likely to report a strong motivation for 'socially useful' work.

The barriers to men considering an education studies course are therefore probably related to perceptions of teaching. The most common career route after graduating with an undergraduate degree in education studies is into teaching (see Section 4 of this book for more on this), and students very often choose to study the subject because they can imagine themselves in a teaching role one day. The high numbers of women on education studies degrees is partly explained because teaching, especially in Early Years and Primary settings, involves focusing on children's development and care, and it is a stereotypical yet common assumption that women are well-suited to this work. This constructs a barrier to men considering this area of study. Moreover, in a patriarchal society, work that is associated with women – that involves children, care or community – has a weaker status and is less financially rewarded because of underlying perceptions that it is 'natural' for women to be able to do and therefore requires less skill development (see Spencer, 1997; Williams, 1995). You may not hear this discriminatory and debunked view expressed directly or so bluntly, yet it underpins how we perceive and reward different occupations. Hence, for men considering entering this field via undergraduate study, we see some quite rigid barriers in the shape of essentialist gender ideas tied up with concerns about weaker status and lower financial rewards than other sectors.

For men who *do* make the choice to study education or other women-majority courses (such as social work and nursing), these gendered associations can affect their study experiences. The extent of this is indicated by data showing that men are more likely to drop out of courses that have a higher proportion of women and, conversely, to make better progress on courses that traditionally attract men (Schaub, 2015). Considering this pattern, research with men studying to become teachers, social workers and nurses highlights a range of common issues linked with notions of masculinity and occupational identities – see Cruickshank, Kerby, and Baguley (2021), Schaub (2015) and Myklebust (2021) for overviews of findings in their respective areas. These issues include:

- Regular challenges from others (including friends and family) about their degree and career choice, because of
    - expectations that men would choose a higher status/higher paid profession
    - questions about their sexuality
    - concerns about men as sexual predators or paedophiles leading to unfounded allegations against them
- Social isolation and a feeling that there is no-one like them on the course
- Pedagogic environments that are not gender-inclusive
- Uncertainties about how they will fit into and cope in their chosen career

Taken collectively, it is perhaps easy to understand how these 'identity bruises' (Foster and Newman, 2005) affect men who have chosen to study in traditionally female terrain. In seeking coping strategies, men may be drawn to construct themselves as 'properly masculine' (Francis and Skelton, 2001) in situations where their identity feels precarious; as Warin and Dempster (2007) note in their study of male undergraduate students, in periods of uncertainty (such as at the beginning of a new academic year) we are likely to depend on entrenched aspects of our self-concept, of which gender group membership is one. Hence established ideas of gender and related patterns of interactions become crutches to steady ourselves, yet this can of course amplify many of the problems because it can emphasise assumed gender difference rather than highlight our commonalities.

This leads us to consider why examining men's experiences on undergraduate education degrees is particularly important. Whilst acknowledging that all students can face challenges in their studies for a host of reasons, based on the discussion above there is a clear rationale to pay attention to men who can face a *bruising* time on women-majority courses. A greater understanding of this experience can help to address it. In turn, this might attract more men to study undergraduate education studies courses; many men value and aspire to work in education and with children and young people, but can feel this is not an option because of the issues outlined above. In confronting men's experiences on undergraduate education courses, we may come to see that there is a key role to play in embracing, facilitating and promoting forms of masculinity that are unashamed to champion social issues and prioritise the care and development of children and young people – that it is possible to eschew career and life choices that align with a more competitive and hierarchical form of masculinity. Moreover, as much as there is a need to support women into higher-wage fields such as in business, science and engineering, there must be an equivalent drive to shape pathways for men into careers that have been seen as 'women's work' to help redress perceptions of gendered roles. Education studies courses can be an important platform and gateway in this respect.

There is also a wider point about the need to interrogate gender within education programmes and support all students to challenge the limits that this can place on them. Women continue to earn less than men and are less likely to occupy positions of power and influence, and attitudes rooted in essentialist notions of femininity and masculinity are woven into the fabric of many work environments (see Eden, 2017). This is very much the case in schools and other educational environments, despite the numbers of women employed in those settings (Acquaro and Stokes, 2016). Understanding how ideas of masculinity and femininity play out in our university experiences, career aspirations and early professional development – including critical consideration of gendered assumptions about our capabilities, characteristics and roles – can help all students understand and challenge established patterns of gender inequality.

> **Questions to consider**
>
> Think about the people who identify as male on your degree programme. What do you think their experience on the course has been like?
> In what ways do you see traditional or stereotypical ideas of gender difference being affirmed or disrupted on your course (you could consider the module content and teaching sessions, but also reflect on how people engage with each other, what are the friendship groups, how are people involved in the wider life of your course, etc.)? What is the *hidden curriculum* of gender on your course?

Our experiences as men on undergraduate education degree programmes

In this section, we focus on our own experiences as men on undergraduate degree programmes. Following emails and discussion, each of the five student authors – Ryan, Abdullah, Rowan, Shenghao and Taiwo – provided an extended written account about their degree choice and motivations, (gendered) experience of studying, and masculinity in higher education. Mark's role was to bring these accounts together and build the chapter around them. Although the chapter provides an inevitably partial view of men's experiences of studying for an undergraduate degree in education and cannot claim to be representative, the five student authors offer their perspectives from a range of social and cultural positions, not least in terms of nationality, ethnicity, religious belief, sexuality, and age. Below, we discuss the issues that resonate in all our experiences and consider their implications. We have not used lengthy quotations and nor do we attribute comments to any one of us because the purpose of the chapter is to outline the broader, collective concerns. The sections below cover *the reactions of friends and family; experiencing the course as 'not for men'; and the silence around students' gender (especially masculinity) on education studies courses.*

The reactions of friends and family

Our experiences match many of the issues listed in the section above. It seems to be the pervasive view of people outside of education that it is 'strange', 'odd', 'anomalous', 'surprising' and even a 'joke' for men to study education at undergraduate level. We have stories of family and neighbours being taken aback at our choice of subject, often because they expect men to study degrees that have a 'high reputation' and better salary prospects, enabling them to take the 'breadwinner' family role. Friends have often challenged us most, although less about our future role as a *family man*. Our peers' reactions instead tend to challenge our current gender identity; we must often navigate questions about our course – and therefore about ourselves – because they perceive education studies to be a more 'feminine' or 'softer' subject. We find this interesting in relation to ideas about masculinity, because surely studying a key feature of all societies, developing our own philosophies of education, enhancing our personal-professional capabilities, and championing the principles of social justice, diversity and inclusion should not be women-only concerns?

Here, it is important to address the relationship between an increasingly instrumentalised view of higher education (that sees the main purpose of taking a degree being to get a job), and prominent notions of masculinity associated with subjects such as science and engineering. The discourses of aspiration that are produced in this context can narrow the range of futures and identities that are imaginable for young men (Spohrer and Stahl, 2017), making education studies a less likely choice. We can see that deciding to study education at degree level may be doubly stigmatised, therefore: first, teaching continues to be underpaid and undermined as a career and routes other than teaching after studying education are somewhat ambiguous. Second, aligning oneself with a subject that is inherently interested in social issues, the development and flourishing of others (especially children and young people), and that foregrounds collective responsibilities for education, care and wellbeing, is a challenge to the gender hierarchy because these perspectives are constructed as 'female' and 'soft' and in that way symbolically framed as of secondary importance. The side-lining, and even denigration, of these topics can tell us a lot about the contemporary social and political environment.

Experiencing the course as 'not for men'

Despite reactions from friends and family, within our education studies courses we have had mostly positive and affirming experiences. However, we are aware of our privileged position as men on woman-majority courses, knowing that this would perhaps not be the case for women on courses with mostly men. Overall, our on-course experiences have been characterised by rarely being interrupted or even openly disagreed with in seminars, regularly leading group tasks, and our names are often remembered by lecturers. This enables more interactions with academic staff and often leads to opportunities for academic support or other positive experiences, such as acting as Course Representative. Being one of only a few men on an education studies course, against a background of policy and public discourse that unquestioningly asserts the need for more men in education, creates the conditions for this privileged position.

Despite this overall positivity, a sense from all our experiences is that the social aspects of our course – how strong our sense of belonging is and how authentic our inclusion feels – can be a little more difficult. Most of us have felt isolated, lonely, nervous and even embarrassed at times. These feelings often come from being the only man in a group or not feeling very connected with the few other men, and sometimes because of uncertainty about how to navigate situations where it feels that representing *the view of men* falls to us. This brings up questions about our relationship to some of the issues that are discussed in seminars and our voice in those debates. Our perspectives on this seem to come in two forms: first, there is a view of being 'outnumbered' when theories such as feminism or issues such as women's rights are encountered, which are seen as of more concern to women than men. Second, that women should have a space to discuss their experiences and that speaking up as a man in those environments can feel 'almost wrong' because 'it's their space not mine'. Both versions highlight how men can feel pushed to the side-lines in education studies taught sessions, either through self-policing to avoid taking airtime from women or from feeling disenfranchised and even alienated from the topics of conversation. In different ways, these both foreground the importance of connecting the topics with men's experiences and men's assumed social roles – in short, that issues of gender discrimination and inequity are concerns for everyone, including those who might experience it less often or in different forms, and that facilitating open, inclusive discussions about privilege is key to future change. This perspective resonates with the other chapters in this section and connects with calls for a higher education pedagogy that is both critical and relational, and curricula that are co-constructed with and for all students.

It is important to raise the point here that the reactions of friends and family to men choosing a degree in education studies, and men's experiences on the course, are not related to gender alone. Other facets of our identities inflect these experiences and have shaped others' perceptions of how well we 'fit' with education studies. The intersections of gender with age, sexuality and ethnicity all factor in how we understand ourselves as students and future educators, shaping our motivations and our relationships with course mates. For example, being a gay man in the education field draws a different set of associations than being a black man, generating different experiences and revealing various social stereotypes and prejudices – yet converging on the sense that men are *out of place* and that some masculinities are constructed as problematic and challenging in education (see Odih, 2002; Phoenix, 2004; Pullen and Simpson, 2009). Where the discourses of contemporary schooling variously construct the ideal learner/teacher as white, female, middle class and heterosexual, men are required to consciously manage their identity practices and negotiate their (mis)alignment with the norm. This can be seen in the experiences of the five student authors during their undergraduate education degree studies.

The silence around students' gender (especially masculinity) on education studies courses

The discussion above highlights the importance of helping men in education studies better understand their social identities in relation to the field of education. Although several of this chapter's authors described being 'comfortable' with their own masculinity and noting that this gave them a certain resilience or confidence when it came to dealing with challenges about their choice of degree subject, they projected concerns for other men who may not feel this way. They report limited opportunities on their courses to discuss masculinity and its relationship with education, and a general silence around gender in their experience as students. As such, they highlighted how beneficial it would have been to discuss this as a topic of academic study, as well as considering gender/masculinity as a part of their own learner identity. Interestingly, one of our comments raised the issue that male identity had only really been discussed in terms of 'toxic masculinity', and therefore addressing what 'healthy masculinity' might look like would be beneficial. This ties with the views expressed from the men above about feeling disenfranchised from some seminar discussion topics and of sometimes feeling they had to represent or even justify *men's views* – circumstances that may create a defensiveness and indeed emphasise the homogeneity of people assumed to fit into binary gender groupings, rather than promoting a more nuanced understanding. It is possible to imagine that with greater opportunities to critically reflect on gender as part of learner identities, and masculinities in education more broadly, gender-inclusive learning environments can develop further in education studies.

Conclusion

This chapter has examined the experiences of five men on education studies programmes and shows that binary ideas of gender and traditional notions of men's social role shape others' attitudes towards their degree subject choice. This may be a *bruising* experience for men's identities as they fend off claims that education studies is 'feminine' or 'soft' compared to other undergraduate courses that tend to attract more men and appear to offer more 'masculine' career prospects. Assumptions about gender are also present on their courses, where they tend to stand out and be noticed (or feel noticeable) as one of just a few men. Although this generally brings positive academic experiences, their sense of belonging may be compromised by staid ideas of gender differences that can segregate them from others and sometimes side-line them in taught sessions. The men understand their privilege and that their relative uniqueness in the field of education may reap rewards (such as in the teacher job market), yet their undergraduate experience can include feelings of loneliness, uncertainty and even marginalisation in spaces where they don't always feel they belong.

This highlights how important it is to break down notions of binary gender difference that are so pervasive and normalised in and around education. As Myklebust (2021) points out, our self-understandings and accounts of our gender identities tend to be heterogenous – they are multiple, varied and sometimes incoherent – and yet notions of gender as fixed and dichotomous in the institutional discourses and practices of education maintain the heteronormative and patriarchal hierarchy. As such, it is vital to see how gender, in its interplay with other social categories and institutional norms, is *actively produced* in practice – in everyday interactions and uses of space, for example – and therefore can be reshaped and made to mean something different and less restrictive (Hicks, 2015). Since we all anticipate that others will judge us based on assumed cultural norms around gender identity, we tend to act accordingly whether we support those norms or not. The extent to which we adhere to these cultural norms, however, depends on how much the social context makes them seem important or relevant (Myklebust, 2021) – hence it is in our power to actively address our role in the production of gender difference in education studies.

Therefore, to finish the chapter we have started a list of actions towards achieving this goal. We encourage you to add ideas to this list, to share these with your peers and to discuss with your tutors.

- Involve everyone in seminar discussions and group activities; avoid assuming people have (or don't have) a view based on what we perceive their gender identity or experiences to be.
- In group work, rotate roles so that different people lead and feedback ideas; avoid assuming that certain roles are best suited to people (including ourselves) because of perceptions about gender attributes (such as leadership, organisation, intellect, confidence).
- Actively dislodge any gender segregation by sitting and talking with different people in seminars.
- Call out gender stereotypes where you encounter them, including in the 'banter' of casual interactions.
- Critically engage with the resources and discourses that are made available around gender – for example, when studying boys' and girls' educational attainment, consider how the data used and common explanations given can present a fixed or essentialist idea of gender, and think about what can be done to challenge that.

- If education studies classrooms do feel like 'women's spaces', think about which women this might centre and what concerns are prioritised; how can a wider range of experiences be given voice in these spaces?
- Pay attention to the way that gender intersects with other social categories (ethnicity, sexuality, age, social class, dis/ability, nationality and so on) to avoid generalising about groups of people; recognise the range of circumstances that generate multi-faceted lived experiences.
- Become conscious of how in new social circumstances and transition periods (such as at the start of a new module), we are especially likely to rely on assumed norms of gender to help ease new interactions – think of ways to break down some of those expectations in yourself and support others in doing so, too.
- If we feel comfortable doing so, find ways to discuss our own sense of gender and our gendered experiences (accepting that diverse, varied experiences and complex feelings are typical rather than unusual).
- Actively embrace and highlight forms of masculinity and men's gender practices that champion social issues and prioritise the care and development of children and young people; consider education studies as a platform to promote these.

Recommended reading

Burn, E. and Pratt-Adams, S. (2015) *Men Teaching Children 3-11: Dismantling Gender Barriers.* London: Bloomsbury. http://dx.doi.org/10.5040/9781474219433

This book unpicks the range of 'barriers' that men may face as teachers of young children, offering a number of strategies to help dismantle them. It provides a wide-ranging and critical take on the 'male teacher scripts', including as role model, classroom disciplinarian, sportsman and senior manager. It is useful for thinking about men on undergraduate education degrees because we can consider the relevance of these 'scripts' to their experiences and identities – how are these scripts modified or added to by men (or on men's behalf) on education studies degrees?

Elliot, K. (2020) *Young Men Navigating Contemporary Masculinities.* Cham: Palgrave Macmillan. https://doi.org/10.1007/978-3-030-36395-6

This book explores how young men in Australia and Germany navigate masculinities in neoliberal times. It examines intersections of whiteness, class privilege, heterosexuality and masculinity, charting how more open and egalitarian forms of masculinity emerge alongside expressions of traditional or regressive masculinity. It argues that care and openness amongst men is a means to achieve change at individual, collective and structural levels. Elliot suggests that possibilities for masculinities are fostered 'in the margins' – and so, because we could say that men on undergraduate education studies degrees are somewhat marginalised, it invites the question of what possibilities we can begin to open up.

Pullen, A. and Simpson, R. (2009) Managing difference in feminized work: Men, otherness and social practice. *Human Relations*, 62(4), pp. 561–587. https://doi.org/10.1177/0018726708101989

This academic paper reports on research with men who work in nursing and in primary school teaching. Using the idea that gender identity is dynamic and fragmented, emerging in social context, the paper argues that these men manage being 'other' in their working environments by appropriating elements of femininity (such as care for children) so that masculinity is both partially subverted and partly maintained. This is useful for thinking about how men might navigate their gender identities as undergraduate students in education often prior to working in the field, where practices such as caring might be less easy to demonstrate.

References

Acquaro, D. and Stokes, H. (2016) Female teacher identities and leadership aspirations in neoliberal times. *International Studies in Educational Administration*, 44(1), pp. 129–144. http://hdl.handle.net/11343/294138

Chevalier, A. (2002) Education, motivation and pay of UK graduates: Are they different for women? *European Journal of Education*, 37(4), pp. 347–369. https://doi.org/10.1111/1467-3435.00115

Cruickshank, V., Kerby, M., and Baguley, M. (2021) How do pre-service male primary teachers cope with gender related challenges? *Australian Journal of Teacher Education*, 46(1). http://dx.doi.org/10.14221/ajte.202v46n1.5

Davies, P., Mangan, J., Hughes, A., and Slack, K. (2013) Labour market motivation and undergraduates' choice of degree subject. *British Educational Research Journal*, 39(2), pp. 361–382. http://dx.doi.org/10.1080/01411926.2011.646239

Eden, C. (2017) *Gender, Education and Work: Inequalities and Intersectionality*. Abingdon: Routledge. https://doi.org/10.4324/9781315673165

Foster, T., and Newman, E. (2005) Just a knock back? Identity bruising on the route to becoming a male primary school teacher. *Teachers and Teaching: Theory and Practice*, 11(4), pp. 341–358. https://doi.org/10.1080/13450600500137091

Francis, B. and Skelton, C. (2001) Men teachers and the construction of heterosexual masculinity in the classroom. *Sex Education*, 1(1), pp. 9–21. https://doi.org/10.1080/14681810120041689

HESA (2021) Higher education student statistics: UK, 2019/20 – subjects studied. Available: https://www.hesa.ac.uk/news/27-01-2021/sb258-higher-education-student-statistics/subjects (Accessed 23 September 2022)

Hicks, S. (2015). Social work and gender: An argument for practical accounts. *Qualitative Social Work: Research and Practice*, 14(4), pp. 471–487. https://doi.org/10.1177/1473325014558665

Myklebust, R.B. (2021) Gendered repertoires in nursing: New conceptualizations of educational gender segregation. *Gender and Education*, 33(3), pp. 322–336. https://doi.org/10.1080/09540253.2020.1765993

Odih, P. (2002) Mentors and role models: Masculinity and the educational 'underachievement' of young Afro-Caribbean males. *Race Ethnicity and Education*, 5(1), pp. 91–105. https://doi.org/10.1080/13613320120117216

Phoenix, A. (2004) Neoliberalism and masculinity: Racialization and the contradictions of schooling for 11- to 14-year-olds. *Youth & Society*, 36(2), pp. 227–246. https://doi.org/10.1177/0044118X04268377

Pullen, A. and Simpson, R. (2009) Managing difference in feminized work: Men, otherness and social practice. *Human Relations*, 62(4), pp. 561–587. https://doi.org/10.1177/0018726708101989

Schaub, J. (2015) Issues for men's progression on English social work honours and postgraduate degree courses. *Social Work Education*, 34(3), pp. 315–327. http://dx.doi.org/10.1080/02615479.2014.997698

Spencer, D. (1997) Teaching as women's work. In B. Biddle, T. Good and I. Goodson (Eds) *International Handbook of Teachers and Teaching. Springer International Handbooks of Education*, vol 3. Dordrecht: Springer. https://doi.org/10.1007/978-94-011-4942-6_5

Spohrer, K. and Stahl, G. (2017) Policy logics, counter-narratives, and new directions: boys and schooling in a neoliberal age. In G. Stahl, J.D. Nelson and D.O. Wallace (Eds) *Masculinity and Aspiration in the Era of Neoliberal Education*. New York: Routledge. https://doi.org/10.4324/9781315649108

Warin, J. and Dempster, S. (2007) The salience of gender during the transition to higher education: male students' accounts of performed and authentic identities, *British Educational Research Journal*, 33(6), pp. 887–903

Warin, J., Ljunggren, B. and Andrä, M (2020) Theoretical perspectives on men's choices to remain and to leave. In D.L. Brody, K. Emilsen, T. Rohrmann and J. Warin (Eds) *Exploring Career Trajectories of Men in the Early Childhood Education and Care Workforce*. Abingdon: Routledge. https://doi.org/10.4324/9781003048473

Williams, C.L. (1995) *Still a Man's World: Men Who Do 'Women's Work'*. Berkeley: University of California.

20 Rebalancing power relations in teacher–student co-creation

Rosi Smith, Robyn Wall, Lucinda White, Emma Wright and Melissa Vernon

SUMMARY POINTS

- This chapter describes a co-creation project at a post-'92 widening participation university in the midlands in 2020–2021. The project re-designed the final-year Special Educational Needs and Disabilities (SEND) module on our BA Education Studies programme, starting from the priorities and perspectives of disabled people along with those of families and practitioners.

- It is written by the 'steering group': three students and two lecturers, who all have lived experience of disability, neurodivergence, mental health and/or special educational needs.

- Together, we developed a research study to gather the views of these groups about what new educators need to know to become inclusive practitioners.

- Questionnaires, focus groups and interviews produced a powerful body of evidence.

- Finally came the difficult part: using this data and our combined expertise to construct the new module – making decisions. This was 'the difficult part' because it meant challenging normal student-teacher power relationships. The rest of the chapter describes and reflects on the process we used to do this.

What is co-creation?

Co-creation (or co-production) is where different groups work together as equals to make decisions and create outcomes. It has been used most frequently and powerfully by disabled people in areas like health and social care. Co-creation is about professionals recognising the people they work with as experts-by-experience (Meriluoto, 2018) and doing things *with them* and *not to them*.

DOI: 10.4324/9781003296935-23

Why co-create?

Universities are making more use of co-creation, but this is too often limited to feedback and 'quality assurance' through 'student voice' (Cook-Sather,2020), reinforcing the student-as-customer dynamic fostered by tuition fees, league tables and the anxiety-inducing precarity experienced both by students and by their teachers (Maisuria and Cole, 2017; Hall, 2021). Cook-Sather notes, however, that where genuine pedagogical partnership is in place, deeper respect for these voices can emerge. This is particularly important 'when your identity isn't affirmed' within your institution or community (Cook-Sather, 2020: 886).

This lack of affirmation is palpable for disabled and neurodivergent people in the UK. Their rates of employment, economic security and well-being continue to lag behind those of their non-disabled peers (Carmichael and Clarke, 2020; ONS, 2021). This has been compounded since 2010 by government persecution of disabled people in the form of cuts to vital services and the instigation of demeaning, punitive assessments to access basic support (Grover, 2014; Hansford et al., 2019), requiring them to constantly and publicly re-state and re-justify their contested disabled identities.

This can also be the case within higher education (HE). Our own research (Wright et al., 2021) supports findings, such as those of Vaccarro et al. (2015) in the US and Osborne (2019) in the UK, which show disabled students' university experiences to vary greatly in terms, not only of support, but also of acceptance, belonging and validation. In our study, while some students spoke of empathetic lecturers, support staff and peers, many had also been disbelieved, had their experiences minimised and heard neurodivergence and hidden disabilities ridiculed or denied. Others were told outright that their differences in learning meant university was not the place for them. All this means that disabled students cannot be confident that their particular 'student voice' will be heard, much less acted upon.

Education Studies modules that develop students' understanding of SEND are absolutely necessary, especially given its insufficient coverage on teacher training programmes (Coates et al., 2020). Being the subject of teaching, however, risks 'othering' disabled students: theorising or pathologising their experiences, or treating their needs as 'problems' for educators to resolve. Disability activism has a longstanding answer to this problem – 'Nothing about us without us' – and this co-creation project aimed to make clear that the 'us' creating the module, the 'us' teaching the module and the 'us' studying the module all included and foregrounded disabled people.

> **Questions to consider**
>
> So, good co-creation empowers students, affirms marginalised identities and draws on a broad range of expertise and experience. Do you feel that teaching on your university course is done *with* you or *to* you?
> What opportunities do you have to shape your studies?

The steering group

Trying to address these power imbalances, we recruited a steering group of disabled and neurodivergent student co-creators to re-design the module with their lecturers.

Emma Wright, Lecturer in Education Studies.
Former teacher of a specialist SEND class in mainstream primary.
Emma has anxiety and is parent to a child with special educational needs.

Lucinda (Lucy) White, final year student, BA Education Studies.
Lucy wrote her dissertation on the experiences of dyslexic teachers.
She is dyslexic and has anxiety and depression.

Rosi Smith, Lecturer in Education Studies.
Experience working on alternative provision, literacy and English as an Additional Language in secondary and further education.
Rosi is dyspraxic and has anxiety.

Melissa Vernon, final year student BA Speech and Language Therapy.
Melissa wrote her dissertation on the experience of obtaining an autism diagnosis in adulthood.
She is autistic.

Robyn Wall, final year student BA Education Studies.
Robyn wrote her dissertation on the use of physical resources to support children with SEND.
She is autistic and dyslexic.

Questions to consider

Students were selected for the steering group using their written statements (alternative formats were available). They were kept anonymous so that the people selecting them couldn't be biased. But... the (brilliant) students selected didn't reflect the ethnic diversity of our student body. Across the applications, neurodiversity and specific learning differences were much more represented than physical disability.

Do you think it's more important to ensure anonymity or representation? What would be the fairest way of selecting participants?

What did we do to try to equalise power relations between students and teachers?

To collaborate meaningfully, we had to consider how to mitigate the unequal power relations often seen as inevitable between students and lecturers (Symonds, 2020). This was especially vital because those power relations mirror the position of disabled people in an ableist society, where 'expert' knowledge from doctors, educators and psychologists continually receives greater credence than disabled people speaking for themselves.

These are some practical measures we put in place:

Inequality	Solution
Lecturers select the students for co-creation.	The selection panel was made up of one lecturer, the chair of the university's Spectrum Society and the Students Union Equalities Officer, so students were in the majority.
Students from marginalised groups (such as disabled/neurodivergent students) can be 'othered' by more privileged staff when speaking from that marginalised identity.	Lecturers on the steering group also had lived experience of disability/neurodivergence, and shared those experiences and their impacts on their working lives with their student collaborators.
University co-creation often just asks students to add ideas or comments, leaving lecturers to make the real decisions.	The steering group were viewed as experts-by-experience and were involved at every stage, from setting priorities and parameters, through conducting research, to writing and signing off detailed teaching plans and assignment briefs. They proposed actions and made decisions, rather than just improving a curriculum authored by lecturers. No decisions were made without going back to the group.
Lecturers are paid professionals, which gives them higher status.	Students on the steering group were paid, which is still not standard in co-creation (Lubicz-Nawrocka and Bovill, 2021), and their hourly rate was the same as their lecturers', a move aimed at emphasising our identity as colleagues, each bringing *different* but *equally valuable* expertise.

Questions to consider

What other inequalities might exist between students and lecturers?
Could they all be addressed in co-creation or are some of them beyond lecturers' control?

But why are equal power relations so difficult to achieve?

While these practical changes facilitate less hierarchical working, they cannot be transformative without much more difficult attitudinal shifts on all sides.

From a lecturer's perspective

Genuinely regarding lived experience as expertise challenges academics' identities; after all, their traditionally certified expertise is literally what they are paid for. Many lecturers feel threatened even by consulting their students, listening to their ideas and adapting in response (Cook-Sather, 2020; Symonds, 2020). This may be reasonable within neoliberal HE, where students are positioned as judges of the quality of provision. This same audit-driven culture makes lecturers reluctant to hand over real power for decisions that they will be solely accountable for – if results or student feedback slip, their jobs could be at risk. More importantly, lecturers' professional identities are closely associated with the modules they lead and have often crafted over years. With more and more of their time monitored and controlled, module design is, for many, a final space of autonomy that is jealously guarded.

From a student's perspective

If it is hard to give up control, it is also hard to take it, especially for students accustomed to respecting their teachers' traditional knowledge, and reliant on the good opinion of the same teachers they are collaborating with for grades, references and validation (Symonds, 2020). With many university students coming straight from school or college, it is understandably difficult for these students to then be seen as, and expected to be, on an equal level with their tutors. Despite this, students on the steering group had seen universities embrace some aspects of collaboration to an extent, through student organisations, such as students' unions, and through course representatives. These feedback routes for student input are often limited by the huge power imbalance embedded into them, whereby universities maintain total control of whether to implement/respond to students' opinions. Therefore, new avenues, outside of these university-wide structures, must be explored both by tutors and by students to foster true co-creation.

So, did it work?

The decision-making phase of the project took place over three intensive weeks in June–July 2021. By that time, we had already established strong working relationships while designing, conducting and analysing our research. In the next section, we describe four key days from those weeks.

For each day, we include:

- The main decisions we needed to take.
- How we worked.
- What we accomplished.
- Extracts from the reflective notes we made along the way.

They offer a grounded, practical account of how far our ways of working managed to reduce power imbalances and create genuinely collective outcomes.

Day 1: Deciding how to make decisions

In response to the research findings, everyone shared in turn their priorities for the module.

We need to focus on how educators can respond to/work round inflexible systems to offer child-centred education. – Emma

We need to think about intersectionality and about neurodivergent students' lives beyond the classroom and into adulthood. Could we look at teachers with SEND? – Lucy

Communication seems to be a key focus in the research. I'm keen to cover non-verbal communication and AAC (Augmentative Alternative Communication). – Robyn

I've been thinking about how to make accessible documents and model good practice on the module. – Rosi

It would be great to create a video for the beginning of the module to show a range of disabled voices and challenge stigma. – Melissa

Then came a discussion of availability (tough for a neurodivergent group with lots of other commitments!).

Rosi presented the decisions that we needed to make and the paperwork we needed to do. We deliberately put this after the priorities discussion so as not to limit our thinking.

We created a structure (shown below) to use for decision-making in the rest of our meetings.

Finally, we decided what tasks to work on before the next meeting.

Our agreed decision-making process

Working together to decide how to make decisions was essential for real collaboration. *Listening* to everyone's contributions equally is only meaningful if everyone is able to *make* those contributions equally. That means being able to take in and process information, develop ideas and communicate those ideas in ways that meet each individual's needs and utilise their skills.

We settled on this structure for all major decisions. The idea was to create space both for detailed group discussion and for individual thinking and processing time.

1 Sharing the decision that needed to be made.	We did this verbally and in writing, making sure we had a shared understanding and agreed on the main points to consider.
2 Having individual time to reflect on our own stance.	We all had different processing speeds and different ways of breaking down and assimilating information. This allowed us to work through our ideas in our own way.
3 Coming together for a group discussion to share our thoughts.	We used a lot of different tools to facilitate these discussions. Online collaboration tools allowed people to add text, images, links and recordings, instead of always having to communicate verbally.
4 Asking an individual or small group to create the outcome.	Tasks (e.g. writing an assessment brief or scheme of work) were allocated depending on people's interests, skills and capacity. We had time to focus on drawing together everything from the discussions, using the visual, written and audio records.
5 Final discussion to ensure we were all happy with the result.	Although we communicated well, there were always some alterations to make. These were often to longest discussions and the ones where student co-creators' recent experiences of navigating confusing course information were hugely valuable.

Co-creator reflections

I felt unprepared for the meeting; marking, plus family, COVID and mental health, meant I hadn't created a 'space' for myself to reflect on everything so far. – Emma

It was the first time seeing the virtual learning environment from the teacher's side – how can we start to make it accessible? I left the meeting feeling good, we got a lot done and I felt there was a plan in place for the rest of the process. – Robyn

I really liked that people were able to state so clearly what their preferences were in terms of process. I wish more work activities were consciously built around how the people doing them work best... Listening back, I talk too much, which I knew, but it's worse than I thought – should I ask someone else to facilitate the next one? – Rosi

I think this was the first time I've properly seen myself as a professional. – Melissa

Day 2: Agreeing the module outcomes

Our first challenge: When creating the module's learning outcomes, general discussion proved ineffective – lots of ideas but not enough clarity.

We resolved this by breaking up and using an online live collaboration platform to write and then group our ideas for what students needed to 'know', 'understand' and 'do'.

Our first real debate: Our research participants had disagreed on how much to focus on individual SEND and how much to think in terms of broader themes. The same divisions existed in our group, especially because Melissa's discipline is speech and language therapy, while the rest of us have educational and social science specialisms.

Discussion of assessment ideas related to the outcomes. We agreed on the nature of the assignments relatively easily. We spent a lot more time discussing how to make the briefs clear and accessible and how to make sure students could submit work in a format that suited them. Freedom of choice vs clear, unambiguous instructions was a key discussion, informed by our own range of neurodiverse preferences.

What came out of the meeting?

A new set of learning outcomes covering the following areas:

1. Examining biases;
2. Critically examining policy and theory;
3. Awareness of educational strategies and forms of communication;
4. Understanding a range of SEND;
5. Assessing the inclusiveness of SEND resources';
6. Understanding the power of language;
7. Communicating effectively and accessibly.

> **Questions to consider**
>
> Co-production involves acting on the expertise of people with lived experience.
> What should researchers and educators do when, as in this case, there is disagreement among people within that group?

Co-creator reflections

I need to be mindful of the research participants' responses and make sure I feed them into the discussions. I want to make sure we don't lose sight of all that data in the discussions. – Emma

I offered to lead this meeting. I felt proud of myself for stepping up, which is something I would have shied away from a couple years ago. Despite this, I did find it quite difficult because I wasn't familiar with the outline for the meeting. I tend to find that if I'm not confident about what I'm doing or saying, or if I have a lack of clarity in my head about things, I get quite overwhelmed. – Robyn

> In general, these meetings haven't caused me the same stress as a normal speech meeting or a university meeting, half because I think that we have a sort of an underlying sense of understanding of each other. We understand when people make mistakes; we're not critical of each other, and there doesn't seem to be a lot of judgement. And I think with us all being female as well… we're the ones that are under-researched in terms of lots of different neurodivergences and disabilities. – Melissa

Day 3: Thinking about the module's assessment approach

We began with a check-in because lots of us were under pressure and stress. We made sure everyone knew they could change their workload if they needed to.

We hadn't all had time to read through the detailed assignment briefs that Rosi had created from our discussions last time. We split up for two hours to give people time to read, reflect and comment.

We also had some time to record our reflections on the process so far.

We checked and finalised the outcomes designed last time.

We had a long discussion of the brief for each assignment, making adjustments and balancing the need to meet the learning outcomes with the clarity and accessibility of each assignment. We also had to make sure that the views of current students were reflected in the timing and weighting of the new assignments.

We had intended to discuss the detail of content but had to move this to a later meeting.

What came out of the meeting?

By the end of this meeting, we had decided how the module would assess the students. The criteria were broken down into three main assessment points.

Assignment One (20%)	Assignment Two (50%)	Assignment Three (30%)
Communicating a key theory / concept for SEND in an 'easy read' format.	Creating a resource (podcast, game, comic strip, leaflet…) for a specific audience about one aspect of SEND, along with the student's choice of a written or verbal rationale.	Identifying potential sources of support for a specific student based on a case study written by someone with parallel lived experience. Again, the student could choose whether to present this verbally or in writing.

Co-creator reflections

I've been thinking around the 'Not Fine in School' website, produced by a former BA Education Studies student now doing her PhD… There are many stories of policy negatively impacting children, young people and their families here, which is why I wanted to include issues with policy in the module, having personally experienced parent-school relationships and policy issues, as both a parent and a teacher… It's so valuable that we all have varied lived experiences as part of the steering group. – Emma

This was where the module as a whole came together and became more tangible to me. Despite writing things down, there were still a couple of times I got lost, particularly discussing the learning outcomes, because language had to be quite broad and formal. Unless it was already written down, I struggled to pick up and formulate the spoken words as a sentence into my head. – Robyn

I have two really conflicting aims:

- Allow people autonomy to make decisions that don't start from me.
- Take care of people and make sure their inclusion needs are met.

I am constantly thinking about how to balance these and I worry that I don't do it well. – Rosi

Day 4: Deciding on the module's content

After catching up on admin, we did a final check of the briefing documents for assignment three.

We then shared the preparatory work we had done on the week-by-week content for the module, which included our own priorities, the material needed for the assignment, guest speakers with experiences different from our own and the concrete suggestions from our interview data.

Most of the rest of the meeting was a long discussion of that weekly content, reorganising and re-prioritising as we went and talking a lot about our own experiences. Much of the conversation centred on how to fit the personal and political priorities of disabled people together with the preparation that our students needed to go into the real education system.

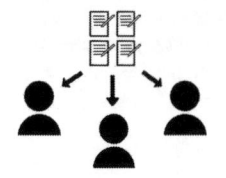

Finally, we shared out the tasks to be completed and checked in future, smaller meetings.

What came out of the meeting?

A content plan for 22 weeks, which we broke down into three main blocks, each of which prepares the students for one of the assignments.

Big ideas in SEND.	*Diversity and inclusion*	*Reality check: Policy and practice.*
The history of disability with a focus on disabled people's activism. Concepts of anti-oppressive practice, models of disability, labelling and intersectionality.	Neurodiversity, person-centred practice, inclusive theories of autism and specific learning difficulties. Guest speakers on intersections of gender, ethnicity and disability; social/sexual identity and disability; alternative and non-verbal communication; and being a neurodivergent teacher.	What current policies say should be happening in education vs what's really happening on the ground. The teacher's role in identifying SEND and supporting students; later-life vs early identification of SEN; the physical, sensory and psychological environment of schools; SEND and exclusion; real services available locally; autonomy, independence and transition into adulthood.

Questions to consider

How is this way of working different to other meetings or workshops you have seen? What are its strengths and weaknesses?

Co-creator reflections

I found the meeting tricky – my child struggled with me being in a meeting during his downtime and found it difficult not to spend time with me, so I got quite distracted in parts. I felt Melissa (who wasn't at this session) was missed; having another viewpoint outside of education would have been useful. – Emma

The same argument around wanting to be an ally towards disabled and neurodivergent people, but also having to be realistic about what polices will allow classroom teachers and headteachers to change in terms of ethos and philosophy of the individual school... the module must make clear that what *should be* and what *is* do not align. – Lucy

I felt good that I was able to share some sensitive stuff in a safe space without dwelling on it too much. It was also good to revisit earlier 'disagreements' and talk through those, because we were more able to come to a consensus after having more time to think about things. – Robyn

I had thought that, by the end, we'd have quite clear topics and I'd just be kind of tweaking that. What actually happened was that we mostly centred on the most important themes and conflicts to address. People spent a lot of time talking about their own experiences and why certain elements were important to them. I didn't realise how good that was until I left, spent time trying to pull those together and saw how rich the discussion was. I realised that it wasn't the list of topics that was important; it was the ethos and the feeling behind them. – Rosi

Final reflections

Initially I was worried how truly collaborative the process would be with the lecturer-student power dynamic, especially after the first meeting. By the end of the project, though, I felt we were genuinely a co-creation group – that hierarchal relationship had disappeared and we had created a safe space for ourselves. We had shared so much of our experiences to contextualise the research we were doing and had become confident in communicating both our needs and our ideas to each other...Our lived experiences, our fears, our half-formed ideas – all of the things that as lecturers we don't always have space to share. I really felt I could be myself during this project; I could talk about my own struggles and triumphs and reflect on them with people who understood. I learnt so much from the other participants. As a former school teacher and now a HE lecturer, hearing the experiences of students on their educational journeys allowed me space to reflect and think about what is important in my own practice.....and it highlighted the importance of all practitioners being involved in collaborative projects like this with their learners – whatever the age. It wasn't always easy – time constraints, caring responsibilities and hearing or reliving my own or others' past traumas – but it was important work. It was invaluable to have those conversations and to build something meaningful, something that is not harmful and is conducive to the learning and well-being of all involved. I think collaborative co-creation projects are absolutely key to inclusive practice – Emma

Please scan the QR code to the left to hear Lucy speak about her reflections on the project.
Below are some of Lucy's thoughts taken from her recording.

- Genuine co-production: students at the forefront of data gathering;
- Characterised by 'love', 'care' and 'work';
- Neurodiversity seen as a strength;
- Use previous challenges constructively and productively.

"We have only been able to co-produce because we are all neurodivergent people… we all have some idea of what our neurodiversity means to us and what it could mean for other people."

Please scan the QR code to the left to hear Rosi speak about her reflections on the project.
Below are some of Rosi's thoughts taken from the recording.

- Balancing the roles of co-creator, teacher and managing the project;
- Anxiety and imposter syndrome;
- What is reasonable to ask of people?

I'm not a natural co-creator. I'm a highly anxious, neurodivergent woman, and I really like to control all sorts of aspects of my environment. And that includes my teaching… I was worried that I would be resistant to people's input because of that.

For context, Melissa started a new job around the same time as the intensive, decision-making phase of the project.
It's a fact that I am predisposed to stress and anxiety and, despite wanting to be a part of the project more, my experience with my new job was challenging. I feel the experience with my job outside of the project perfectly represents the lack of education and support for people who are like us and have unique struggles. The job role was high pressure, with little support, I received disciplinaries for reasons I couldn't understand – e.g. inappropriate social tone and sensory overload causing me to step out and leave other staff struggling. Because I am neurotypical passing, I was held to expectations I could not meet.
In this role, I feel I have been given space and given responsibilities that don't add to the growing burnout and stresses. The team has been supportive and truly has embodied the ethos of inclusiveness. I've felt I can contribute to the project in my own way. I've also felt free to stim and begin to unmask while working on our project and during discussions. This balance is absolute magic for getting the best work out of me!
There is also an unspoken level of understanding and compassion in the co-creation group that I've never felt elsewhere. All in all, the dynamics of the group reflect our goals for the module – and this is the most important aspect for me. – Melissa

Coming into this project, I already knew most of the participants due to already being on the Education Studies BA program as a student, allowing me to be able to feel more comfortable about discussing ideas. However, two other participants were also tutors on the degree course, initially causing me to revert into the role of a student rather than an equal participant. This, although it did not last more than a few months, did initially cause some power imbalance.

However, when we arrived at the co-production stage, these feelings had dissipated, enabling me to feel equal to the other participants. This encouraged my self-confidence in conveying ideas and opinions to the group, likely due to the amount of time we had spent together discussing and researching ideas for the project. Despite this, reflecting on our meetings, there were times when I was slightly lost, and I perhaps could have asked for more clarity on what was confusing me. However, if I were to repeat this process, there is extremely little I would have done differently, as I felt that I was able to say things and contribute as we went along. Even though some distressing memories were raised as part of our discussions regarding past experiences, it felt like we had created a safe environment to discuss topics such as these, allowing me to continuously feel comfortable and supported in discussions. – Robyn

Recommended reading

Emma recommends:

Not Fine in School (n.d.). Available at www.notfineinschool.co.uk (Accessed: 15 February 2022). An organisation which researches and campaigns around school avoidance and the potential barriers to school attendance.

Lucy recommends:

Burns, E. and Bell, S. (2011) Narrative construction of professional teacher identity of teachers with dyslexia. *Teaching and Teacher Education*, 27(5), pp. 952–960. A study which shows teachers experiencing their dyslexia as a positive element of their professional identities.

Melissa recommends:

Piepzna-Samarasinha, L. (2018) *Care work: Dreaming disability justice*. Vancouver: Arsenal Pulp Press. Available in visual, auditory and online formats, this is a 'celebration of the work that sick and disabled queer/people of color are doing to find each other and to build power and community'.

Robyn recommends:

MacLeod, A., Allan, J., Lewis, A. and Robertson, C. (2018) 'Here I come again': the cost of success for higher education students diagnosed with autism. *International Journal of Inclusive Education*, 22(6), pp. 683–697. This qualitative study resonates with my own experiences of navigating higher education.

Rosi recommends:

Autistic Self Advocacy Network (2012) *Loud hands: Autistic people, speaking*. Washington: Autistic Press. Written by more than forty autistic contributors, this book of essays combines testimony, polemic and analysis, and shows the diversity and nuance that can be achieved by projects that are genuinely disabled-led.

References

Carmichael, F. and Clarke, H. (2020) Why work? Disability, family care and employment. *Disability and Society*. https://doi.org/10.1080/09687599.2020.1848802

Coates, J. K., Harris, J., and Waring, M. (2020) The effectiveness of a special school experience for improving preservice teachers' efficacy to teach children with special educational needs and disabilities. *British Educational Research Journal*, 46(5), pp. 909–928. https://doi.org/10.1002/berj.3605

Cook-Sather, A. (2020) Respecting voices: How the co-creation of teaching and learning can support academic staff, underrepresented students, and equitable practices. *Higher Education*, 79(5), pp. 885–901. https://doi.org/10.1007/s10734-019-00445-w

Grover, C. (2014) Atos healthcare withdraws from the work capability assessment: A comment. *Disability and Society*, 29(8), pp. 1324–1328. https://doi.org/10.1080/09687599.2014.948750

Hall, R. (2021) *The hopeless university: Intellectual work at the end of history*. Liverpool: Mayfly.

Hansford, L., Thomas, F., and Wyatt, K. (2019) The impact of the work capability assessment on mental health: Claimants' lived experiences and GP perspectives in low-income communities. *The Journal of Poverty and Social Justice: Research, Policy, Practice*, 27(3), pp. 351–368. https://doi.org/10.1332/175982719X15637716050550

Lubicz-Nawrocka, T. and Bovill, C. (2021) Do students experience transformation through co-creating curriculum in higher education? *Teaching in Higher Education*, https://doi.org/10.1080/13562517.2021.1928060

Maisuria, A. and Cole, M. (2017) The neoliberalization of higher education in England: An alternative is possible. *Policy Futures in Education*, 15(5), pp. 602–619. https://doi.org/10.1177/1478210317719792

Meriluoto, T. (2018) Case study – experts-by-experience in Finnish social welfare. In T. Brandsen, T. Steen, and B. Verschuere (Eds) *Co-production and Co-creation: Engaging citizens in public services* (pp. 294–296). Abingdon and New York: Routledge.

Ons.gov.uk. (2021) *Coronavirus and the social impacts on disabled people in Great Britain – Office for National Statistics*. [online] Available at: https://www.ons.gov.uk/peoplepopulationandcommunity/healthandsocialcare/disability/articles/coronavirusandthesocialimpactsondisabledpeopleingreatbritain/february2021 (Accessed 12 July 2021).

Osborne, T. (2019) Not lazy, not faking: Teaching and learning experiences of university students with disabilities. *Disability and Society*, 34(2), pp. 228–252. https://doi.org/10.1080/09687599.2018.1515724

Symonds, E. (2020) Reframing power relationships between undergraduates and academics in the current university climate. *British Journal of Sociology of Education*, 42(1), pp. 127–142. https://doi.org/10.1080/01425692.2020.1861929

Vaccarro, A., Daly-Cano, M., and Newman, B.M. (2015) A sense of belonging among college students with disabilities: An emergent theoretical model. *Journal of College Student Development*, 56(7), pp. 670–686. https://doi.org/10.1353/csd.2015.0072

Wright, E., Smith, R., Vernon, M., Wall, R., and White, L. (2021) Inclusive, multi-partner co-creation for the teaching of special educational needs and disabilities in higher education. *Journal of University Teaching and Learning Practice*, 18(7), 25–40. https://doi.org/10.53761/1.18.7.03

Section 4
The personal and professional in education studies

Ross Purves

The chapters in this section offer critical perspectives on the notion of 'employability' and the role that the undergraduate study of education – together with placement, professional, family and personal experiences – can play in your graduate future. Authors touch on many of the issues and debates introduced in earlier chapters, particularly the relationship between undergraduate education programmes and initial teacher education, and tensions regarding higher education as a functional pathway to the workplace versus an opportunity to evaluate and shape the world around us through academic engagement. The re-appraisal of these issues places the reader firmly at the centre of things, highlighting the potential for personal and professional transformation through the undergraduate study of education. We hope that you should be able to see yourself in at least some of the following pages.

In Chapter 21, David Menendez Alvarez-Hevia and Alexandra Hay survey the various debates regarding the nature of employability and consider ways in which education studies degrees can help prepare students both for teaching and other-than-teaching careers. In doing so, the authors help us understand how those teaching and leading these undergraduate programmes have responded to the 'employability agenda' in contemporary higher education via curriculum and pedagogy.

In Chapter 22, Catherine A. Simon considers the distinct and powerful contributions which can be made to students' development through work-based learning, and in particular placements. Using a range of theoretical positions, she illustrates the importance of remaining critical and reflective about the nature of the placement being undertaken. She also highlights the increasing significance of alternative forms of work-based learning, including virtual and technology-mediated opportunities. Both Chapters 22 and 23 remind us that work placements should be regarded as far more than simply 'dress rehearsals for future jobs' – instrumental exercises driven by contemporary neoliberal higher education discourse. Instead, in the context of the complex legacies and identities associated with undergraduate education degrees, placements have potential to help students understand not only what they want to *do* but also – and, arguably, far more importantly – who they *are* and who they might *be*. In Chapter 23, Gisela Oliveira traces complex, 'consequential' transitions students can experience as they navigate paths between university studies and the workplace. In describing the experiences of Julie, Oliveira emphasises that we do not travel these paths in one direction. She invites us to re-consider our expectations of placement experiences and re-assess their formative value in our learning and student identity.

DOI: 10.4324/9781003296935-24

170 *The personal and professional in education studies*

The book's final chapter, by David Thompson, Rachel Higdon and Charlotte Barrow, is a manifesto for your potential to contribute to the world as a graduate of education. It ends our book with an engaging, upbeat and unashamedly positive assessment of how you, as an individual student of education, can bring together all that you have learned and experienced – both from within your degree and beyond – to thrive in complex and rapidly changing social and employment landscapes.

21 Employability and pedagogies for employability in education studies

David Menendez Alvarez-Hevia and Alexandra Hay

SUMMARY POINTS

- Employability is a complex concept that needs to be critically examined. How we approach issues about employability will have a deep impact on how we conceptualise, organise and practise education.
- When exploring career options associated with education studies programmes, we find two employment pathways. The most popular and visible pathway is to a career in teaching. On the other hand, modern education studies programmes also prepare students for a wide range of careers related to education. These programmes emerge as a good choice for those interested in education and young people but who also want to keep their professional options open.
- There are many different approaches education studies programmes can take to embed employability into their courses. Some examples are through placements, innovations in curriculum planning and the use of guest speakers.

What is employability?

In recent years, there has been an increasing interest in how education prepares people for work. This discussion is more relevant for some levels of education than others. While compulsory education (e.g. primary and secondary education) is more oriented to provide opportunities for young people to acquire the basic knowledge and skills that they will need to become members of society and thus become active citizens, post-compulsory education (e.g. vocational training, further education and higher education) puts more emphasis on preparing and qualifying people for work. In this chapter, we explore this debate in the context of higher education, bearing in mind that discussions about employability have influenced institutional, teaching and organisational practices in higher education. We start by introducing and critically analysing the concept of employability before going on to explore in more depth how this idea is approached in education studies.

The concept of employability has been defined in many different, yet often related, ways. Pegg et al. (2012) suggest two definitions of employability that are useful to 'illustrate the continued tensions that exist when engaging with the employability agenda in HE' (p. 5). The first definition is from Yorke (2006):

DOI: 10.4324/9781003296935-25

.... A set of achievements – skills, understandings and personal attributes – that makes graduates more likely to gain employment and be successful in their chosen occupations, which benefits themselves, the workforce, the community and the economy.

(p. 8)

This second definition is proposed by Harvey (2003):

Employability is more than about developing attributes, techniques or experience just to enable a student to get a job, or to progress within a current career. It is about learning and the emphasis is less on 'employ' and more on 'ability'. In essence, the emphasis is on developing critical, reflective abilities, with a view to empowering and enhancing the learner.

(n.p)

These two definitions help us to move from a traditional or narrow view of employability that focuses on the development of skills and attributes to a broader, sustainable, and comprehensive approach to employability (Hinchliffe and Jolly, 2011). This approach to the concept of employability connects to education by considering both personal and social imperatives. Inherent in this idea is the development of abilities, skills and knowledge required to perform a job, but more importantly, it also involves learning how to navigate the labour market by developing complex personal and social abilities.

More recently, Römgens et al. (2020) considered different definitions and models of employability and developed an integrated approach that focuses on six common dimensions:

1. (Applying) disciplinary knowledge
2. Transferable generic skills
3. Emotional regulation
4. Career development skills
5. Self-management
6. Self-efficacy

We need to be cautious when talking about employability in higher education. Ideas and initiatives related to employability need to be unpacked, critically analysed, and contextualised to gain a better understanding of their implications for education (Brown et al., 2003; Sin and Neave, 2014). There are risks associated with putting too much emphasis on employability elements when taking decisions about education. If not carefully considered, a strong orientation towards employability can produce an even deeper impact. We may find that the purpose of education is reduced to acquiring basic skills or abilities but without including a critical understanding of the area of knowledge and its relation to the social world. In other words, a good graduate should not only be educated in how to do things, but also in how to situate themselves within a complex and changing social world.

> **Questions to consider**
>
> To what extent do you think that employability matters should be at the centre of the purpose of higher education?
> What do you think will be missed if higher education is solely oriented to prepare and qualify people for work?

Employability in education studies

As noted in Chapter 2, academic studies in education in the form of undergraduate or teacher education programmes emerged in the UK from the 1960s onwards. However, it was not until the late 1990s that courses with names like BA Education Studies made an appearance. For Bartlett and Burton (2006), these courses emerged as a response to the changes introduced in initial teacher education. As these authors explain, the transformation of teacher education into a form of training resulted in the loss of critical ideas and theoretical elements from the content of the course. Whilst teacher training courses were more oriented to school practices and preparing teachers to work in schools, the new education studies courses were more open. They were intended to prepare students to explore different educational contexts and engage with critical and theoretical perspectives.

Generally, education studies programmes do not provide Qualified Teacher Status (QTS) so graduates need to complete a Postgraduate Certificate in Education (PGCE) or take another teaching training route (e.g. postgraduate teaching apprenticeship, Teach First) if they want to teach in a maintained school or non-maintained special school in England. Therefore, the option of becoming a primary school teacher is open to all education studies graduates if they complete a PGCE in primary education. In some circumstances, there is a possibility of undertaking a PGCE for secondary school teaching, but this generally requires undergraduate-level knowledge related to a National Curriculum subject.

Teaching is still today one of the preferred career options when students choose to study a degree in education studies. However, as explained in the study carried out by Menendez Alvarez-Hevia and Naylor (2019) many education studies students discover through their undergraduate journey that the flexibility of the course allows them to explore other career pathways more suitable for them within the educational, social or caring sectors. For Hodkinson (2009), this programme flexibility and openness to multiple employability possibilities served to differentiate education studies from the vocational approach of teacher training courses. Nowadays, this argument is still used as a way of illuminating debates about employability in education studies.

As a result, discussions about employability in education studies have been articulated around two main options or employment pathways that are explained below.

Employment pathway associated with teaching

A career in teaching is the most popular and visible option when considering studying education studies. It is chosen by those students who aspire to become schoolteachers. The different providers of undergraduate education studies programmes offer them an alternative preparation for teaching that puts emphasis on developing an open understanding of education but without forgetting that schooling is at the centre of modern education. The main challenge associated with this option is to show the value of an education studies degree as the basis for a teaching training route that requires further study to obtain QTS.

Although it is possible to teach in independent schools, academies, and free schools without QTS, it is desirable to obtain QTS to work as a teacher. It is worth noting that QTS is a requirement to teach in many state schools in England and non-maintained special schools. In some instances, not having QTS might have implications for salaries and career progression.

Employment pathway associated with other careers

Education studies programmes are designed to assist students in the development and acquisition of a range of skills and knowledge that are useful for a wide range of careers. Most of them are commonly associated with the social, administration and caring sectors. This option has always been less popular, although in recent years there has been increased interest in it (Menendez Alvarez-Hevia and Naylor, 2019). The challenge here is to make visible those career possibilities that are not directly linked to teaching and include them when planning, teaching and studying in education studies programmes.

Table 21.1 represents the most significant examples of alternative career possibilities that education studies degrees offer to their graduates. The table associates main blocks of education studies content with examples of jobs in which that type of knowledge is valuable or can provide a foundation. It is worth noting that further qualification or study will be needed to access some of these roles (e.g., social work or youth work).

Education studies courses are a good choice for those who want to keep their professional options open. They offer a good foundation for those interested in becoming teachers, but are also conceived to prepare for other jobs in which knowledge about educational issues is highly valuable. We should bear in mind that the educational sector has grown and expanded very rapidly in the new century, leading to an increased complexity that comes with new possibilities (Facer, 2011). For example, education is now recognised as a lifelong process, so professionals of education are not only required to work with young people in schools. They will work with people of all ages, in private, social or public settings doing tasks that involve more than teaching.

The employability debate is not only about exploring professional pathways. It is also about discussing the best ways of nurturing the skills, competencies and knowledge that future graduates in

Table 21.1 Alternative careers and content of education studies programmes

Content of education studies programmes	*Examples of alternative careers*
Education and society Knowledge about the nature, purpose and role of education in society. Understanding of questions related to education and social inequality.	• Social work • Youth work • Prison education • Charity sector • Inclusion officer
Policy and practice Knowledge about educational policies and ideologies, how policy affects our lives/life chances, the relationship between policy and practice. Understanding of how educational practice can shape or change society.	• Political advisor • Local authorities • Research jobs
Learning and learners Knowledge of the nature of learning, factors that affect learning, spaces for learning and the politics of learning.	• SEN assistant/support • Mentors (e.g., in pupil referral units) • Administration (e.g., schools, universities) • Hospital education • Human resources • Educational consultant • Student support services • Education officer

education studies will need. The focus is on preparing students to negotiate their employability transition, envisage new possibilities and build their identity as critical, informed, and flexible professionals.

> **Questions to consider**
>
> Find the unit/module descriptions of your programme of study.
> Identify the title of each unit or module and, if possible, look for the key content.
> Using Table 21.1, match your units or modules against a category in the first column (content of education studies programmes). You may find that sometimes a unit or module could be in more than one category.
> Consider how those units or modules help to prepare students to develop the associated careers.
> Can you expand the table adding more examples of alternative careers? What additional qualifications or training would be needed to progress from an education studies programme into these careers?

Teaching and learning about employability in education studies

There are many different approaches education studies programmes can take to embed employability. As mentioned earlier in this chapter, Harvey (2003) argues that employability is not just about getting a job, it is also about students developing their abilities.

Many education studies programmes take the traditional placement route, offering students different work experience settings. The placement coupled with a reflective piece of work or journal will go towards module/unit credit. Placement settings can vary from traditional schools and early years settings to hospital education, pupil referral units, forest schools, museums and art galleries. Enabling the student to actively engage with the job and setting can be useful as they evaluate future career plans. It can also help them build relevant skills and attributes, for instance, developing their teamwork and other abilities.

In recent years, there has been a move towards partnership working between universities and work settings (Stokes, 2017). For example, at universities that sponsor their own academy schools, students on placement often provide a mutually beneficial service, perhaps managing a creative outdoor project or developing a new library system. This allows students to work with young people in a non-teaching role, and might inspire them to pursue other avenues of employment, for instance, within pastoral support or youth work.

There are other curriculum-based ways in which employability skills can be developed. For example, some modules/units are designed to enable students to reflect on their goals and aspirations, or to develop certain skill sets including teamwork or confidence. Encouraging students in the first year of their studies to reflect upon their career goals is also a useful task, as steps can be identified early to help them achieve them. In addition, those who need more support and guidance can be directed to the careers service. In recent years, career services have expanded their activities including support to students at all the stages of their university journey (even after graduation). They have created opportunities to gain skills and experiences which assist students to develop a better understanding of themselves, their aspirations and possibilities (Dey and Cruzvergara, 2014).

Guest speakers can also be used to advertise the range of different options to students. Former students often make the greatest impact, as can tutors discussing master's or PGCE courses. Inviting professionals from outside of the university, for example, educational welfare officers, speech and language therapists, educational psychologists, human resources consultants and those involved in marketing will also demonstrate the breadth and range of careers available.

> **Questions to consider**
>
> Which of the approaches above would work best to develop your employability skills? Why is this do you think?
>
> Employability is also your responsibility; do you know where to seek out additional opportunities? University-based clubs or societies and your students' union would be good places to start.

Pedagogies for employability

Pegg et al. (2012) suggest employability should be woven into teaching, learning and curriculum design to equip students with professional skills for their future careers. One way to do this is via links to classroom practice or wider educational settings. Students should also be encouraged to be proactive during their degree, seeking out experiences that help apply theory to practice, and to highlight influences and approaches in relation to schooling and the experience of being educated. This could be done via wider reading or volunteer work, for example.

One example of a module/unit designed to embed employability is described below.

Module/unit example: Introduction to educational theory

Ways to promote employability in a module/unit about educational theory:

1. Ensure there are strong links back to classroom practice.
2. Ensure that wider policy context is understood by students.
3. Ensure students are encouraged to develop transferable skills such as reflexivity and critical thinking.
4. Ensure a range of education related professions are represented and students are provided with opportunities to independently investigate these.

Assessment – case studies used to link theory, practice and professional roles

As part of the assessment for a module/unit like this, you may be asked to link a theory to a child focused case study. This will enable you to contextualise the theory not only within the wider policy context but also the actual lived experience of being educated. The case study may include a combination of:

- A report on a child from an educational welfare officer or educational psychologist.
- An excerpt from an Ofsted report concerning the school the child attends.

- A quote from the child's class teacher or teaching assistant.
- Minutes from a head of year or curriculum leader's meeting concerning the child.
- An excerpt from the child's school report.
- A quote from the child themselves or their parents/carers.

The assessment task will then require that theory be used to interpret the case. For example, constructivists such as Piaget and Vygotsky may provide insight into the child's developmental needs, or philosophical theories such as progressivism may highlight issues with the design of schooling. Students will also be expected to research the roles of the professionals involved, their specific skill sets and expertise, the levels of training required and ways in which their roles interlink with others.

By completing assessment tasks such as this, students will not only gain insights into applying theory to practice, but also develop criticality and reflexivity through consideration of the pros and cons of each theory in the context of the case. They will also reflect upon the range of professionals, policies and practices that interact to inform a child's daily experience. This, in turn, will increase student confidence and understanding of the demands of the education profession. An awareness of the wider impact of their professional actions will provide further employability awareness.

Questions to consider

Have you completed a module/unit similar to the one described above?
Were you aware that employability was (or could be) embedded in this way?
Were you aware of the range of professionals involved in education and the diverse set of skills, knowledge and experience utilised?

Conclusion

The idea of embedding employability into degree programmes is, for some, controversial (Tomlinson and Holmes, 2016). There is an argument that it may 'dumb down' the intellectual offering of the subject and over instrumentalise student learning experiences at university. By embedding employability into the curriculum, the university faces the prospect of fundamentally changing its role in society which was traditionally to 'educate the intellectual elite' (Ward, 2014: 99).

However, as university education becomes more widespread, and students demand a return for their investment in tuition fees, arguably universities must offer some form of careers advice or links to the wider world of work. This is particularly pertinent in a degree such as education studies, where the need to link to the professions it represents is paramount. There is a careful pedagogic balance to be struck between the academic and theoretical content which marks such a degree out as distinct from teacher education and the vocational links back to practice required to develop student employability. There must be a recognition that the students enrolled on education studies degrees are future educational professionals of some kind, and as such should graduate equipped with skills and professional understandings to enable success in the field. Students should play an active role in building their professional journey. However, if they find themselves on an education studies programme where employability debates do not recognise the multiple possibilities on offer, they are encouraged to investigate further using the information provided in this chapter.

Recommended reading

Ward, S. (2014) University knowledge: The market and the state. In W. Curtis, S. Ward, J. Sharp and L. Hankin (Eds) *Education Studies an Issues-Based Approach* (3rd Ed). London: Sage.
This chapter provides an overview of this history of university education and some arguments concerning its educative role and purpose in society. It considers the role of universities in employability.

Routes into Teaching. Available at: https://www.prospects.ac.uk/jobs-and-work-experience/job-sectors/-teacher-training-and-education/routes-into-teaching (Accessed 23 September 2022).
This is a useful resource for those considering gaining QTS following graduation from an undergraduate degree in education studies. This web source provides brief and clear information on the different routes into teaching, including entry requirements.

Student Employability Profiles. Available at: https://www.advance-he.ac.uk/knowledge-hub/student-employability-profiles.
Pages 73 and 74 of this guide, published by Advance HE, describe the abilities that a graduate in education studies is expected to develop. This is helpful to enhance understanding of the subject and what it offers.

References

Bartlett, S., and Burton, D. (2006) The evolution of education studies in higher education in England. *Curriculum Journal*, 17(4), pp. 383–396. https://doi.org/10.1080/09585170601072635

Brown, P., Hesketh, A. and Williams, S. (2003) Employability in a knowledge-driven economy. *Journal of Education and Work*, 16(2), pp. 107–126. https://doi.org/10.1080/1363908032000070648

Dey, F., and Cruzvergara, C. Y. (2014). Evolution of career services in higher education. *New Directions for Student Services*, 2014(148), pp. 5–18. https://doi.org/10.1002/ss.20105

Facer, K. (2011) *Learning Futures Education, Technology and Social Change*. London: Routledge. https://doi.org/10.4324/9780203817308

Harvey, L. (2003) Transitions from higher education to work. Available at: http://bit.ly/oeCgqW (Accessed 26 May 2021).

Hodkinson, A. (2009) Education studies and employability: How do students and graduates define the subject and what they perceive its vocational relevance to be? *Educationalfutures*, 2(1), pp. 14–30.

Hinchcliffe, G., and Jolly, A. (2011) Graduate identity and employability. *British Educational Research Journal*, 37(4), pp. 563–584. https://doi.org/10.1080/01411926.2010.482200

Menendez Alvarez-Hevia, D., and Naylor, S. (2019) Conceptualising routes to employability in higher education: The case of education studies. *Journal of Education and Work*, 32(4), pp. 407–419. https://doi.org/10.1080/13639080.2019.1649376

Pegg, A., Waldock, J., Hendy-Isaac, S., and Lawton, R. (2012) *Pedagogy for employability*. York: The Higher Education Academy. Available at: https://www.advance-he.ac.uk/knowledge-hub/pedagogy-employability-2012 (Accessed 27 May 2021).

Römgens, I., Scoupe, R., and Beausaert, S. (2020) Unravelling the concept of employability, bringing together research on employability in higher education and the workplace. *Studies in Higher Education*, 45(12), pp. 2588–2603. https://doi.org/10.1080/03075079.2019.1623770

Sin, C., and Neave, G. (2014) Employability deconstructed: Perceptions of bologna stakeholders. *Studies in Higher Education*, 41(8), pp. 1447–1462. https://doi.org/10.1080/03075079.2014.977859

Tomlinson, M., and Holmes, L. (Eds) (2016) *Graduate Employability in Context: Theory, Research and Debate*. London: Palgrave Macmillan. https://doi.org/10.1057/978-1-137-57168-7

Stokes, P. J. (2017). *Higher Education and Employability: New Models for Integrating Study and Work*. New York: Harvard Education Press.

Ward, S. (2014) University knowledge: The market and the state. In W. Curtis, S. Ward, J. Sharp and L. Hankin (Eds) *Education Studies an Issues-Based Approach* (3rd ed, pp. 94–105). London: Sage.

Yorke, M. (2006) *Employability in Higher Education: What It Is – What It Is Not*. York: Higher Education Academy. Available at: https://www.advance-he.ac.uk/knowledge-hub/employability-higher-education-what-it-what-it-not (Accessed 27 May 2021)

22 Career identity, employability and placements in education studies

Catherine A. Simon

SUMMARY POINTS

- Placements and work-based learning (WBL) in education studies provide important opportunities to interrogate theoretical understandings in practical, real world settings.
- Theories of authentic learning and assessment, and of restrictive and expansive learning, suggest that placements and WBL yield rich and invaluable environments in which to explore educational issues, personal characteristics and career dispositions.
- There is a diversity of education contexts in which placements can take place and these can be extended through online platforms and virtual environments. The Covid-19 pandemic opened up opportunities for virtual placements and enhanced equality of access for some students. It demonstrated how WBL might be reconceptualised for future education studies courses.
- However, virtual placements rely on students having access to secure and stable broadband and computer facilities, and lead to implications for pedagogy and learning. These cannot be ignored and thus provide scope for future research and practice.

Introduction

Graduate employability is recognised as one of the central issues that drive the current mission of higher education institutions (HEIs) (Small et al., 2018), so as to make education and training more relevant and better prepare students for the transition from education to the workplace. The alignment of higher education and employability has been strongly influenced by government policy over a number of decades, evidenced in England by reports such as the Leitch Review of Skills (2006) and the Government White Paper, *Skills for Growth* (BIS, 2009). The result is a tripartite relationship between HEIs, employers and employees leading to a plethora of career-based qualifications. Such policy is set against a background of the growth in the knowledge economy, and the post-war transition from a largely manual workforce to one requiring the new industry skills of technology and creativity. Furthermore, in the years following the Covid-19 pandemic and its foreshadowing of a global recession, opportunities to prepare students for the brave new world of employment became even more essential elements of undergraduate degree courses. This chapter explores the role of the professional education placement in education studies degrees and considers different theoretical models of work-based learning (WBL). Finally, based on primary research during 2021, the chapter reports on ways in which education studies programmes have

DOI: 10.4324/9781003296935-26

adapted to new technologies such as online video conferencing, made possible through high-speed internet access.

Background

Placements have formed an integral part of undergraduate and postgraduate education studies degrees from their introduction to the UK higher education landscape in the late 1990s. As with many of the social sciences, education studies is both career and practice-orientated. By engaging in professional education placements, students of education studies are able to experience workplace contexts first hand, in order to glean valuable material for personal, professional and academic reflection. Such engagement enables an understanding of the skills and personal attributes required for professional practice in the field. Real life experience of educational practices provides students with opportunities to critically engage in educational theory and question the perceived role of education in wider society. The Quality Assurance Agency (QAA) Subject Benchmark Statement for Education Studies argues that the role of learning in the workplace is to achieve 'knowledge, understanding and critical analysis' (QAA, 2019: 2). Whilst the majority of education studies students may look to schools and classrooms for their placement experience, growing numbers are interested in allied professional education settings such as local government, heritage and cultural industries, special needs support services, youth work, education administration, international education development and local, national and international policy-making.

Career orientation of education studies courses

Education studies emerged in the late 1990s as a response to greater government involvement in the teacher training curriculum which had considered university based teacher training 'too theorised' (see Chapter 2). In the intervening decades, education studies has become established as a subject in its own right, and the curriculum has developed to be both deeper and wider in scope. At the same time, as indicated above, HEIs have developed an 'institutional narrative' around employability and embarked on initiatives that are intended to prepare students for their professional practice in a labour market dominated by uncertainty and change (Small et al., 2018: 2). Thus, education studies 'is seen as a very useful area of study for students planning careers that involve a range of roles in relation to learning, whatever the context' (QAA, 2019: 5).

There is, of course, an inevitable tension for HEIs in meeting the demands of the employer (which may also swiftly change according to market trends) and maintaining the academic and critical integrity of their courses. Employers look for graduates with more than mere technical knowledge and skills related to a specific profession, favouring a range of transferable skills such as creativity, communication, team working and analytical abilities that will equip employees for economically productive work in the global marketplace. Thus, education studies placements provide students with the opportunity to navigate the complex and intersecting spaces defined by academic critical analysis and (pre) professional learning whilst also acting as a self-managing, self-directed learner (Lester and Costly, 2010). In this manner, students are able to 'try out' and 'try on' potential professional education roles and to relate professional experiences to critical understandings of educational contexts and processes. Placements and WBL thus support the development of career and professional identity.

> **Questions to consider**
>
> How important was the offer of placements and work-based learning in your selection of an education studies degree?
> Why?
> In what ways has your experience of the workplace contributed to your career identity and choice of profession?

Theoretical underpinning of placements and work-based learning

This section explores a number of theoretical perspectives that underpin WBL. Engaging in WBL is a purposeful human activity. Placements in education studies programmes enable students to understand different forms or the *practice* of education in different settings. How much access a student may be given to different roles and contexts within the workplace will depend in part on the focus of the placement setting.

WBL perspectives

No two workplaces are alike. Nottingham (2011), for example, identified a typology of WBL perspectives. The *discipline centred model* ensures curriculum design is linked to associated workplace skills and competencies, supported by a professional mentor as in the case of training courses for teaching, engineering or health. The *employer-centred model* is more directly focused on continuous professional development courses, relating as it does to employer staff development priorities. Finally, the *learner-centred model* permits the interests of the learner to take priority. WBL often involves a complex intersection of these approaches, and these are not always clearly defined. It is for the student to negotiate and navigate these boundaries using critical engagement to understand the personal and (pre-) professional assumptions emerging from day-to-day incidents in the workplace. To this extent, as Nottingham notes, WBL represents an interdisciplinary field for the generation of knowledge, one that identifies the generic priorities of work and professional practice as a site for academic learning.

Authentic learning

Authentic learning 'focuses on designing real-life tasks and creating environments which reflect the manner in which the knowledge will be used in real-world contexts' (Ornellas *et al.*, 2018: 113). Furthermore, Ornellas *et al.* posit a broadened notion of authentic learning, one which 'incorporates not only the epistemological dimension – what students are expected to know and be able to do, but also the ontological – who students are becoming or learning to be' (2018: 109). Characteristics of authentic learning include:

- An authentic context that reflects the way knowledge will be used in real life
- Engaging in authentic activities
- Access to expert performances and modelling of processes
- Experience of multiple roles and perspectives

- Collaborative construction of knowledge
- Reflection
- Articulation
- Authentic assessment

Authentic assessment means that students are able to demonstrate, via meaningful performance, their knowledge and skills in real world situations. Whilst education studies students are rarely assessed on their work in the placement, they are often called on to reflect on their learning in seminar discussion or the writing of a report.

Education placement experiences therefore provide opportunities for students to engage in authentic learning depending on the purposeful intersection of programme, placement and student aims.

Restrictive and expansive learning

To help identify the type or character of the workplace environment encountered on placement, Hordern (2017) uses an adapted version of Fuller and Unwin's (2004) 'expansive - restrictive' framework. The more expansive the factors, the greater the opportunity for higher quality learning. For example, being permitted to engage with numerous communities of practice within the workplace, a placement where team-working and prior knowledge is valued and where students are encouraged to engage in off-site learning and reflection is more likely to result in quality learning. More restrictive work environments would find greater control of learning by the employer, barriers to learning new skills and a lack of organisational recognition of, or support for, employees as learners.

> **Question to consider**
>
> Think of a placement you have undertaken recently.
>   How do the theoretical models listed above help you make sense of your experience?

Reconceptualising the placement experience

The Covid-19 pandemic brought unprecedented disruption to teaching and learning institutions across the globe. Furthermore, in the UK as elsewhere, Government restrictions meant that opportunities for on-site placements were limited. Many HEIs introduced temporary changes to their advertised courses and offered alternative learning opportunities to the placement experience. In other words, HEIs were by necessity encouraged to make full use of the advances in teaching and learning technologies already available and apply them more consistently across courses. One small-scale research project undertaken by the author in 2021 (Simon, unpublished) indicated the breadth of opportunities afforded by HEIs during the time of pandemic. Such alternatives included virtual, online placements; the use of practitioners in residence, e.g. for question and answer sessions with students; webinars, reflective dialogues, studies of film footage of practice and virtual internships. Other online materials also supplemented teaching, including attendance at online educational conferences, observations of online taught courses and support of home-schooling.

Whilst many of these interventions were devised for the short-term, respondents reported positive feedback from students about these experiences and were enthusiastic about incorporating some of the online alternative measures into their programmes going forward concluding, as one course leader stated, 'I think virtual/online placements are the future and can offer a more inclusive experience' (Simon, unpublished). Indeed, the potential for alternative placement experiences has been realised, with implications for future course development. Above all, virtual experiences have demonstrated their ability to address issues of inequality in terms of access to physical workplaces, be that for economic, health or other reasons. The caveat here is suitable access to faster and reliable broadband and appropriate devices for online working.

However, the consequences of pivoting the placement experience online, like all e-learning, have implications for both pedagogy and the disposition of the learner (Herrington et al., 2010). As education studies placements are reconceptualised, it would be pertinent to consider the nature and authenticity of virtual placements, new approaches to pedagogy and the long-term implications for future employability.

Recommended reading

Carter, J. (2021) *Work Placements, Internships and Applied Social Science*. London: Sage.
This book provides a practical and theoretical view of placements and internships for social science students, with an emphasis on experiential learning. Written with the social science researcher in view, the book has valuable contributions from students in a range of placements and internships which are of value for any student of education studies.

Hordern, J., and Simon, C.A. (Eds) (2017) *Placements and Work-based Learning for Education Studies: An Introduction for Students*. Abingdon: Routledge.
This book is based on the teaching and learning of staff and students on the Education Studies courses at Bath Spa University. It explores various theoretical approaches to placements and on-the-job learning as well as exploring the student experience on placement, how to prepare for placements and what to do if placements 'go wrong'.

Medwell, J. (2015). *Training to Teach in Primary Schools: A Practical Guide to School-Based Training and Placements*. (3rd Edition). London: Learning Matters.
Designed for those on QTS courses in England, the book addresses issues for student teachers on placement in primary schools and in early years' settings.

References

BIS Department for Business, Innovation and Skills (2009) *Skills for Growth: The National Skills Strategy*. Norwich: HMSO.

Fuller, A. and Unwin, L. (2004) Expansive learning environments. In H. Rainbird, A. Fuller and A. Munro, (Eds) *Workplace Learning in Context*. Abingdon: Routledge, pp. 126–144.

Herrington, J., Reeves, T.C., and Oliver, R. (2010) *A Guide to Authentic E-learning*. London: Routledge.

Hordern, J. (2017) The context of placement and work-based learning. In J. Hordern and C.A. Simon, (Eds) *Placements and Work-based Learning for Education Studies: An Introduction for Students*. Abingdon: Routledge, pp. 13–21.

Leitch Review of Skills (2006) *Prosperity for All in the Global Economy – World Class Skills*. Final report. December. Norwich: HMSO.

Lester, S., and Costly, C. (2010) Work-based learning at higher education level: Value, practice and critique. *Studies in Higher Education*, **3**(5), pp. 561–575. https://doi-org.libproxy.ucl.ac.uk/10.1080/03075070903216635

Nottingham, P. (2011) *An Exploration of How Differing Perspectives of Work-Based Learning in Higher Education Influence the Pedagogies*. Adopted. PhD dissertation, Middlesex University.

Ornellas, A., Falkner, K. and Edman Stålbrandt, E. (2018) Enhancing graduates' employability skills through authentic learning approaches. *Higher Education, Skills and Work-Based Learning*. https://doi.org/10.1108/HESWBL-04-2018-0049

QAA (2019) *Subject Benchmark Statement for Education Studies for Higher Education* (fourth edition). Gloucester: Quality Assurance Agency.

Small, L., Shacklock, K., and Marchant, T. (2018) Employability: A contemporary review for higher education stakeholders. *Journal of Vocational Education and Training*, **70**, pp. 148–166. https://doi.org/10.1080/13636820.2017.1394355

Simon, C. A. (unpublished). Reconceptualizing the Education Studies Placement.

23 Placements as mediational transitions

An opportunity for negotiated, identity-shaping make-belief experiences

Gisela Oliveira

SUMMARY POINTS

- Employability is a frequently used concept to interpret what happens in the transition between university and the workplace. It focuses on the acquisition of skills and the adaptation to the world of work.
- Consequential transitions form a sociocultural theory of transfer of learning that offers four different types of transition: lateral, collateral, encompassing and mediational. These can be used to enrich the interpretation of students' placement experiences beyond traditional notions of employability.
- Julie's placement experience in a research centre at the university where she is a student is presented as an example of a mediational transition. This highlights the challenges of having to adapt to a placement as a familiar setting and the benefits of interpreting placements as safe locations to role-play professional identities.

Introduction

The transition from university to the workplace is often perceived as the entry into a graduate position where students will transfer academic knowledge, skills and attributes to a professional setting. This transition is generally conceptualised as a crucial moment to focus on employability, where a typical definition would include developing 'a set of achievements – skills, understandings and personal attributes – that make graduates more likely to gain employment' (Yorke, 2004: 4). Supported by such definitions largely based on the principles of human capital theory (Dalrymple et al., 2021), employability has grown to become a dominant discourse in higher education (Gracia, 2009; Jackson, 2014). Work placements in particular are presented as the main way students can develop those achievements (e.g., Pereira et al., 2020).

This chapter starts from a critical view of discourses on the transition between university and the workplace, and the development of employability as the mere possession of skills (Holmes, 2013). It then uses King Beach's (1999, 2003) sociocultural theory of consequential transitions to describe placements as 'sites of possibility' (Urrieta, 2007: 109) and agency. The main argument here is that students' experiences might not reflect the expected successful development of employability, but still be a valuable experience to trial and test emergent professional identities and even reinforce a student identity (Oliveira, 2017).

DOI: 10.4324/9781003296935-27

Consequential transitions: What are they and why are they relevant for students going on placements?

Consequential transitions form a sociocultural theory of learning transfer that gives particular importance to the individual, the context, and how they develop and shape each other across time and space. Due to this focus, they are well-placed to enable an in-depth analysis of the multifaceted transition between university and the workplace. According to Beach (1999: 102), their main aim is to improve understanding of 'how we experience continuity and transformation in becoming someone or something new – a student, a machinist, a bartender, a shopkeeper, or a teacher'.

As a framework, consequential transitions study generalization – how knowledge, skill and identity are maintained and transformed when applied to different social encounters (Beach, 1999, 2003). In the context of placements, they allow the analysis of students' transfer of learning as the application of prior learning, the transformation and creation of new learning, and as the development of individual identities (Oliveira, 2017). They are transforming, developmental, often struggled with (Beach, 1999, 2003) and provide insight into a range of lived experiences that add nuance to typical views of placements as promoters of employability as a set of achievements. A key point with consequential transitions is that they are never easy, as at their core is individual transformation regarding identity (e.g., transition from student to teacher), learning and agency (e.g., transition from learner to creator of knowledge). Beach (1999: 114) explains that consequential transitions are struggled with because they ultimately change the individuals' 'sense of self and social positioning'.

There are four types of consequential transitions: lateral, collateral, encompassing and mediational (Beach, 1999, 2003). Lateral transitions require progression within two related activities, much like an education student progressing from first to second year at university. To access the second year at university, participation in the first year is essential and therefore there are underlying notions of progress and unidirectionality in lateral transitions. Collateral transitions require simultaneous participation in two or more related activities. They are more frequent, multidirectional and do not explicitly imply progress or development like lateral transitions. An example could be an education student volunteering in a school while completing their degree, as the placement might not have a developmental impact in terms of better grades or helping the student becoming effective or independent. Encompassing transitions require participation in a social activity that is changing or where the individual is changing. A possible example includes the use of new technology or processes in a specific activity, like the move to online learning during the Covid-19 pandemic, where teaching and learning was greatly transformed for both teachers and students. Like in lateral transitions, there is a clear sense of progress in the way the individual adapts to the changing elements, although still within the same activity. Finally, mediational transitions require participation in activities that simulate the real activity that the students have yet to experience. They are perceived as role-play activities in which individuals get to explore elements of the real social activity in a 'what if' scenario, allowing for the development of knowledge, skills and modes of action.

All four types of consequential transitions can be applied to the transition between university and the workplace based on context, but more importantly, based on the student experience of the transition. For example, an education studies student can interpret their placement in a school as a clear progression from their degree to becoming a teacher, focusing on the opportunity to advance their knowledge, skills and behaviours (lateral transition). However, the same student can also interpret their placement as an opportunity to role-play being in a school as a teacher, a teaching assistant, a counsellor, thus focusing on negotiating what role suits them better in that instance (mediational transition). Whether a placement is experienced as a lateral or a mediational transition, will depend on many factors (e.g., the student's perceptions of the new role); but more importantly, it will have clear implications for the student and the contexts involved. Indeed, a student interpreting the placement as a lateral transition might have a strong desire to engage with the placement's practices or develop enough confidence to propose new ways of working or projects. However, a student interpreting the placement as a mediational transition might be focusing on exploring how the placement aligns with their professional and academic aims (Oliveira, 2017).

Overall, literature on placements seem to portray them as lateral transitions, focusing on their multiple benefits in the acquisition of skills and knowledge and enabling a smoother transition from school to work in a progressive manner (e.g., O'Donovan, 2018; Thompson, 2017). However, it is likely that not all students experience their placements in this way, especially when placements are understood as events that can lead to a negotiation of emerging identities (Inceoglu *et al.*, 2019). Therefore, it is important to address the developmental nature of this transition without imposing lateral notions of progress.

Questions to consider

As a student going on a placement, do you think of your experience as 'becoming employable'? Why?

In your opinion, would a lateral transition be the best type of placement experience? Or would one of the other types of transition (collateral, encompassing or mediational) be more effective? Why?

Meet Julie

This is a real job, but you know, I'm still a student.

(Julie)

Julie is a second-year management student at a university in the UK. She has two older siblings who also studied management and, when they started applying for jobs, employers highlighted their lack of 'experience'. So, Julie knew it was important to have some real work experience before completing her degree.

However, Julie was not interested in a placement in a corporate setting, and it was only when a research placement became available in her own university faculty that she decided to apply. In the end, Julie got the placement and spent one year researching sustainability and corporate responsibility. Interacting with professionals in different organisations, she developed research skills in data analysis, writing and delivering presentations. She also became more confident and independent. Still, during the placement experience she struggled with her professional identity and often chose to work in computer clusters surrounded by students instead of her office, with her colleagues. She also continuously felt like a student at the placement and around her supervisors, except when she went on field trips to organisations. At the end of the placement, she was 'eager to go back' (Julie) to university, not as a researcher or professional, but as a student.

Questions to consider

Are students' motivations to have a placement relevant to how they will experience the placement? Why?

Considering Beach's consequential transitions, how would you characterise Julie's experience? Why?

Was Julie's placement choice relevant to how she experienced the placement? Why?

Discussion and conclusion

It is possible to argue that Julie experienced her placement as a mediational transition. She described it as 'not a proper work environment' (Julie), but a balance between university and the workplace. From the start, she was not interested in a placement in a corporate setting and part of her motivation to pursue a placement was due to her siblings' experiences of applying for jobs after graduation. Therefore, in a negotiation between a need to be 'employable' and to continue being a student, Julie chose a placement where she could role play being a professional.

During the placement experience, Julie continuously negotiated her participation (Lave and Wenger, 1991) to remain in the margins of her new role as a researcher. She worked with other students, felt like a student and self-identified as a student. In doing so, Julie did not experience the placement as a lateral transition (Beach, 1999, 2003) where she progressively became a professional or a 'master practitioner' (Lave and Wenger, 1991: 111). Instead, she experienced an identity confrontation (Tanggaard, 2008) between being a student and a professional. In this make-belief context she became a 'marginal-stranger – people who sort of belong and sort of do not' (Tanggaard, 2007: 460).

Following mainstream views of employability as becoming 'successful in the labour market' (Tholen, 2015: 767), Julie's placement experience might be characterised as unsuccessful. Indeed, as presented earlier, Julie often made decisions that removed her from the placement setting and from interactions with colleagues. In addition, most of the skills and knowledge that Julie developed during the placement were framed in the context of being relevant to her final year back at university. This meant that Julie's actions and intentions in the placement were very far from a desire to progress to that new role (researcher) and new context (the university as a workplace). However, what Julie's placement experience offers is an opportunity to reflect on how students' reasons for having a placement and the context of the placement might shape their experience. In this case, Julie's extrinsic reasons to have a placement to accommodate for outdated views of employability were a weak starting point. Moreover, her prior knowledge, interactions and identity within the placement setting created a barrier for the full development of a professional identity.

However, as a mediational transition, Julie found the placement to be a safe setting to test an emergent professional identity as a researcher, and reject it, while also taking valuable experiences, knowledge and skills from the placement. She was able to negotiate her level of engagement and participation to suit her personal trajectory and still return to university with a renewed understanding of the value of her degree beyond the classroom, despite the lack of a clear progressive trajectory. To conclude, consequential transitions can offer important options to interpret students' placement experiences by validating less linear and less traditionally progressive experiences. For students in transition between university and the workplace, consequential transitions and mediational transitions offer a framework for action based on the value of the interactions between the students and the setting and how they shape each other.

> **Questions to consider**
>
> Given that placements as part of education programmes tend to be in educational settings (e.g., schools, universities), what can we learn from Julie's experience regarding possible challenges in adapting to a familiar setting as a placement?
>
> With their focus on placements as safe opportunities to role-play different roles, approaches to work and ways to develop knowledge within the workplace, can mediational transitions offer a useful framework to present placements to education students? Why?

Recommended reading

Beach, K. (1999) Consequential Transitions: A Sociocultural Expedition Beyond Transfer in Education. *Review of Research in Education*, **24**(1), pp. 101–139. https://doi.org/10.3102/0091732X024001101

Beach, K. (2003) Consequential Transitions: A Developmental View of Knowledge Propagation. Through Social Organizations. In T. Tuomi-Grèohn and Y. Engeström (Eds) *Between School and Work: New Perspectives on Transfer and Boundary Crossing*. Bingley: Emerald Group Publishing.

These two sources are useful for an in-depth analysis of consequential transitions and the empirical research supporting this theory.

Dalrymple, R., Macrae, A. and Shipman, S. (2021) *Employability: A Review of the Literature 2016–2021*. York: Advance HE. https://www.advance-he.ac.uk/knowledge-hub/employability-review-literature-2016-2021

This is useful for an in-depth analysis of employability theories and studies. It can complement the use of Beach's framework to interpret students' experiences of the transition between university and the workplace.

References

Beach, K. (1999) Consequential Transitions: A Sociocultural Expedition Beyond Transfer in Education. *Review of Research in Education*, **24**(1), pp. 101–139. https://doi.org/10.3102/0091732X024001101

Beach, K. (2003) Consequential Transitions: A Developmental View of Knowledge Propagation. Through Social Organizations. In T. Tuomi-Grèohn and Y. Engestrèom (Eds) *Between School and Work: New perspectives on transfer and boundary crossing*. Bingley: Emerald Group Publishing, pp. 39–61.

Dalrymple, R., Macrae, A. and Shipman, S. (2021) *Employability: A Review of the Literature 2016–2021*. York: Advance HE. https://www.advance-he.ac.uk/knowledge-hub/employability-review-literature-2016-2021

Gracia, L. (2009) Employability and Higher Education: Contextualising Female Students' Workplace Experiences to Enhance Understanding of Employability Development. *Journal of Education and Work*, **22**(4), pp. 301–318. https://doi.org/10.1080/13639080903290454

Holmes, L. (2013) Competing Perspectives on Graduate Employability: Possession, Position or Process? *Studies in Higher Education*, **38**(4), pp. 538–554. https://doi.org/10.1080/03075079.2011.587140

Inceoglu, I., Selenko, E., McDowall, A., and Schlachter, S. (2019) How Do Work Placements Work? Scrutinizing the Quantitative Evidence for a Theory-Driven Future Research Agenda. *Journal of Vocational Behaviour*, **110**, pp. 317–337. https://doi.org/10.1016/j.jvb.2018.09.002

Jackson, D. (2014) Testing a Model of Undergraduate Competence in Employability Skills and Its Implications for Stakeholders. *Journal of Education and Work*, **27**(2), pp. 220–242. https://doi.org/10.1080/13639080.2012.718750

Lave, J. and Wenger, E. (1991) *Situated Learning: Legitimate Peripheral Participation*. Cambridge: Cambridge University Press. https://doi.org/10.1017/CBO9780511815355

O'Donovan, D. (2018) Bilateral Benefits: Student Experiences of Work-Based Learning during Work Placement. *Industry and Higher Education*, **32**(2), pp. 119–128. https://doi.org/10.1177/0950422218761273

Oliveira, O. (2017) *Transfer of Learning between Higher Education and the Workplace*. Ph.D. thesis, University of Leeds.

Pereira, E., Vilas-Boas, M., and Rebelo, C. (2020) University Curricula and Employability: The Stakeholders' Views for a Future Agenda. *Industry and Higher Education*, **34**(5), pp. 321–329. https://doi.org/10.1177/0950422220901676

Tanggaard, L. (2007) Learning at Trade Vocational School and Learning at Work: Boundary Crossing in Apprentices' Everyday Life. *Journal of Education and Work*, **20**(5), pp. 453–466. https://doi.org/10.1080/13639080701814414

Tanggaard, L. (2008) Learning at School and Work: Boundary Crossing, Strangeness and Legitimacy in Apprentices' Everyday Life. In V. Aarkrog and C. Jorgensen (Eds) *Divergence and Convergence in Education and Work*. Berlin: Peter Lang AG, International Academic Publishers, pp. 219–239.

Thompson, D. (2017) How Valuable Is 'Short Project' Placement Experience to Higher Education Students? *Journal of Further and Higher Education*, **41**(3), pp.413–424. https://doi.org/10.1080/0309877X.2015.1117601

Tholen, G (2015) What Can Research into Graduate Employability Tell Us About Agency and Structure? *British Journal of Sociology of Education*, **36**(5), pp. 766–784. https://doi.org/10.1080/01425692.2013.847782

Urrieta, L. (2007) Figured Worlds and Education: An Introduction to the Special Issue. *The Urban Review*, **39**, pp. 107–116. https://doi.org/10.1007/s11256-007-0051-0

Yorke, M. (2004) *Employability in Higher Education: What It Is - What It Is Not*. York: The Higher Education Academy. https://www.advance-he.ac.uk/knowledge-hub/employability-higher-education-what-it-what-it-not

24 More than your degree title

Transferable skills, employability and diverse opportunities for education students

David Thompson, Rachel Higdon and Charlotte Barrow

SUMMARY POINTS

- Education falls within the social sciences; as such it potentially offers a wider range of career opportunities than narrowly defined notions of education, such as schooling.
- Education graduates have many transferable skills, assets and experiences that make them highly employable.
- Strategic reflection upon the skills that students of education have, and need to develop, may expand thinking about job roles, destinations and 'value' in employability terms.
- You are unique. Learners should try to be confident in identifying their own individual assets, presenting these assertively and positively for future employers and development opportunities.
- It is important to recognise the value of creativity, and how this may be seen in skills such as flexibility, complexity and problem solving. This is something that many students may feel does not have a place in their studies.

Introduction

This chapter encourages learners to think about more diverse definitions of employability, challenging the assumption that all graduates of education-related subjects will become teachers. In Part 1, David Thompson reminds us that education – its study and its value to society more broadly – does not only occur in classrooms, and that graduates need to be flexible when thinking about career planning. Part 2, by Rachel Higdon, begins to equip learners with the confidence to think beyond simplistic and outdated ideas about employability, and highlights particular skills that learners should seek to develop. The final part, by Charlotte Barrow, aims to enable learners to confidently identify and articulate assets gained not only through their studies, but also life experiences that make graduates of education more employable, unique, and resilient in the world of work. The chapter acts as an important reminder to scholars of education studies that the discipline offers more than a narrowly defined career route into teaching. Within the field of social sciences, the diversity of such programmes of study enables graduates to pursue many career paths and encourages them to be flexible in responding to future employment demands.

DOI: 10.4324/9781003296935-28

Part 1: Education as a social science discipline – using your studies to broaden your horizons and open up diverse opportunities

'Shift Happens' (Fisch and McCleod, 2008) was a video that went viral with over 250,000 views. Fisch and McLeod presented a series of statistics and propositions that provided 'a wake-up call to educators and their students' (Corcoran, 2018), maintaining that students would experience a very different world once they had entered the workforce. International organisations have elaborated on this; a report by the World Economic Forum (2016) on the future of jobs and skills suggested the most in-demand occupations did not exist ten or even five years before and possibly up to 65 per cent of children entering primary school today will end up working in new job types that do not currently exist.

For the moment at least, there are some professions that seem relatively secure in the longer term. We need farmers to grow food for our daily sustenance and, even with the advent of artificial intelligence (AI), we still need teachers to educate our young people and nourish them intellectually. It would be a mistake to assume that education and schooling are not evolving, but there is a 'relevance gap' as schools have trouble keeping up and catching up with the digital, global, hyper-connected, information landscape (McLeod in Corcoran, 2018). The nature of the skills and education needed for a rapidly changing world present philosophical and practical discussions about people's development at all stages in their lives, and about what society expects. There are important implications for all graduates in a world where the future cannot easily be predicted.

There are still colleagues in education that assume education studies and teacher training are one and the same; nothing could be further from the truth. We concur with many of the comments made in the preceding chapters in this book; it is important to remember that education takes place beyond narrowly defined representations of schooling. Education and lifelong learning occur in many settings both formal and informal; including charities, hospitals, private businesses, families and communities, social work, counselling, prisons, museums, training organisations and just about anywhere there is an opportunity for learning and professional development to take place. To narrow one's career prospects to purely teaching in schools is limiting in terms of aspirations, career development and employability. Broadly speaking:

> Education studies is concerned with understanding how people develop and learn throughout their lives, and the nature of knowledge and critical engagement with ways of knowing and understanding. It offers rigorous analysis of educational processes, systems and approaches, and their cultural, societal, technological, political, historical and economic contexts.
>
> (QAA, 2019: 4)

Students of education studies are not necessarily being trained to teach. They are engaging with all the academic rigour and transferable skills of other subject areas in the social sciences as they pursue the study of education, not only as an academic exercise but also whilst gaining practical experience through placements and work-based learning. They will:

> contest changing discourses, exemplified by reference to debate about values, personal and social engagement, and how they relate to communities and societies (developing) their critical capabilities through the selection, analysis and synthesis of relevant perspectives, and to justify different positions.
>
> (QAA, 2019:4)

We can conclude that such studies are not about being trained to do a specific job; this pair of quotes represents a callout to challenge our ideas about the world, society and the way education develops and the policies that affect it. We need to address the challenges that society faces; this includes a consideration of how we have arrived at the education system of the present day, how we respond to policy and solve educational problems, and – importantly – what vision we have for the future of education. Education studies students can take their skills and qualifications in many different directions, some may not directly relate to the teaching profession and can easily be transferred to careers outside the sphere of education.

However, there is a debate on the future of work and just how much we can predict what will happen. There may be 'multiple futures of work' (Malton, 2017), so staying flexible is important. While the traditional 'employability skills' of team working, problem solving, analytical skills, etc. are valued by employers, others point to what might be just as valued in the future, including decision-making, ideas, creativity, originality and reasoning skills. A range of skills will be required if organisations are to respond to future demands. These skills could be applied to teaching, management, support and guidance, or any aspect of complex education institutions and other organisations serving communities across diverse locations.

It has been argued that transferable skills gained in social sciences are attractive to employers across different sectors (SAGE, 2019). Education studies is located in the field of social sciences; the content is constantly evolving, sometimes controversial, and open to debate. It can be applied both locally and globally, and relates to societies, families, communities and even nations. Therefore, it is about the policies and interventions that contribute to better outcomes for society. Hard questions are asked, and supporting evidence sought, to shape the future. The goal is to provide 'education that is fit for the challenges we face today and social science graduates have plenty to offer as employees, as citizens and as entrepreneurs' (Craig, 2019). Looking at education studies from this perspective provides a refreshing alternative that offers agency and potentially empowers students; an antidote to today's mechanistic and instrumental accountability culture that encroaches on education and other careers more generally. This diverse interpretation of education studies therefore offers rich and diverse career directions and increases employability.

Questions to consider

A report about social sciences and the future of the workforce cites important challenges to humanity. 'Addressing these challenges will need not just technological solutions, but the understanding of human behaviour and how to achieve social and cultural change' that social sciences provide (The British Academy, 2020: 25). A selection of these global challenges is listed below.

What education-related perspectives might be applied to each challenge? Consider the skills and contributions that students with expertise in education studies can offer in finding solutions to the following. Can you think of others to add to the list?

- Climate change
- Global pandemics
- Artificial intelligence
- Sustainable growth
- Inequality
- Ageing societies
- Poverty and hunger

Part 2: Living an individual experience within a graduate career

This section discusses graduate mind-sets and the need to evaluate what you have learnt in your education degree and recognise your own, *unique* offer in the world of work.

What does the word 'employability' mean to you? Governments in the United Kingdom (UK) in recent years have viewed employability as skills that you learn in education, training and 'on the job'. In the UK, skills training is promoted by government policy as imperative to economic productivity and is linked to human capital (Gov.uk, 2022a, 2022b). Certain skills fit with a certain type of job. Government policy around skills and upskilling infers that when an individual obtains the 'right skills', they are rewarded with a job that fits with these skills. This is a simplistic way of looking at recruitment and the job market. A more helpful perspective, as students in education, is to understand that you seek your own individual experience. You are not aiming for one job after graduation, with a limited set of skills attached to it. Instead, you should strive for a graduate career. In your individual experience, you will use your own personal attributes and skills development to seek a range of roles throughout your working life. You should see this as an exciting prospect.

Of course, we should acknowledge that social and economic factors make the process of access, participation and inclusion for all a complex issue. The financial, cultural and social capital that we each have affects what we have access to and what we can participate in (Higdon, 2018). For example, money (financial capital) is needed to obtain high level qualifications and also to support ourselves (with accommodation and food, etc.) while undertaking work experience and placements (which can be low paid or even unpaid). Employment opportunities and jobs often come from knowing people in the relevant business and making connections through who you know (social capital). Students who have parents in senior level professional jobs are far more likely to regard education as a priority, go to university and aspire to high status professions for themselves (cultural capital). Employability is far more complicated than just having the skills to get the job.

Intersectionality around age, gender, ethnicity, disability and nationality will also play a part in the diversity of selection and recruitment. Human resources processes aim to eliminate direct and indirect bias in job recruitment and access (Equality Act 2010: Guidance, Gov.uk, 2022c). However, through our critique of institutions, policy and processes as students of education, we can see that this bias is not always eradicated (Higdon, 2014).

Rather than focus on finite skill sets and specific jobs and worry whether we can access them straight after graduating, it is important to change the way we view work. We need to recognise that as students and graduates it is better to see our working graduate lives as a continuum of many opportunities with different paths and routes that we can take. There is no wrong way or wrong path to take. It is likely that we will have many jobs and our careers will be shifting all the time. As suggested in Part 1 of this chapter, many of the jobs that exist now will have evolved into something else in ten years' time. So, we should think about graduate skill sets, rather than employer specific skill sets, which can restrict us. We should ask ourselves what can we do or have the potential to do and what is our own self-agency?

The World Economic Forum (2022) views graduate work, across all sectors and across all countries, as having many similarities. It stresses that creativity and problem solving are the key to any graduate employment. The Forum identifies ten top key skills that graduates should have for work in a global, technological world. Employer skill sets (that are probably best taught on the job) are replaced with self-agency and the key skills of a graduate mindset. These key attributes lead to graduate work in many sectors and employment throughout the world. Some of the top key skills include:

- Complex problem solving
- Critical thinking
- Creativity
- People management
- Coordinating with others
- Emotional intelligence
- Judgement and decision making
- Negotiation
- Cognitive flexibility

These attributes are regarded to promote the growth mindset necessary to be able to adapt, evolve and remain resilient in multifaceted and diverse environments. They can inspire us to be more ambitious and help prevent students/graduates from self-limiting by viewing their potential only in a local sense, a parochial way or in a narrow field. Specific employer skills sets are secondary to these key graduate attributes. Creativity is seen as not only arts-based, but an important part of education and work. STEAM (Science, Technology, Engineering, Arts and Mathematics) education acknowledges that arts and creativity are crucial parts of science, technology and mathematics. We need inventive and creative scientists. We also need inventive and creative teachers, with innovative methods to teach, to engage and to motivate learners to be self-reliant, curious, critical thinkers and problem solvers in their own lives and jobs.

Your degree in education helps build your own self agency, problem solving and creativity. You learn to be curious and look at issues in new ways, to unpack them and look for alternative solutions and outcomes. This is the graduate mindset that is important in your own life.

As educators, we believe it is more valuable for students in education to look at themselves critically. That is not to see yourself with a critical, negative view but to evaluate what you like doing: jobs should be enjoyable and not drudgery. All jobs will have high and low points but, essentially, they should be in areas that you find attractive to work in. Human beings are unique. Look at your own **qualities**. We are each different and this is something we can celebrate.

Questions to consider

What do you enjoy doing?
   What are your own personal qualities?
   What do you believe in?
   What do you value in the world?
   Look back over your own experiences in education and in work (if you have completed any). What has interested you?
   What have been your favourite activities or projects at school, college and university?
   Look at the World Economic Forum's (2022) top skills above. Think about where you have experienced each of these skills in your course and in any work experience. You will have knowledge of all of the areas to some extent. For example, working on team presentations and within study groups will give you skills in people management.

Part 3: The assets students bring to their studies

This section will enable you to take a step back and consider characteristics of yourself and your life that are valuable assets. Being able to articulate these can make a difference when thinking about how to present yourself for future employment and opportunities.

Students of education often bring with them diverse backgrounds and varied circumstances. For instance, education consistently attracts a higher proportion of female students and is amongst the top three subjects most likely to attract mature students (HESA, 2020). So, for example, a student in her 30s with two children will already have years of valuable experiences, despite perhaps feeling somewhat disconnected from education after time out of studying. Education students are also more likely to have a known disability. Some learners therefore may be adept at approaching their studies in a different way, for example, having to organise time in order to liaise with support workers, having to access materials differently, or using organisational tools for time management. These individual characteristics or experiences bring with them a likelihood of increased responsibilities and complex experiences which are often unrecognised as an asset.

Many authors in the field of education have written around the idea of capital, to try and distinguish what assets individuals may hold that could make them more, or less, successful in their educational experiences and longer-term careers. The most well-known types of capital education students will probably come across stem from the work of Pierre Bourdieu, and over the years his original ideas around the concept of capital have been developed significantly. As mentioned in Part 2 of this chapter, the capital an individual possesses can impact directly upon their opportunities for participation and progression in education and employment.

> **Questions to consider**
>
> Donald et al. (2019) and Tomlinson (2017) recognise a number of different types of capital in which individuals may have the most agency. These include *social*, *psychological* and *cultural* capital. Work your way through these types of capital, reading the examples below. Identify assets, experiences, or elements of your life that could be viewed as 'capital'.

Social capital: think here about *who* you know, or indeed who *they* know. Friends, their parents, neighbours, team-mates, people in the community, clubs, any organisations you are a member of, anyone you have helped, people you used to work with – a list of social contacts can be extensive. Recognising the value of this might be important: for example, asking to be put in touch with a contact in a particular industry to pursue work experience. This is also an area where social media and online connections can be useful: do you follow certain individuals, people in the community, relevant professional organisations or former colleagues? Be sure to follow guidelines about passing on personal information in line with data protection legislation and good practice. Always be respectful and ask permission for a contact or referee to vouch for you or make a recommendation.

Psychological capital: think here about your *self-efficacy* (belief about your own capabilities), *resilience* (the extent to which you can recover, or 'bounce back'), *grit* (your passion and persistence) and aspects of yourself that you've drawn upon in certain life experiences. Have you ever started from scratch and committed to learning something new? Have you re-located and built new networks at any age or stage of your life? Have you had a time when, in spite of varied pressures, you showed determination and completed a particular task, or flourished when circumstances were difficult? Whilst job applications or CVs are not the place to document detailed personal experiences, it can be possible to present challenging times in your life as instances where you have employed particular strategies or mindsets to help you cope.

Cultural capital: think beyond the traditional interpretations of this concept, and don't be quick to dismiss less well known, recognised or regarded types of 'culture'. Have you learned a new language? Do you seek out music of a particular genre? Do you enjoy watching or participating in certain sports or pastimes? Are you an avid reader or cinema-goer? Are you drawn to a certain country's culture, or do you aspire to travel to a certain part of the world? Here, you can also think about the kinds of cultural capital you draw upon online as well: do you follow particular social media accounts that help you to learn more about something in particular? These are all types of cultural activities that feed into our health and wellbeing or provide us with immersive, sensory or aesthetic experiences. In turn, they help us to make meaningful contact with other people and learn more about the lives of those outside our immediate circles, broadening our knowledge.

Education studies is a subject that tends to attract particularly diverse learners. Those studying in this area have often included people from 'non-traditional', or 'widening participation' backgrounds, for example, learners from some minority ethnic groups, or those from lower socio-economic backgrounds. Parutis and Kandikoo Howson (2020) acknowledge that students from higher socio-economic backgrounds may be better at both generating and utilising their capital. Donald et al. (2019) refer to several studies which find that males are likely to have an increased self-perception of their own employability compared with the views females hold of themselves. Studies like these tell us that inequalities in relation to *actual* and *perceived* capital still persist. This is why it is even more important to think about a range of attributes you may hold yourself, and the ways in which different types of capital can be used and presented to the outside world as transferable assets that could make you more employable.

To finish, here are a few examples of circumstances that could be instrumental in developing capital, qualities or experiences that are specific to yourself. Whilst society might sometimes focus on the challenges, deficits and difficulties associated with such circumstances, consider that they may be opportunities to recognise and promote your own unique transferable skills and qualities.

- Juggling **caring responsibilities** for children, neighbours, or family members who may need you to act as an advocate for them. Perhaps you needed to become an expert in a particular condition, type of medical treatment or provision, or had to get to grips with complex legal rules and determine how to apply these?
- Any kind of **previous job** (whether paid or voluntary) carries with it certain responsibilities, requirements and opportunities. Were you charged with being the face of the company or organisation, meeting and greeting customers, and therefore directly impacting upon the kinds of reviews people leave online? Has a placement enabled you to make contacts with professionals within the field in which you would like to work? Have you had to develop particular organisational skills to juggle and prioritise varying demands?
- Perhaps you have had to learn how to manage a **special educational need or disability** (such as attention deficit hyperactivity disorder, being on the autistic spectrum, or a specific learning difficulty such as dyslexia). Recognising your neurodiverse strengths and 'marketing'

these could be worth considering. Silberman's (2015) text Neurotribes recognises that some companies are beginning to understand the potentially huge benefits of employing neurodiverse individuals because of their unique ways of thinking, analysing and problem solving.

Conclusion

We hope that reading this chapter has expanded your notions of employability. This is your opportunity to take the skills, knowledge and understanding of your educational experiences into diverse settings and to understand that there is not just one route or destination (i.e. teacher training).

Remember, in addition to your formal education degree, the assets and skills you have gained all contribute towards a creative approach to your career that you can present positively.

By foregrounding your individual and unique nature in a competitive employment market, you will be better placed to progress and flourish with the lifelong opportunities that will come your way.

Recommended reading

It is important to remember that studying education makes you part of a global community of education students, researchers and practitioners. Expand your social network by following these organisations:
British Education Studies Association (BESA) https://educationstudies.org.uk/
British Education Research Association (BERA) https://www.bera.ac.uk/
European Educational Research Association (EERA) https://eera-ecer.de/
Many other education-related organisations exist!
James, S.J., Houston, A., Newton, L., Daniels, S., Morgan, N., Coho, W., Ruck, A. and Lucas, B. (2019) Durham Commission on Creativity and Education. Available at https://www.dur.ac.uk/creativitycommission/ (Accessed 25 September 2022).
This report recognises the economic and social value of creativity and creative thinking in education and work. The report advocates creative thinking across all disciplines including the arts, sciences and humanities and argues the education system should support the development of this self-agency.
Redmond, P. (2010) *The Graduate Jobs Formula: How to Land Your Dream Career*. Bath: Trotman Publishing.
This book gives information and analyses the graduate job market. It gives advice on graduate employment and a range of career opportunities that students may not know about.

References

British Academy (2020) *Qualified for the Future. Quantifying Demand for Arts, Humanities and Social Science Skills*. London: British Academy.
Corcoran, B. (2018) Has 'Shift' Happened? Revisiting a viral video from 2008. EdSurge. Available at:https://www.edsurge.com/news/2018-11-06-has-shift-happened-revisiting-a-viral-video-from-2008 (Accessed 7 March 2022).
Craig, J. (2019) Benefits of Studying Social Sciences. Leeds School of Social Sciences. Available at: https://www.leedsbeckett.ac.uk/blogs/leeds-school-of-social-sciences/2019/10/benefits-of-studying-social-sciences/ (Accessed 7 March 2022).
Donald, W.E., Baruch, Y. and Ashleigh, M. (2019) The Undergraduate Self-Perception of Employability: Human Capital, Careers Advice, and Career Ownership. *Studies in Higher Education*, 44(4), pp. 599–614. https://doi.org/10.1080/03075079.2017.1387107
Fisch, K. and McLeod, S. (2008) *Shift Happens*. Available at https://www.youtube.com/watch?v=FdTOFkhaplo California State University. (Accessed 7 March 2022).
Gov.uk (2022a) *National Skills Fund*. Available at: https://www.gov.uk/guidance/national-skills-fund (Accessed 6 January 2022).
Gov.uk (2022b) *Support for Employers on Education and Skills*. Available at: https://www.gov.uk/guidance/-support-for-employers-on-education-and-skills (Accessed 6 January 2022).

Gov.uk (2022c) *Equality Act 2010.* Available at: https://www.gov.uk/guidance/equality-act-2010-guidance (Accessed 6 January 2022).

Higdon, R. (2014) Why Do Creative Industries Still Favour the Privileged? *The Guardian,* 26 February 2014. Available at: https://www.theguardian.com/careers/creative-industries-privileged-job (Accessed 6 January 2022).

Higdon, R. (2018) From Employability to 'Complexability': Creatour – A Construct for Preparing Students for Creative Work and Life. *Industry and Higher Education,* 32(1), pp. 33–46. https://doi.org/10.1177%2F0950422217744721

Higher Education Statistics Agency, HESA (2020) *Who's Studying in HE? Personal Characteristics.* Available at:https://www.hesa.ac.uk/data-and-analysis/students/whos-in-he/characteristics January 13th 2022 (Accessed 11 March 2022).

Malton, C. (2017) The Future of Work - What Do We Know? WONKHE. Available at: https://wonkhe.com/blogs/-the-future-of-work-what-do-we-know/ (Accessed 7 March 2022).

Parutis, V. and Kandiko Howson, C. (2020) 'Failing to Level the Playing Field: Student Discourses on Graduate Employability' *Research in Post-Compulsory Education,* 25(4), pp. 373–393 https://doi.org/10.1080/13596748.2020.1846312

Quality Assurance Agency (2019) Subject Benchmark Statement. Education Studies. Gloucester: QAA.

SAGE campus (2019) What Do Future Social Science Graduates Look Like? Available at: https://campus.sagepub.com/blog/future-social-science-graduates (Accessed 7 March 2022).

Silberman, S. (2015) *Neurotribes.* New York: Avery.

Tomlinson, M. (2017) Forms of Graduate Capital and Their Relationship to Graduate Employability. *Education and Training,* 59(4), pp. 338–352. https://doi.org/10.1108/ET-05-2016-0090

World Economic Forum. (2016) *The Future of Jobs. Employment, Skills and Workforce Strategy for the Fourth Industrial Revolution.* Global Challenge Insight Report. Available at: http://reports.weforum.org/future-of-jobs-2016/chapter-1-the-future-of-jobs-and-skills/#view/fn-1 (Accessed 6 January 2022).

World Economic Forum. (2022) *The 10 Skills You Need to Thrive in the Fourth Industrial Revolution.* Available at: https://www.weforum.org/agenda/2016/01/the-10-skills-you-need-to-thrive-in-the-fourth-industrial-revolution/(Accessed 6 January 2022).

Index

academic performance 60, 62, 63, 64
active learning 51
Africa 18, 69, 71, 120
anxiety: student 49, 53, 54, 79, 166; young people's 48
Aristotle 41
artificial intelligence 192, 193
arts education 42, 96–102, 195
Asia 18, 69, 120; Central 70
attention deficit hyperactivity disorder (ADHD) 197
Augustine, St 41
Australia 18, 19, 69, 151
autism 155, 164, 167; autistic spectrum 197
autonomy: of learners 55–64, 163; of lecturers 157

Bakhtin, M. 25
Baltic states 22
Bath Spa University 9, 10, 183
BBC (British Broadcasting Corporation) 107
BEd degree 8, 9, 12, 13
belonging 50, 61, 78–79, 80, 90, 104, 119, 121, 124. 148, 150, 154
Bentham, J. 42, 43; Chrestomathic School 42; panopticon concept 43; utilitarianism 42, 43
Bernard, J. 139
biodiversity 88
biophilia 88
Birmingham, University of 119
Bishop Grosseteste University 9
Bourdieu, P. 77, 196
Brazil 43, 69
Bridgewater College 89
British Education Research Association (BERA) 198
British Education Studies Association (BESA) 3, 10, 198
Bruner, J. 36

Canada 16, 17
capital 197; cultural 194, 197; financial 194; human 70, 185, 194; psychological 196–197; social 76, 194, 196

careers and career planning 31, 41, 53, 68, 75, 78, 117, 141, 144–150, 169, 170–177, 179–183, 191–198; other than teaching 12, 21, 23, 171, 174–175; in teaching 2, 11, 15, 68, 171, 173; see also employability
Chester, University of 10
Chile 16, 18
China 18, 19, 40, 69, 71, 75, 124
citizenship 20, 68, 107
class: middle 42, 149; social 43, 70, 106, 110, 115, 138, 139, 151; working 120, 131
climate change 88, 100, 105, 107, 108
co-construction of knowledge 63, 104
co-creation (co-production) 51, 124, 153–167
collectivism 64
communication 42, 79, 108, 124, 141, 161, 164, 180
Comparative and International Education Society (CIES) 72
Complexity in learning and education 5, 34, 36, 37, 58, 77, 83, 124, 174, 191
constructivism 35, 38, 40, 44, 46, 83, 85, 177
Coronavirus (Covid 19) pandemic 26, 48, 89, 108, 112, 122, 160, 179, 182, 186
Council for the Accreditation of Teacher Education (CATE) 8
creativity 41, 62, 63, 76, 101, 179–180, 191, 193–195, 198
critical disability theory 43
critical gender theory 43
critical pedagogy 43, 109, 128, 130, 132, 134, 135
critical race theory 43
critical reflection 130, 134, 135
critical sexuality theory 43
critical theory 43
critical thinking 125, 195,
Cuba 71
culture 74, 80, 108, 138
curricula, education studies 8–11, 16, 103, 116, 119, 121, 140, 149; university 68
curriculum: hidden 77, 147; planned 24; received 24; school 9, 10, 42

da Vinci, Leonardo 41
dance 96, 99, 100, 101
decolonisation 100, 119, 120, 121, 122, 125, 126
democracy 62, 103, 105–112
Denmark 89
Department for Education (England) 8, 48
deprivation 115, 139
Dewey, J. 40, 42, 44, 83, 86, 87, 90, 98, 103, 108, 109; Laboratory School 42
dialogic education 25, 28
digital storytelling 31, 40, 44, 45
diglossia 79
disability 17, 43, 48, 71, 104, 117, 122, 137, 138, 141, 153–156, 158, 162–167, 194, 196, 197; rights 107
discourse 116, 129, 130, 135, 148, 149, 150, 169, 185, 192
discrimination *see* prejudice and discrimination
diversity, cultural 42, 76, 128; within student body 74, 75, 129, 155; in teaching and learning 24, 51, 63, 81, 116, 125, 131, 137, 148, 191
drama 96, 100, 101
Durham Commission on Creativity and Education 42, 198
dyslexia 167, 197

early years 17, 18, 25, 89, 145, 175, 183
economics 8, 12, 23
educational culture 25, 74, 76, 77, 125, 157, 193
educational psychology 17, 18
educational sciences 22
educational theory 8, 16, 17, 91, 176, 180
Eisner, E. 97, 98
emotional intelligence 91, 195
emotional labour 140, 142
employability 41, 46, 52, 54, 122, 124, 169, 171–198; *see also* careers and career planning
empowerment, student 31, 43, 53–54, 59, 84, 100, 117, 121, 172, 193
England 5, 21, 22, 41, 42, 106, 173, 179
English Outdoor Council 42
entertainment 107
environmental issues 43, 88–90, 92–94, 103
epistemology 15, 86, 181
Equalities Act 2010 116
equity and equality 26, 100, 104, 114, 133, 141
ethics 100, 142, 125
ethnicity 34, 129–131, 137–141, 147, 149, 151, 164, 194
ethos, education studies course 2, 31, 48, 49–54, 165–166
Eton College 41

eurocentrism 120, 124
Europe 1, 7, 16, 19, 20, 22, 41, 67, 69–71, 75, 76, 77, 120; Eastern 70
European Network of Information Centres in the European Region 20
extrinsic motivation 59, 60, 62

Feminism 148
Forest School Association 89
formative feedback 26
Frankfurt School for Social Research 106
Fraser, N. 107, 112–118
Freire, P. 43, 109, 130, 132, 134, 135; banking model of learning 25, 130, 132, 134
Fröebel, F. 42, 90
Further and Higher Education Act 1992 68

games 91, 101
gay men *see* LGBT and LGBTQ+
gender pay gap 140
Germany 16, 69, 106, 151
Giroux, H. 46
Global South 72, 123
globalisation 67–72, 75, 114
Greece, Ancient 16, 40, 41
growth: of education studies 7, 9, 10, 11, 137; of the individual 49, 59, 195

Habermas, J. 103, 105, 106, 107, 111
Harrow School 41
health 49–50, 84, 88, 89, 106, 153, 160, 181, 183, 197; mental 48–50, 54, 88, 92, 153
heteronormativity 116, 150,
heterosexuality 137, 149, 151
Higher Education Funding Council for England (HEFCE) 9
Hirsch, E. D. 25
holistic: learning 58, 62–64, 89; wellbeing 52–53
Holt, J. 39
Honneth, A. 106
Horkheimer, M. 43
human rights 71, 100, 113
humanism 31, 48–51, 54–55

identity: career 179–183; cultural 126; education studies subject 1, 2, 5, 21–28, 169; individuals' 2, 61, 63, 77, 78, 80, 99, 103, 104, 107, 121, 132–133, 137–142, 145, 146–151, 154, 156, 157, 164, 167, 175, 185–189
imagination 41–44, 98, 109
inclusion 78, 79, 81, 86, 100, 103, 107, 110, 113, 122, 134, 148, 163, 194
indigenous groups 43, 70
individualism 26, 64, 103

inequity and Inequality 2, 69, 70, 71, 84, 103–104, 112, 114, 119, 121, 123, 130, 137, 138, 141, 147, 149, 156, 174, 183, 197
innate: curiosity 89; motivation 91
Instagram 108
intellectual elite 177
international students 32, 69, 70, 75–82, 123
intersectionality 104, 117, 138–140, 151, 158, 164, 194
intrinsic motivation 59, 60, 62, 63, 64, 90
Islamophobia 132–133

James, E. 9
Japan 35, 71, 75

Kaizen philosophy 35
Keele University 119
Kingston University 119, 125
knowledge economy 179
Korea, South 75

labelling 78, 79, 80, 81, 164
language 63, 70, 74, 76, 78–80, 98, 101, 123, 126, 139, 163
Latin America 69
learning technologies 182
learning theory 35, 36, 64; see also theories by name
lecturers 51, 53, 63, 71, 104, 128, 131–131, 137, 141, 148, 154, 156–165
LGBT and LGBTQ+: intersectionality and 117, 149, 167; knowledge and 120; pupils 116; rights 107, 116, 117, 120
Lincoln, University of 9
Lippmann, W. 108, 109
locus of control 50, 52

Malaysia 75
Manchester Grammar School 9
Mandela, N. 43
marginalised groups 120; see also minority groups
masculinity 104, 144–152
Maslow's Hierarchy 49
mathematics 100
medieval period 41
memorisation 41
mental health see health
metacognition 78, 85
metaphor 84, 85, 87
Mezirow, J. 109
Middle East 19, 67, 69
mindfulness 91
minority groups 74, 75, 116, 120, 121–125, 129, 137, 139–140, 197; see also marginalised groups
modelling 36, 81, 181

Montessori, M. 42, 70, 90
Morra, S. 44
music 17, 44, 45, 96, 97, 101
Muslim experience 124

National Academic Recognition Information Centres in the European Union (NARIC) 20
National Curriculum 9
National Student Survey (NSS) 49
National Union of Students (NUS) 140
nature 41, 88, 90–93
Neil, A. S. 90
neoliberalism 23, 27, 28, 109
Netherlands 124
neurodiversity 153–167, 197, 198
neuroscience 34
neurotypical 166
Nigeria 18, 19
North America 17, 69
nursing 145, 146, 151

Oceania 18
OECD (Organisation for Economic Co-operation and Development) 42, 43, 69, 71
Office for Students (OfS) 48
Ofsted (Office for Standards in Education, Children's Services and Skills) 8, 176
originality 35, 51, 193

parents 42, 63, 163, 177, 194, 196
patriarchy 140, 145, 150
pedagogy 8, 16–18, 25–28, 31–32, 40, 43, 46, 48, 50–54, 70–71, 83, 90–91, 93, 97, 101, 104, 109, 119, 121–122, 124, 130, 132, 134–135, 139, 146, 149, 154, 169, 171–178, 179, 183; see also critical pedagogy
personal tutoring 51, 52
Pestalozzi Method 41
Peters, R.S. 8
PGCE (Postgraduate Certificate of Education) 9, 10, 21, 22, 25, 100, 173, 176
Piaget, J. 177
play, learning through 41, 90, 91
poetry 101
policy: educational 10, 23, 70, 74, 77, 92, 97, 116, 174; makers of 97; school 116
Polytechnics 68
Portugal 16, 17
post-1992 universities 68
power and power relationships 2, 84, 90, 103–104, 105, 107, 115–116, 120, 121, 131–134, 138–139, 141, 146, 153–167
pragmatism 32, 85, 86
prejudice and discrimination 109, 125, 130, 131, 134, 135, 138, 139, 141, 149
primary schools 89; placements in 183; teaching in 151, 173

privilege and privileging 2, 27, 43, 103, 104, 120, 131, 132–134, 144, 148–151, 156
problem solving 191, 193, 194
professional development 17, 181, 192
professional practice 25, 91, 139, 180
Programme for International Student Assessment (PISA) 42
progressivism 177
psychology 31, 34, 57–64, 88, 164, 196

QTS (Qualified Teacher Status) 8, 9, 10, 11, 12, 173, 178, 183
Quality Assurance Agency (QAA) 9, 11, 20, 113, 180
queer *see* LGBT and LGBTQ+

race 71, 104, 106, 110, 117, 128–135, 138–142
racism and anti-racist approaches 43, 120–121, 128–137, 140–143
reasoning skills 114, 193
Rée, H. 9
reflexivity 27, 84–87, 103, 176, 177
religious belief and values 19, 41, 42, 131, 147; intolerance 43; practice 139
Renaissance period 41
research methods 16, 83–87
research proposal 84–86
Rhodes, Cecil and Rhodes Must Fall movement 68, 119, 126
Robbins Committee/Report 7
Rogers, C. 49–50
role play 100, 185, 186, 188, 189
Rome, Ancient 41
Rousseau, J. 41, 42, 43
Rugby School 41
Russia 70

scaffolding 36
Scandinavia 71
scientific method 97
self-agency 54, 76, 103, 185–186, 193–198
self-determination theory (SDT) 31, 57–64
self-efficacy 53, 54, 78, 172, 196
Seneca 41
sex, biological attributes of 145
sexism 43, 140, 141
sexuality and sexual orientation 106, 116, 138–139, 141, 146, 147, 149, 151, 164
Shotwell, A. 128, 132; and chapter 17 generally
situated learning 35–36, 38
skills, acquisition of 185, 187
social justice 16, 17, 19, 76, 103, 112–117, 125, 139, 148

social life 106, 114, 115
social media 108, 196, 197
social mobility 112
social network theory 72
social science 34, 87, 180, 183, 191–193
social work 145, 146, 174
social world 78, 172
socio-economic status 197
sociology and sociologists 8, 9, 11–12, 16, 18, 28, 34, 43, 77
South Africa 119, 126
South America 18
Spain 16, 17
special educational needs and disabilities (SEND) 16, 17, 18, 70, 71, 104, 116, 153–155, 174, 197; *see also* chapter 20
STEAM (Science, Technology, Engineering, Arts and Mathematics) 195
Steiner Schools 42
STEM (Science, Technology, Engineering and Mathematics) 42, 43
stereotypes 78, 79, 80, 116, 125, 144, 149–150
students, East Asian 75, 76, 79, 80
summative assessment 37, 85
sustainability education 10, 32, 88, 89, 92, 93
Sustainable Development Goals (SDGs) 70–71, 88–89, 92–93

Tanzania 71
Teach First 173
teacher education (training) 1, 7–9, 10–13, 19, 22, 23, 70, 99, 113, 129, 130, 135, 154, 169, 173, 177, 180, 192, 198
Teacher Training Agency (TTA) *see* Training and Development Agency for Schools
testing, pupil 39, 46, 90
TikTok 108
Training and Development Agency for Schools (TDA) and Teacher Training Agency 8, 10
transferable skills 1, 2, 176, 180, 191, 192, 193, 197
transformative learning 50, 84–85, 110, 128, 134
travel 67, 77, 78, 197

UCL (University College London) 119
UNESCO 42, 116
United Kingdom 67, 137, 194,
United States of America (USA) 1, 16, 18, 43, 69, 154
Universities UK 119, 140

Valenzuela, G. 124
vocabulary 77, 116

vocational education and experience 5, 17, 171, 173, 177
Vygotsky, L. 36, 53, 177

wellbeing 3, 31, 32, 48–50, 52, 54, 57–64, 77, 78, 81, 88, 89, 99, 140, 148, 154, 165, 197; *see also* health
whiteness 104, 131, 132–134, 151
widening participation 81, 197
wisdom 41

Woodhead, C. 9
work 172, 179, 192; future of 193; and market forces 23, 180, 188
work based learning (WBL) 179–181; placements 179, 182
World Alliance for Arts Education 42

York, University of 9

Zone of Proximal Development 36, 53

Printed in Great Britain
by Amazon